# Social Media Marketing

Githa Heggde • G. Shainesh
Editors

# Social Media Marketing

## Emerging Concepts and Applications

palgrave
macmillan

*Editors*
Githa Heggde
Director
IFIM Business School
Bangalore, India

G. Shainesh
Professor - Marketing
Indian Institute of Management
Bangalore
Bangalore, India

ISBN 978-981-10-5322-1 ISBN 978-981-10-5323-8 (eBook)
https://doi.org/10.1007/978-981-10-5323-8

Library of Congress Control Number: 2017962122



Printed on acid-free paper

This Palgrave Macmillan imprint is published by Springer Nature
The registered company is Springer Nature Singapore Pte Ltd.
The registered company address is: 152 Beach Road, #21-01/04 Gateway East, Singapore 189721, Singapore

# Preface

Social media has emerged as the defining trend in the last decade and continues to restructure communication and interactions between individuals, communities, government and businesses. Researchers and marketers are grappling with the profound impact of the rapidly evolving social media on viral user-generated content, its impact on shaping consumer perceptions and the constantly changing landscape for developing business cases to proactively engage with stakeholders. The increasing opportunities to listen to customers on company managed channels as well as third party review sites, including social media pages, across the digital space are accompanied by the challenges of responding, real-time, to these conversations. This requires a huge shift in the way marketing functions engage and dialogue with customers.

Our book focuses on the role of social media as the next big game changer. We had hosted the first international conference on 'Social Media Marketing in Emerging markets' as a platform to bring together a distinguished panel of speakers from academia and the corporate world. The conference provided a forum for practitioners and researchers to discuss, debate and share their insights and research findings. This book is a collection of selected papers submitted by researchers and managers and offers additional inputs from corporate experts and business leaders who have shared case studies. It focuses on the impact of social media on marketing, from brand building, communications, and advertising to customization and customer engagement.

The book is divided into four sections.

## Part I: Conceptual Issues in Social Media

This section charts the evolution of social media research and attempts to identify the underlying conceptual issues in social media. The section affords insight into how social media impacts marketing media, giving a peek at the future of marketing media and how social media is not just a platform but is transforming how businesses work. The collection of papers in this section is quite eclectic in subject matter, ranging from integrated marketing communication to a technology platform stack, legal aspects, and lifecycle of information the web. A model for developing an integrated perspective on communication through traditional and social media is proposed. The concept of an integrated stack of four technology service platforms—social, mobility, analytics and cloud (SMAC)—is an example of this new-age convergence. The section also includes discussions on the lifecycle of information in the context of social networks, covering key concepts including nodes, ties, triadic closure, bridge, strength of a tie, and diffusion. The last topic in this section emphasizes the dark side of using social media, which could have larger ramifications for stakeholders and hinder the peaceful co-evolution of professional and public good in this digital ecosystem. Hence it needs a deeper examination.

## Part II: Understanding Digital Consumers

This section attempts to understand the digital consumer and his/her influence in emerging markets. Consumer behaviour is a multidimensional facet and digital proliferation makes it more complex. The papers in this section focus on challenges and opportunities for marketers to ensure customer engagement by identifying determinants of customer engagement in social media and the impact of customer engagement on customer loyalty. The consumption value for digital devices like smartphones integrates concepts from literature outside the traditional marketing domain to develop a framework for user experience. The changes that have occurred in communication technologies have extensively affected how 'digital natives' receive and disseminate information. Having been born in the digital environment where the use of various social media platforms has proliferated, the section also emphasizes how the digital natives have become an important market segment.

The section presents an understanding how infusing innovative social media techniques is beneficial as compared to conventional media spend and also proposes a theoretical model for social media integration.

## Part III: Integrating Social Media into Marketing

This section highlights the role of social media in specific business areas including advertising, marketing communications, customer service and public relations. There is an increasing emphasis on opportunities available and challenges faced by marketers in adopting social networking sites for marketing, including the development of a cost-effective social media strategy for small businesses. Some of the critical issues discussed in this section are companies' understanding of the benefits to be derived from social media, focusing on the return on investment (ROI) of social media efforts. A good number of organizations are engaging customers in their new product development activities via social media platforms. The section also focuses on social change and the influence of social media on corporate social responsibility, relevant social media strategies for each social media tool, and identifying gaps, and provides recommendations for making future CSR attempts effective. The future of the world will drive us all to that economists' utopia of perfect competition, as everyone will soon have access to every bit of information. This is due to the scale of social media interventions which this section highlights. Another area focuses on the development of a conceptual framework that posits salespersons' use of social media as an antecedent to the creation of social capital. The goal is to provide a foundation for subsequent empirical investigation aimed at helping managers appreciate the use of social media in multinational organizations.

## Part IV: Social Media Applications and Case Studies

The papers focus on the emergence and increasing use of social media across sectors and markets. This section highlights the adoption of social media in various industries such as health care, automobile, and so on. The emergence of social networking sites globally has brought in a paradigm shift in word-of-mouth communications, thus enabling users to observe, interact, and exchange information. The segment also attempts to examine the existing legal framework in the Indian context with respect to information to be provided by online portals to their customers on their websites. Inference is also drawn from some of the international best practices adopted in upholding consumer trust and confidence in online shopping.

The case studies in this section explore how social media can be used to convey the responsible marketing intent and activities of companies through ongoing online conversations in real-time situations.

## Intended Audience

This book is intended for academicians, professionals and managers who wish to gain insights on the impact of social media marketing. It will be valuable to marketing practitioners and brand custodians as they explore social media outreach to their target customers and engage with individual customers and other stakeholders. Researchers and managers will find this book to be a handy reference on social media in emerging markets.

Bangalore, India Githa Heggde

Bangalore, India G. Shainesh

# Acknowledgements

We thank Mr Louis D'Mello, President, IDG Media, and his team; Mr Sudhir Kamath, Mr Rupesh Sreedharan, and Mr Siddharth Singh for partnering with us in conducting the International Conference on Social Media Marketing and supporting Conference communications and promotional materials from which select papers form part of a few sections. Thanks also go to Ms Margaret D'costa for helping with the preparation of the conference kit, brochures and promotional material. The production team of IDG, for helping with the smooth conduct of the Conference. We thank the Academy of Indian Marketing(AIM) for partnering with us, and Mr Jayant Shah, Director of AIM, for his continued support. Additionally we thank all authors who have contributed to this book.

# Contents

# Notes on Editors and Contributors

## Editors

**Githa S. Heggde** is Director, IFIM Business School, Bangalore, India. She is also a member of the editorial board of *International Journal on Emerging Markets* (Emerald), Core member at the Centre for Emerging Markets, IIM, Lucknow (India), and Faculty resource, MDP, IIM, Kozhikode, India. She is the vice chairperson, CII-IWN, Karnataka (India), and has over 27 years of teaching, consultancy, and industrial experience. Her papers have been awarded best research papers at the Association of Indian Management Schools (AIMS) conventions. Several of her articles on marketing, supply chain, sales and distribution have been published in international and national journals. She was part of the team at "Global colloquium on participant-centered learning" at Harvard Business School, Boston, and worked on teaching with case studies and developing curriculum for management courses. She has conducted several training programs for senior marketing and sales executives at Airtel, ITC, Infosys, Murugappa group, Pricol, HDFC, EY, and Biocon. She has been engaging in consultancy and research with companies such as Logitech (USA), iWatt (USA), Reliance (India), BEL (India), and so on. She was the chairperson, FICCI Ladies Organization, southern region.

**G. Shainesh** is Professor of Marketing at the Indian Institute of Management Bangalore (IIMB). He has over two decades of research and teaching experience in India and abroad. He has conducted research and teaching assignments at the Goteborg University (Sweden), the University of St. Gallen (Switzerland), Audencia Nantes and IESEG (France), Vienna University and MCI Innsbruck (Austria), Bocconi University (Milan), Curtin University of Technology (Perth), and the American University of Armenia (Yerevan). His research focuses on CRM, services marketing, and service innovations. At IIMB, he leads the cross-functional research initiative on consumer insights. His book titled *Customer Relationship Management—A Strategic Perspective* (Trinity Press/Laxmi Publications) is a prescribed textbook for CRM courses at several business schools. He is also the co-author of a book on CRM titled *Customer Relationship Management—Emerging Concepts, Tools and Applications* (2017). His papers on services and relationship marketing have been published in the *MIS Quarterly*, *Journal of Service Research*, *Journal of International Marketing*, *Journal of Services Marketing*, *International Journal of Bank Marketing*, *International Journal of Retail and Distribution Management*, *International Journal of Technology Management*, *Journal of Relationship Marketing*, *International Marketing Review*, among others.

## Contributors

**Raj Agnihotri** is the John Merrill Endowed Professor in Consultative Sales and Associate Professor of Marketing at the University of Texas—Arlington. He was formerly Robert H. Freeman Professor of Sales Leadership and Chair of the Marketing Department at Ohio University. He also served as Director of Research at Ralph and Luci Schey Sales Centre at Ohio University. Before entering academia, Raj held a number of sales and marketing positions with start-up ventures to major corporations.

**Joyeeta Chatterjee** is Professor of Marketing and Dean (Academics)—PGDM at IILM Institute of Higher Education, New Delhi, India, and has been into academics for the last 22 years. She teaches MBA/PGDM students and conducts MDPs/Corporate Training Programs. She is also passionate about Soft Skills Training and involves herself actively in training programs for Developing Business Etiquettes, Effective Team Building and Service Excellence, Motivational Strategies, Leadership Challenges, Excellence Through Effective Communication, and so on. She has conducted several training series for executives. She has an MBA with dual specialization in marketing and HRM from the Department of Business Administration, Guwahati University, and is an economics graduate from

Cotton College, Guwahati, Assam, India. She holds a PhD in marketing from Banasthali Vidyapeeth, Rajasthan, India.

**Nathalie Chinje** is Founder and Director of UPbeat Marketing, a marketing consultancy based in Johannesburg, South Africa. Chinje also serves as the executive director for WEConnect International—South Africa, a corporate-led non-profit that empowers women business owners to succeed in local and global markets. She is a faculty member at Wits Business School and Duke Corporate Education, South Africa, where she teaches marketing and customer centricity.

**Richard Chinomona** is an associate professor in the School of Economic & Business Sciences at the University of the Witwatersrand, Johannesburg, South Africa.

**Sameer Deshpande** is an associate professor of marketing at the Faculty of Management, the University of Lethbridge, Canada.

**K. Ganesh** is Chairman—Portea. Ganesh is a successful serial entrepreneur with four successful greenfield ventures and exits. His last venture, TutorVista, was acquired by US- and UK-listed education leader Pearson for $213 m. He was among the top five nominees for the Economic Times Entrepreneur of the Year 2012 Award. His current venture, Portea Medical, provides technology-led home health care to the Indian consumer. He actively mentors, incubates and funds start-ups and is a strategic investor and promoter of several Indian consumer Internet and ecommerce companies, including Bigbasket.com—India's largest egrocery company, Bluestone.com—leading online jewelry company, and Avagmah.com—India's fastest-growing online higher education company.

**Aswinraj Govindaraj** is Program Manager at Hewlett-Packard. He is an alumnus of the University of Cincinnati Carl H. Lindner College of Business and Anna University, Chennai, India.

**Easwar Krishna Iyer** is an associate professor at the Great Lakes Institute of Management. He has worked as an associate professor at Amrita School of Business (ASB) and Vice Chair of the EMBA Program jointly run by ASB and the State University of New York, Buffalo. Prior to that, he had done extensive research in the technology area, with several international publications in journals as varied as *Electronics Letters*, *Microwave & Optical Technology Letters* and *Applied Superconductivity*.

**Ambrish Joshi** is Assistant Vice-President, Healthcare and Lifesciences Analytics, at GENPACT LLC, Bangalore India. He has more than 20 years of experience in designing and developing strategies for pharmaceutical and healthcare businesses and products. He is instrumental in providing decision support to leading global healthcare/pharmaceutical organizations for developed and emerging markets. Joshi's work areas include opportunity identification and assessment, threat assessment, emerging market opportunities, assessment of current and future competition, R&D pipeline analysis, disease/market/competitive landscape, market entry strategy, and assessment of regulatory environment. He played a strategic role within a global pharma organization and was part of brand/marketing teams. He did his MBA with dual specialization in marketing and finance and B. Pharm, both from the University of Rajasthan, India. He also holds a PhD from MLS University, Udaipur, Rajasthan, India.

**Rajiv Kashyap** is Chair of the Marketing and Management Department and Professor of Marketing at the Cotsakos College of Business, William Paterson University, Wayne. His teaching and research focus on strategic marketing and social marketing.

**Prabakar Kothandaraman** is the executive director of the Russ Berrie Institute of Professional Sales and an associate professor of professional sales at William Paterson University. Kothandaraman has held academic tenure-track appointments at Drexel University and the Texas A&M University and research and administrative appointments at the Harvard Business School India Research Center. In his over 15 years of academic experience, he has taught courses in the area of sales and marketing, which include marketing strategy and Panning, industrial marketing and sales, marketing research, business-to-business marketing, product management, principles of marketing and negotiation. Academically, PK has obtained a Ph.D. in business administration from the Pennsylvania State University, an MBA from Xavier Institute of Management, Bhubaneswar (India), and a bachelor of engineering degree from The Birla Institute of Science & Technology, Pilani, India.

**Sudha Mani** is an assistant professor at the Cotsakos College of Business, William Paterson University, Wayne. She focuses on sales management and inter-organizational relationships in her teaching and research.

**Avinash Mulky** is Professor of Marketing at the Indian Institute of Management Bangalore.

**Pratima Narayan** is an advocate and mediator. She has extensively worked in the areas of consumer law, e-commerce and intellectual property rights. She is an empanelled mediator with the Indian Institute of Arbitration and Mediation, Cochin, and Indian Institute of Corporate Affairs, New Delhi. She has worked as a research associate and mediator at Online Consumer Mediation Centre, National Law School of India University, Bangalore, India.

**Rajendra Nargundkar** is Professor of Marketing at the Indian Institute of Management Indore.

**T.M. Prasanna** has been a member of the technical team at Juniper Networks for almost a decade now. He has worked with Tejas Networks. He studied at the Indian Institute of Management Bangalore.

**T.P. Pratap** co-founded QwikCilver Solutions Private Limited in 2006 and serves as its chief marketing officer. Pratap has over 15 years of experience in strategic marketing, product launch initiatives, media campaign management, and public relations. He has experience of the Middle East markets, having handled the marketing function at Kuwait Danish Dairy for GCC markets for over three years. He has been a part of many startup teams across segments and categories—setting up channels of distribution, product development, and growing retail networks. He was involved in the launch of leading brands and companies across sectors in India, such as Timex watches across India, lighting business of Wipro Ltd., and polyurethanes paints business of ICI. Pratap studied engineering at BITS Pilani and MBA at IIM Calcutta, India.

**Ajay Row** is Founder and CEO of LitmusWorld.com. He is an entrepreneur and executive with nearly 30 years of experience globally in database marketing, analytics, loyalty and CRM across industries. His past roles include Executive Director—Aimia India and Vice President CRM—Taj Hotels. Ajay is an alumnus of IIM Calcutta, India.

**H.V. Satyanarayana** is Senior Engineering Manager at Flipkart. In a professional career spanning over a decade, Satya has worked with leading firms, including Yahoo and Talisma. He studied at the Indian Institute of Management Bangalore.

**Shweta Sharma** is a research associate at the NITI Aayog, Delhi, India

**Jagdish N. Sheth** is the Charles H. Kellstadt Professor of Marketing at the Goizueta Business School of Emory University. He is a renowned scholar and internationally recognized thought leader. More than 300 research papers and more than 30 books of his on various disciplines and topics have been published. His insights into global competition, strategic thinking, geopolitics, and emerging markets are considered revolutionary. As a thought leader, Professor Sheth has made hundreds of presentations to business leaders, academic scholars, and public policymakers from around the world. He is frequently quoted and interviewed by *Fortune*, *Financial Times*, *The Economic Times*, *The New York Times*, and *The Wall Street Journal*. He is also a regular guest at and frequent commenter for major news networks: BBC, CNBC India, and CNN.

**Anuragini Shirish** is an assistant professor at the Telecom Ecole de Management (Institut Mines-Telecom), France.

**Supriya Tandon** is Senior Manager, Business Operations Performance, at Hewlett Packard Enterprise, Bangalore, India.

**Harsh V. Verma** is Professor of Marketing at the Faculty of Management Studies, University of Delhi, India

# List of Figures

# List of Tables

PART I

# Conceptual Issues in Social Media

CHAPTER 1

# How Social Media Will Impact Marketing Media

*Jagdish N. Sheth*

## Introduction

The world is changing; technology is ubiquitous and it is impacting society with each rapid change it undergoes itself. A few decades ago, television was the most exciting technological development, and it transformed society in an unprecedented manner. Today, we're seeing a similar transformation via the Internet and the rise of social media. In fact, social media is poised to transform society in an even more fundamental manner.

It is easy to underestimate the true disruptive potential of social media, a moving target which is hard to pin down due to constant innovation. For example, as a consequence of the widespread adoption of social media, the distinction between the public and private spheres of life is quickly eroding. Whether one is a CEO, the president of a country, a member of the British royalty, or a commoner, everything about one is on social media: personal information, likes and dislikes, and other mundane activities. In fact, everything said or done is now a matter of public record, and nothing can remain

The author is grateful to Racchit Thapliyal for his excellent research and editing assistance for this paper.

J. N. Sheth (✉)
Goizueta Business School, Emory University, Atlanta, GA, USA



G. Heggde, G. Shainesh (eds.), *Social Media Marketing*,
https://doi.org/10.1007/978-981-10-5323-8_1

hidden anymore. Besides the doom and gloom surrounding social media because of this lack of privacy, however, there is a bright side as well: social media has led to a drastic increase in transparency in society.

The focus of this paper is on the impact of social media on marketing media. Traditional media, consisting of print, radio and television, offer what can be called a shotgun approach: they represent one to many (passive communication). Therefore, in order to achieve efficiency and effectiveness, segmentation, targeting and positioning strategies are utilized. Social media, on the other hand, are interactive in nature: they represent peer to peer relationships, or what is referred to as many to many (active communication). Additionally, since word of mouth (WOM) is so crucial in marketing, the paper will also discuss how traditional WOM influence will change dramatically in the world of social media.

## Social Media: Platforms and Use

Social media is a blur of "likes," tweets, shares, posts and content (Bullas, 2014). Its use is not limited to youth. Rather, it is universal and embedded in every corner of the web. The numbers are staggering: 72 percent of the all Internet users are now active on social media (Bullas, 2014). Eighty-nine percent of people eighteen to twenty-nine years of age use social media. Eighty-two percent of people thirty to forty-nine years of age are active on social media. Sixty-five percent of those fifty to sixty-four years of age use social media, while, of those over sixty-five years of age, 49 percent are active users (Pew Research, 2014). It is clear that regardless of their age, people are now spending a lot of time on social media, constantly sharing and browsing information.

When it comes to geography, it is US citizens who top the list of time spent on social media with sixteen minutes per hour spent on the Internet. Australians follow them with fourteen minutes and Britons with thirteen minutes (Experian, 2013). The use of mobile technology to access social media is also increasing rapidly, with 71 percent of the users of social media using mobile devices to access it (Bullas, 2014) (Fig. 1.1).

Currently, Facebook is the "biggest kid" on the social media block, with 1.49 billion Facebook users (Statista, 2015) and more than 100,000 web pages are accessed with the Login with Facebook feature (Lafferty, 2014). Twenty-three percent of Facebook users login at least five times a day (Romeri, 2014). Facebook also has a lot of influence on the buying decisions of customers, as 47 percent of Americans say that Facebook is the number-one influencer of their purchasing habits (Romeri, 2014).

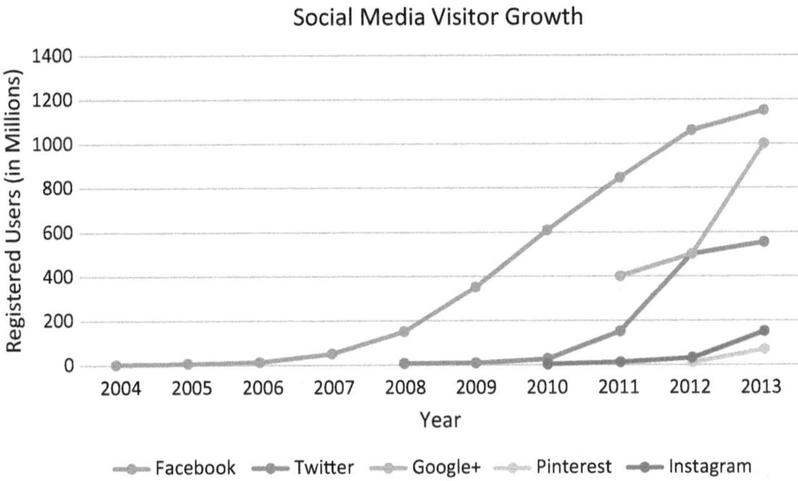


**Fig. 1.1** The growth of social media (Data source: www.jeffbullas.com)

Since Facebook has so much influence on people, it isn't surprising that 94 percent of business-to-consumer (B2C) marketers and 82 percent of business-to-business (B2B) marketers today use Facebook for customer acquisition (Stelzner, 2014).

But Facebook isn't the only large player in the social media space, as there are a number of other platforms that are quickly amassing users. For instance, Twitter, which took the social media world by storm with its 140-character limit, now has almost a billion registered users (Koetsier, 2013) and 316 million monthly active users (Twitter, 2015). As is the case with Facebook, where people spend their time, marketers are soon to follow, and 34 percent of marketers use Twitter to generate leads (Bullas, 2014).

Other popular social media platforms include WhatsApp, Instagram, Snapchat, Pinterest, LinkedIn, YouTube, Vine, Tumblr, and SlideShare. With their impressive user base, these platforms are also gaining more and more attention from marketers.

## Word of Mouth (WOM) Versus Social Media WOM

What follows is a discussion of the WOM phenomenon in both its traditional context and on social media. Specifically, the emergence of WOM, its impact on marketing, and other characteristics are considered in both contexts (Table 1.1).

### *Emergence of WOM*

The origin of WOM communication can be traced to the origin of trade itself. It was most powerful in the agricultural age, when the producer and consumer interacted closely. The milkman who delivered milk to one's home, the butcher who delivered fresh meat daily, and the grocery store delivery person knew everything about their consumer families and their preferences.

The services they provided were characterized by much more than a mere transaction of goods. Family customers confided in these goods and services providers, who knew the family dynamics, and were even privy to the family's finances. In fact, the grocery storeowner often acted as a money lender to the family if they didn't have money to pay for the groceries at the end of the month. This financing service would be underwritten in the "good name" of the family, something akin to the modern credit score. This was a multigenerational relationship, with the children continuing to avail themselves of such services and even taking up unpaid family debts.

With the dawn of the industrial age, however, came the separation of production from consumption, and the rise of middlemen and trading. As a result, the economy became more transactional as opposed to relational, as it had been in the past (Sheth & Parvatiyar, 1995).

Counterintuitively, social media is bringing us back to that bygone agricultural age. In those days conversations were "recorded" by the barber and hairstylist who knew more about anything and anyone in the community. People discussed politics and their religious beliefs at the local diner where everybody got together. It was here that they discussed com-

**Table 1.1** Characteristics of traditional WOM vs. social media WOM

| *Traditional WOM* | *Social media WOM* |
|---|---|
| Local | Global |
| Voice | Text and video |
| Gated community | Viral |
| Trickle down | Circular |
| (Opinion leadership) | (Network effect) |
| Passive recipient | Interactive recipient |
| Marketer in charge (targeting) | Recipient in charge (shot gun) |
| Episodic feedback | Continuous feedback |
| Brand Stewardship | Brand alteration |
| Measurable impact | Diffused impact |

munity events and what was happening in their lives as well. With the rise of social media, we are back to recording conversations today, albeit digitally, and this time it is more tangible and permanent as (almost) nothing is erased from the web.

### *WOM Marketing: The Holy Grail of Marketing*

The explosion of social media services over the last few years continues to have a significant impact on advertising, as consumers' reliance on word of mouth (WOM) in the decision-making process—either from people they know or online consumers they don't—has increased significantly.

According to Nielsen's *Global Trust in Advertising* report issued in 2012, 92 percent of consumers around the world say they still trust earned media, such as recommendations from friends and family, above all other forms of advertising—an increase of 18 percent since 2007 (Grimes, 2012). Online consumer reviews are the second most trusted source of brand information and messaging, with 70 percent of global consumers surveyed online indicating they trust messages on this platform—an increase of 15 percent in four years (Grimes, 2012) (Fig. 1.2).

Today, we can gauge a significant increase in the impact of WOM on social media. Now, let us turn to an overview of the WOM phenomenon in the traditional context as well as on social media.

Traditional media refers to conventional means of mass communication, such as street theatre, television, radio, newspapers, magazines, newsletters, the tax press, and other print publications. Traditional WOM is limited to a local impact. This form of publicity takes place on an ongoing basis when people attend to their daily chores. For example, it is at a park, salon, or supermarket that people are most likely to have conversations about their experiences with, and expectations of, any product or services. Publicity here, whether good or bad, is limited to particular communities that are formed at particular places.

Hence WOM is local and lies within a "gated" community of neighbors. The medium is primarily voice, where one's experience is referred to by every other member within the community. There is a trickle-down effect of one opinion to several recipients (i.e., a one-to-many relationship). A key influencer will influence every other recipient here. Thus, WOM here is driven by a single opinion maker, with the rest being passive

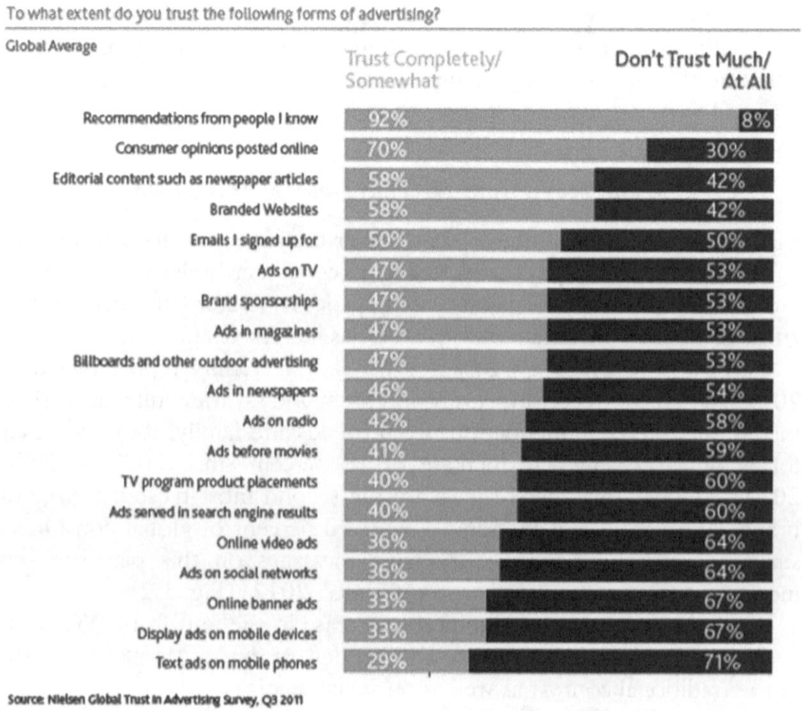


**Fig. 1.2** Consumer trust in advertising

recipients of it. This is reflected by the theory of diffusion whereby a handful of opinion makers in a community influence the masses.

*Who Is in Charge?*

To generate WOM publicity via traditional media, the marketer is in charge of targeting the right audience with the right message about the company and/or its products and services. The feedback in this case is, thus, episodic in nature, where market research is primarily done periodically (for example, a particular Neilson Corporation dataset).

The brand is very closely managed in this case. Marketers are extremely particular about their trademarks and logos so that brand perception is consistent and remains intact in everyone's mind. Moreover, the impact of WOM is easily measurable in this case.

### *WOM on Social Media*

With the growing number of smartphone users and access to the Internet, social networking services have also become increasingly accessible and user friendly. People talk to each other, people make recommendations, and people make suggestions on social media with ease. The global reach and flexibility of social media is indisputable. One can share not only text but also photographs, rich content such as videos and graphics interchange format (GIF) files, and connect with the masses in a very short period of time. WOM on social media is not just restricted to a particular community; it has the possibility of going "viral": it travels all over the world, where neither the sender nor the receiver is necessarily well acquainted with one another or within close proximity.

Social media is highly interactive in nature. In fact, the larger the number of interactive recipients, the larger the number of opinions. Here one sees a network of influencers—a many-to-many, peer-to-peer relationship (as opposed to a one-to-many relationship in the case of traditional WOM). If one communicates with another, the other, in turn, is both influenced and influences the sender; there is no opinion leader or laggard. Thus, WOM in social media is circular in nature and effectively builds a network effect. Networks of different opinions are formed, giving the recipients a better picture of the brand.

#### *Who Is in Charge?*

Unlike traditional WOM, the recipients are in charge of generating WOM on social media. The marketers need not identify the target demographic and then communicate or design the product accordingly. Rather, they can simply devise the product and "throw" it, or disseminate it widely on the web. Somebody will buy it, but the marketer will not have a preexisting idea of who the customer or user of the product or services will be. Consequently, the traditional concept of market segmentation, targeting, and positioning is obsolete here.

A promotional campaign for products or services on social media covers as wide an area or population as possible (i.e., a shotgun approach). Then, it is up to the recipients to initiate, build and hold conversations about them on social media. The conversations are not limited to a certain group of people for a certain time period. Rather, they are open for anyone to react to, give feedback and modify. This means the marketer must constantly react to the feedback on social media. Thus, we have a continuous feedback cycle.

People also express themselves through their possessions (Belk, 1988). In the digital world, one can create one's own avatar and collect digital possessions (such as trophies on Sony's PlayStation network) and, thus, there is no need to acquire physical objects in order to derive happiness or enjoyment (Sheth & Solomon, 2014). Virtual communities such as Farmville have formed online, and about eight million people log in to it daily—one rushes to milk one's cow in time (Sarkar, 2013). That is the nature of the virtual world, where the concept of kinship is almost extinct. People no longer meet their family or neighbors in person. Rather, people are moving toward virtual friendships on social media. The telephone had a similar disruptive effect in the past: one could call one's neighbour over the phone, and talk to one's friends and relatives across the country. The telephone thus displaced conversations in person due to its sheer convenience.

Social media is likely to give rise to brand alteration. Consumers can take liberties with a brand and the company will have a hard time enforcing its intellectual property rights. In the worst-case scenario, there is a possibility of the brand alteration going out of control. This, in turn, would have an impact on marketing, advertising agencies and brand management in general. This impact will be nonlinear by nature and diffused, and, thus, may not be easily measured. And this, in turn, could create anxiety among the marketers. What we have, essentially, is a black box scenario. This is the nature of the diffused impact of WOM on social media.

## The Future of Marketing Media

Marketing media has seen two shifts due to the rise of social media. First, from mass communication (one-to-many) relationships, marketing media has shifted toward the more apt and convenient social media (peer-to-peer network) relationships. Second, traditional media is passive whether print, voice or video, while social media is more interactive. Traditional media is firmly situated in the one-to-many paradigm: It follows the broadcasting model, whereby it transmits the message it wants to convey through broadcast television, print, radio, or signage. Traditional media is thus limited in creating engagement as social media does (Fig. 1.3).

With the shift to the more interactive social media, marketers are now adopting digital marketing tools to market their products and services

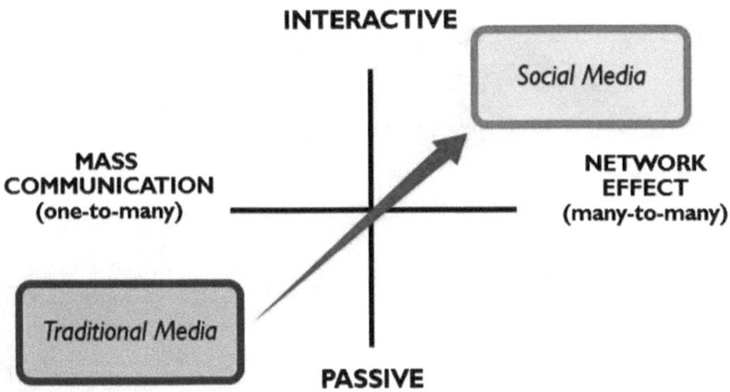


**Fig. 1.3** The future of marketing media

anytime, anywhere and anyhow. Where traditional marketing was limited by location and time, digital marketing has effectively removed these hindrances to present itself as a hassle-free marketing tool.

## Impact on Marketing

As explained above, marketing has been deeply impacted by the advent and widespread adoption of social media. Social media is no longer merely a platform for social interactions. Rather, it is transforming the way businesses work. Marketers are increasingly leveraging social media to influence customer decision making. Some of the specific instances of the impact on marketing are shown in Fig. 1.4. What follows is an elaboration of each of these areas of impact:

### *No More Segmentation, Targeting, and Positioning (STP)*

One of the most important concepts in marketing is segmentation, targeting and positioning (STP) for any product/brand. Together, these enable a marketer to (a) determine the different types of customers, (b) select one of the group of customers that can be served best, and (c) communicate with the targeted group in the best possible manner. Hence it is a "sniper" approach because a "shotgun" approach can prove far too expensive and inefficient when marketing via traditional media.

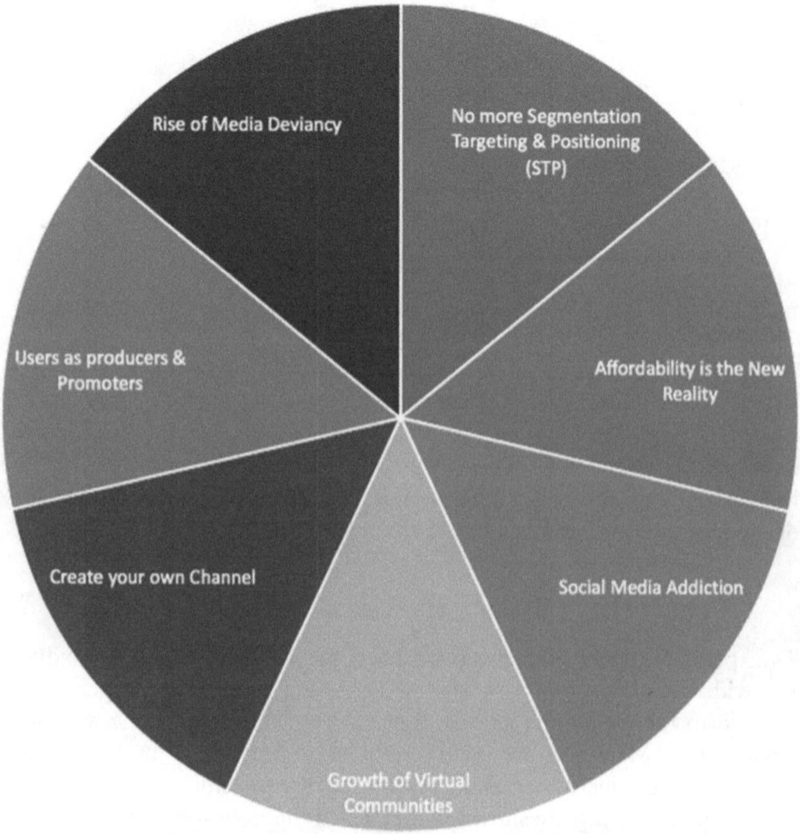


**Fig. 1.4** Impact of social media on marketing

In the digital age, however, a product/brand has a worldwide reach. The Internet is also a very rich and affordable medium. Therefore, the aforementioned factors do not play as much of a role as they did in the past. Thus, traditional marketing is now being replaced by the more cost-effective and result-oriented digital marketing.

Accordingly, the question arises of whether STP will still hold ground or will lose importance in a world where market players are able to communicate the details of their products and also sell their products across demographic or geographic boundaries. Many e-commerce companies, including Amazon and Ali Baba, have amply demonstrated this.

The idea of a "relevant" target market is somewhat obsolete. For example, Apple iPads are used by everyone—from a five-year-old in the United States to a sixty-year-old woman in India. Hence, following the traditional STP tool for marketing might not be beneficial to the next generation of companies.

### *Affordability Is the New Reality*

Social media has also disrupted the paradigm of production and the cost of distribution. In the realm of entertainment, or filmmaking, to be specific, a person today is not as dependent on a producer or a director anymore. A good storyteller is now capable of producing and directing a film of reasonable quality in a quick span of just two to three months, enabled by the hardware and software platforms of Apple and Sony, both of which have been highly affordable and produce good quality digital films. Similarly, in the realm of book publishing, we find that authors today are increasingly choosing to self-publish. A small company can scale up its marketing and offer products and services globally. The Internet is both a rich medium and one that has global reach.

### *Social Media Addiction*

Social media addiction (SMA) refers to a state of mind in which people feel the constant urge to keep track of their social media existence. Though it is not yet recognized as such, this might very well be seen as a mental disorder characterized by a compulsion to constantly check for social media updates, or even "stalk" other people's profiles, among other things. Any kind of addiction is likely to be harmful to a person's mind and body. Researchers at the University of Chicago have recently concluded that SMA can be stronger than an addiction to cigarettes or even alcohol, following an experiment in which they recorded the cravings of several hundred people for several weeks (Wilhelm, Vohs & Baumeister, 2012).

SMA is becoming so common that it is having an impact on social demographics: families are struggling with maintaining relationships as a lot of time is consumed by their "social" lives. Companies are now targeting consumers with "app-only" strategies and are cashing in on the idea that since smartphones are constantly being checked by users, this can be converted into revenue. In order to fight this addiction experts generally advise consumers to limit the number of apps on their phones, and parents to keep a check on their children's smartphone use. The "real estate" on the smartphone has a premium just as retail store goods do.

Some people, however, run counter to this trend. They make the point that despite the fact that people are not interacting face-to-face, social media still remains a platform that facilitates widespread human interaction, which is normal and shouldn't be termed an addiction. Whatever one's view on the matter, social media is indisputably a very addictive medium. Addiction of the mind is very different from addiction to, or consumption of, physical objects. We have acquired knowledge about reducing addiction to consumables such as alcohol and tobacco, but we still need to learn how to effectively control the addiction of "mental consumption" that social media brings about. Digital detoxification and digital rehabilitation might very well be matters of real concern for the future generations.

### *The Growth of Virtual Communities*

A rise of virtual communities can also be observed across the digital world. A virtual community is a social network of individuals who interact through a specific social medium on topics of mutual interest, potentially crossing geographical boundaries. Society has been observing a gradual shift from kinship bonding to friendship bonding. The virtual communities' activities range from forming friendships, learning new subjects, and obtaining opinions on purchases to human experience in general.

Earlier, people had a very limited audience to help them answer their queries, but today the audience is unlimited; anyone can find someone to help solve an issue. People are no longer connected by the proverbial six degrees of separation. Reaching someone by name and location has been reduced to just one or two degrees of separation. Companies are leveraging this opportunity to target audiences. For example, there was a time in India when marriages were arranged with the help of relatives and one's immediate social circle, but today, matrimonial websites are giving families an opportunity to expand their social circle and yet stay within the boundaries of religion, caste, and creed, criteria that continue to dominate the Indian marriage market.

In China, *wang hun*, or online marriage, is a phenomenon in which people become friends online, then become online lovers, and, finally, have an online wedding without meeting in person. This concept is challenging the sanctity of marriage in society, something that has serious consequences for the wedding business. In the long run, more and more people might prefer this type of arrangement over the real experience of a physical wedding, due to sheer convenience.

There are thriving virtual communities such as Second Life and Farmville, which let users access a virtual life satisfying real human emotions and desires. Professional executives have been known to rush home to milk their virtual cows in time on Farmville. These virtual communities satisfy human emotions to the extent that people are gradually shifting to an atomistic or autonomous lifestyle from the earlier nuclear (family of four) lifestyle. This atomistic lifestyle is mostly followed by people with a self-serving and self-sustaining mindset. Whether this phenomenon creates new opportunity for marketers is yet to evolve. Also, we don't know if a highly atomistic lifestyle makes one prone to impulse buying and consumption.

### *Create Your Own Channel*

With the growth and nearly universal availability of high bandwidth, broadband Internet connectivity and other growing technological and communications infrastructures, all individuals today are empowered to put their message out to a larger audience. In fact, individuals have the ability to create their own media channel rather than depend on traditional media such as newspaper, radio, and television to transmit their message. They have the ability to take control of the entire process of production and dissemination. Over the years, we have seen the rise of bloggers, "Twitterati" and other social influencers who have emerged as celebrities in their own right. YouTube has clearly demonstrated this. It is very easy to create and manage one's own YouTube channel, as is evident by the presence on YouTube of celebrities, athletes, religious leaders, such as Pope Francis, and political leaders, such as US President Obama and Indian Prime Minister Narendra Modi.

This democratization of media has also enabled citizen activism. On January 25, 2011, Egyptians started organizing protests against their government and their long-standing leader, President Hosni Mubarak, through Facebook and Twitter. On a global level, not only has media been democratized by the advent of social media but, conversely, social media is also being used as a tool for democratization. Be it Filipinos' demonstrations against their President Joseph Estrada in 2001 or the Jan Lokpal Bill struggle in India, social media is helping change the political scenario worldwide. It has the potential to encourage public policy intervention, as demonstrated by the Maggi quality issues in India and the recent Volkswagen scandal over fuel efficiency.

This has been made possible due to the easy accessibility of a platform where people can raise their voice in unity. There was a time when people used to wait for the morning newspaper to know what was happening in the world, but today, in an instant, YouTube videos, infinite tweets and Facebook updates start "trending" way before the news even makes its way to the newspaper editor's desk.

### *Users as Producers and Promoters*

Cocreation is a very simple idea: it brings together independent parties, such as a company and its consumers, in order to jointly produce a valued product. For example, Nike provides online tools to customers to design their own sneakers. Cocreation is not just limited to product design; it expands to the creation of marketing campaigns as well. Recently, Converse persuaded a large number of loyal customers to come up with their own video advertisements for the brand. Also, Frito-Lay has successfully crowd-sourced from consumers for their Dorritos brand advertising at the Super Bowl. To accomplish such cocreation, companies try to tap consumer insights at the right point in the innovation process.

Cocreation enables brands to leverage consumers' participation in activities that they undertake, for free, to promote as well as produce, and yet the product ownership remains intact. Brands have also started engaging consumers in brand promotions. It isn't a one-sided communication anymore: the consumer has become a part of content creation and brand promotion, similar to the functions provided by advertising agencies. The voice of the customer today is being recognized, appreciated, and leveraged by brands to deliver better products and services, and to promote them.

### *Rise of Media Deviancy*

While social media has placed much power in the hands of users for positive purposes, such as social activism and fandom, it also has also given rise to media deviancy. Every technology has its pros and cons, and social media is no different. When there is too much freedom, as there is on the Internet, security is at risk, especially when there is no one to manage it.

Government and lawmakers have been late adopters of technology and the legal system is slow to adapt to the new technological environment. All this makes the system and its consumers more vulnerable to risk. For instance, recently, multiple cases of fraud and crime have erupted out of social media, making social mediaa more 'social devil'.

## Conclusion

The rise and widespread adoption of social media has changed society dramatically. In just a few years, social media has gone from being a platform for young people to connect with each other to being the lifeline of Internet users. Because of its pervasiveness in society, social media has also affected the way marketers connect with consumers and, in turn, the way consumers connect with brands and products. In fact, social media is a much more powerful force than radio and television. Marketers must learn to swim in these unchartered waters and be sure of how to reach the shore.

Social media will have an enormous impact on shaping the future of consumption culture. While social media benefits society in a number of ways, not all of the transformation it has brought about has been positive. In many ways, it is a double-edged sword, providing both positive value and negative repercussions for society. Social media addiction and deviancy are real issues, which should be addressed.

Marketers should be cognizant of the fact that social media allows users to alter a brand. Marketers must not only respond but also proactively shape social media to be a positive force for society. In sum, marketing media will be permanently transformed by social media.

## References

Belk, R. W. (1988). Possessions and the Extended Self. *Journal of Consumer Research, 15*(2), 139–168. Retrieved from http://www.jstor.org/stable/2489522

Bullas, J. (2014). 22 Social Media Facts and Statistics You Should Know in 2014. Retrieved October 17, 2015, from http://www.jeffbullas.com/2014/01/17/20-social-media-facts-and-statistics-you-should-know-in-2014/

Grimes, M. (2012, October 4). Global Consumers' Trust in 'Earned' Advertising Grows in Importance. Retrieved October 17, 2015, from http://www.nielsen.com/us/en/press-room/2012/nielsen-global-consumers-trust-in-earned-advertising-grows.html

Koetsier, J. (2013, September 16). How Twitter Plans to Make Its 750M 'Users' Like Its 250M Real Users. Retrieved October 17, 2015, from http://venturebeat.com/2013/09/16/how-twitter-plans-to-make-its-750m-users-like-its-250m-real-users/

Lafferty, J. (2014, December 12). Major Websites Are Increasingly Adopting Facebook Login. Retrieved October 17, 2015, from http://www.adweek.com/socialtimes/major-websites-are-increasingly-adopting-facebook-login/301953

Pew Research. (2014). http://www.pewinternet.org/2015/01/09/social-media-update-2014/. Retrieved from December 29, 2017.

Romeri, M. (2014, February 18). New Social Media Statistics You Need to Know. Retrieved October 17, 2015, from http://www.socialmediatoday.com/content/new-social-media-statistics-you-need-know

Statista. (2015). Facebook: Monthly Active Users 2015. Retrieved October 19, 2015, from http://www.statista.com/statistics/264810/number-of-monthly-active-facebook-users-worldwide/

Sarkar, S. (2013, January 4). FarmVille 2 Has 40 Million Monthly Active Users, Amid Other Staggering Numbers. Retrieved October 17, 2015, from http://www.polygon.com/2013/1/4/3837236/farmville-2-infographic-40-million-monthly-active-users

Sheth, J., & Parvatiyar, A. (1995). The Evolution of Relationship Marketing. *International Business Review, 4*(4), 397–418. https://doi.org/10.1016/0969-5931(95)00018-6

Sheth, J., & Solomon, M. (2014). Extending the Extended Self in a Digital World. *Journal of Marketing Theory and Practice, 22*(2), 123–132. https://doi.org/10.2753/MTP1069-6679220201

Stelzner, M. (2014, May 1). 2014 Social Media Marketing Report. Retrieved October 17, 2015, from http://www.socialmediaexaminer.com/SocialMediaMarketingIndustryReport2014.pdf

Twitter Usage: Company Facts. (2015, July 1). Retrieved October 19, 2015, from https://about.twitter.com/company

Wilhelm, H., Vohs, K., & Baumeister, R. (2012). What People Desire, Feel Conflicted About, and Try to Resist in Everyday Life. *Psychological Science, 23*(6), 582–588. https://doi.org/10.1177/0956797612437426

CHAPTER 2

# Social Media Marketing: Evolution and Change

*Shweta Sharma and H. V. Verma*

## Background of the Study

Historically, communication has facilitated the relationship between sellers and buyers, with sellers using words, signs and symbols for drawing the attention of potential customers to their products and persuading them to buy them. While the underlying goals of marketing communications—differentiate, remind, inform, and persuade (Fill, 1999)—remain unchanged, the nature of marketing communications has changed with the development of new media systems, ever-growing in scope and complexity. Web 2.0 technologies, specifically the social media, have added the element of real-time interactivity, removing the traditional restrictions of time and geography.

The most significant consequence of social media has been the *shift of power* from the institution to the individual. Social media gave users a voice, an open platform where they could connect, collaborate and co-create content for themselves and others. This user-generated content is perceived to be more trustworthy and has been found to be a bigger influence on consumer behavior and purchase decisions.

S. Sharma (✉)
NITI Ayog, New Delhi, India

H. V. Verma
University of Delhi, New Delhi, India



G. Heggde, G. Shainesh (eds.), *Social Media Marketing*,
https://doi.org/10.1007/978-981-10-5323-8_2

These shifts in the consumer-brand relationship have thrown up new challenges and opportunities for marketers. Marketers are in a precarious position, where both the offline and online brand-consumer interactions can have immediate, global ramifications due to the viral propagation of information on social media. Nonetheless, social media offers an invaluable opportunity to build sustainable bonds with consumers and to create and facilitate brand advocacy by encouraging positive conversations about the brand among consumers. Thus, these consumer conversations have necessitated reshaping the content of marketing messages and the way they are distributed (Landry, Ude, & Vollmer, 2007).

## Purpose

The prolific success of social media platforms (SMPs) such as Facebook, Orkut, MySpace and Twitter caught the attention of researchers and business practitioners globally. Marketers started looking at social media as a new avenue to create profitable relationships with consumers. Researchers suggest that the online environment can provide brands with structural asset, scale and process advantages in terms of a proactive devoted customer base, online consumer data and new campaign concepts (Edelman, 2007). Recently, brands have started allocating a significant portion of their marketing budgets to social media marketing (SMM).

Despite the exponential growth of SMM, certain issues remain unresolved. Marketers are still unsure of how to measure the impact of their social media strategy and its contribution to the bottom line, and how to use social media to build and sustain value-creating relationships with their customers (Kumar, Hsiao, & Chiu, 2009). Furthermore, social media research is still in its nascent stage and yet to evolve as a separate marketing sub-discipline.

With this thought, we systematically review prior research to discern a coherent pattern in the extant social media literature and present a holistic view of the insights derived. We chart the evolution of social media research and attempt to identify the underlying themes from the communication perspective. Further, we propose a model with an integrated perspective on communication through traditional and social media. We seek to identify the gaps present in the extant literature with the objective of providing structure and direction for future research.

## Methodology

The study involves a systematic analysis of the prior academic research in the area of social media marketing. Fifty-three research papers focusing on social media specifically in the marketing domain were selected. These papers were published between 2001 and 2013 in twenty-eight academic journals and thirteen conference proceedings. Out of the fifty-three papers, eleven were published between 2001 and 2006 while the remaining forty-two (81 percent) were published after 2007 in eminent journals such as *Journal of Advertising Research, Journal of Interactive Marketing* and *Marketing Research*. One-third of the research papers focused on social media in general. Among the SMPs, social networking sites (SNS) were the most researched, followed closely by blogs and consumer opinion platforms. Through a chronological and platform-wise analysis, we uncover six underlying themes. We examine each theme and identify the gaps present in research. This analysis creates a background for investigation of certain crucial unanswered questions pertaining to the role of social media in marketing communications.

## Findings

### *Defining Social Media*

Researchers have yet to arrive at a consensus on what constitute social media, with the definitions centered on three key elements: content, communities and Web 2.0 (Ahlqvist, Bäck, Heinonen, & Halonen, 2010). Parr (2008) highlights the efficiency of message distribution and defines social media as "the use of electronic and Internet tools for the purpose of sharing and discussing information and experiences with other human beings in more efficient ways," while Lewis (2010) adds the cocreation aspect and defines social media as "the current label for digital technologies that allow people to connect, interact, produce and share content." The oft-cited definition by Kaplan and Haenlein (2010) takes social media to be "a group of Internet-based applications that build on the ideological and technological foundations of Web 2.0 and that allow the creation and exchange of user generated content." For the purpose of this study, we use the term *social media* to refer to the online media, enabled by Web 2.0 technologies that allow multidirectional conversations and real-time interactions, and encompass a gamut of platforms such as SNS, blogs, discussions forums, video sharing, content sharing, social bookmarks, podcasts and wikis. The defining characteristic of social media is the user-created personal profile page through which users connect with friends, family, acquaintances or make new connections to share information, news and experiences.

### *Relevance of Social Media in Marketing*

Spurred by the exigencies of enhancing marketing efficiency, increasing market diversity and application of technology, the strategic focus for marketing has moved from being product-centric and segment-centric to being customer-centric and relationship driven (Sheth, Sisodia, & Sharma, 2000). This new relationship-based marketing paradigm requires marketers and academicians to think beyond the elements of the traditional marketing mix and consider the inclusion of interactive elements in their strategy (Grönroos, 1997).

Social media marketing (SMM) has been widely used to refer to the use of online SMPs for the purpose of marketing. Akar and Topcu (2011) have defined SMM as the "use of social media channels to promote a company and its products." This is similar to the definition proposed by Drury (2008) where SMM is the "usage of the existing social media platforms for increasing the brand awareness among consumers on online platforms through utilization of the WOM principles." While these definitions of SMM converge on the "promotional" aspect, they ignore the relational aspect of conversing with consumers on social media and the benefits accrued thereof.

SMM can provide several advantages to companies. In addition to enabling a free exchange of ideas and information among consumers, SMPs allow them to engage in a two-way communication with brands. This helps in reducing consumer prejudice toward brands, thereby enhancing the brand value (Kim & Ko, 2012). By participating actively in online conversations, companies can provide direction and enrich the conversation experience, making the content more meaningful and focused. This allows companies to involve their consumers more closely with brands through collaboration for marketing campaigns, and so on.

In his book *Join the Conversation*, Jaffe (2007, p. 22) highlights the significance of social media as a point of access to "a series of endlessly rich, dynamic, gratifying, robust, authentic and meaningful conversations going out there." Unlike traditional market research techniques, social media offers a real-time glimpse into the consumer mind by listening to consumer conversations as well as an opportunity for the consumer to provide real-time feedback (Chen, Ching, Tsai, & Kuo, 2008). Thus marketers can make changes to their marketing mix, products, services and so on, based on what is working "now" (Edelman, 2007). Precourt (2010) stresses the importance of listening, which can contribute to brand strategy and tactics, help assess competitor risk and deal with public issues, thereby increasing marketing effectiveness.

Traditional targeting techniques do not take into account the influence that the members of a segment have on the purchase decisions of others. This is largely due to the difficulty in accessing the source of interactions that shape and propagate such influence (Richardson & Domingos, 2002). Since communities are at the heart of social media, new improved techniques for targeting and segmentation can be developed from insights drawn from social media. Landry et al. (2007) observed that the age-based segmentation of a "generation" can be reduced to a shorter and more relevant period of three years by observing the social media behavior of different age groups.

To utilize SMPs as effective marketing tools, it is necessary to understand how individuals and user communities use online social interactions for different purposes (Domingos, 2005; Landry et al., 2007) and the perceptions of different SMPs (Chen et al., 2008). It is important for marketers to therefore note that each new social media has built on its predecessors and evolved in an attempt to meet a very specific purpose. The various types of SMPs are classified on the basis of their primary purpose as given in Table 2.1.

### *Understanding Marketing Communication on Social Media*

Kim and Ko (2012) found that communication by brands on social media positively affected brand equity and relationship equity. Value equity was improved by providing novel value to consumers and an opportunity to have two-way communication with brands, while customer equity was improved by strengthening customer relationships and positively affecting purchase intent. Nevertheless, Bezjian-Avery, Calder, and Iacobucci (1998) argued that interactive media may not be necessarily superior to traditional media in all scenarios. Calder and Malthouse (2008) also suggested that advertising could be more effective when ads are experientially congruent with the media vehicle.

**Table 2.1** Typology of social media platforms

| *SMP* | *Definition* | *Primary purpose* | *Characteristics* |
|---|---|---|---|
| Social networking sites e.g., Facebook, LinkedIn | Web-based services that allow individuals to: (1) construct a public or semi-public profile within a bounded system; (2) articulate a list of other users with whom they share a connection; and (3) view and traverse their list of connections and those made by others within the system (Boyd & Ellison, 2007) | Connecting with friends, family and acquaintances | • User profile<br>• Connects with people who share some form of offline tie<br>• Egocentric<br>• Newsfeed |
| Blogs e.g., blogger, Wordpress, Technorati | Personal journals on the Internet arranged in reverse chronological order that facilitate interactive computer-mediated communication through text, images, and audio/video objects (Huang, Shen, Lin, & Chang, 2007) | Producing digital content with the intention of sharing it asynchronously with a conceptualized audience (Boyd, 2006) | • Extension of the blogger in the digital world<br>• Smaller dedicated group of users<br>• Linking |
| Microblogs e.g., Twitter | Micro-blogs are online social networks where the updates or content are limited by characters | Daily chatter, sharing information or URLs and reporting news (Java, Song, Finin, & Tseng, 2007) | • Character limit<br>• Hashtags<br>• Faster, more frequent updates<br>• Trends |
| Consumer opinion platforms e.g., Zomato, Tripadvisor | Virtual communities where users can post questions and comment on others' posts related to common subjects or interests | Share experiences, knowledge, advice, ratings and reviews with other users on a common topic | • "Explicit form of trust," expressed through rating of user reviews<br>• Availability of positive and negative opinions |
| Social bookmarking sites e.g., Digg | Sites that allow users to tag online content | Classify and highlight content for personal and others' consumption | • Users can read, share and promote content |

(*continued*)

**Table 2.1** (continued)

| *SMP* | *Definition* | *Primary purpose* | *Characteristics* |
|---|---|---|---|
| Content sharing platforms e.g., Flickr, YouTube | Sites that allow users to share videos, presentations, documents, audio, pictures and other media with other users | Share content such as videos, documents, audio and photos | |
| Collaboration platforms e.g., Wikipedia | Sites that allow users to coordinate their efforts toward a common goal or task | Coordinate efforts toward a common goal or task | • Crowd-sourcing |

An investigation conducted by Stephen and Galak (2009) revealed that both traditional media and social media contribute value to the marketing performance in different manners and are significantly influenced by each other. While the per-event impact of traditional media was found to be greater than that of social media, SMPs contributed significantly as "information brokers," continuously propagating information, connecting different channels, creating awareness and maintaining interest.

We propose a model offering an integrated perspective on the flows of communication through social media and traditional channels as given in Fig. 2.1.

The proposed model takes into account these multidirectional, interactive conversations from brand to consumer, and consumer to consumer. As can be seen from Fig. 2.1, social media is a channel for both consumer-generated and brand-generated messages as posited by Mangold and Faulds (2009). More importantly, the above model assimilates listening as an important aspect of the communication loop. A brand can communicate with the consumer directly through traditional media and multiple platforms on social media or indirectly through offline conversation and online interactions with other consumers. The company can use its website as a hub for its social media activities or it can connect with consumers on third-party SMPs such as Facebook and Twitter. Consumers can directly access the brand website, visit the brand page on Facebook, follow the brand on Twitter or can come across the information on a friend's social media page or a friend can share the content with them. On the Facebook page, consumers can "like" the company's page to get the latest updates and discounts. They might also share this information with others in their circle.

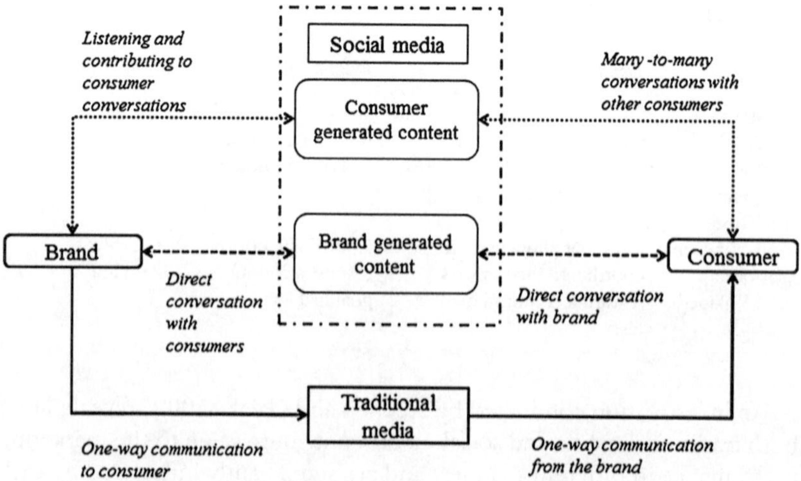


**Fig. 2.1** Communication model for marketing through social media

## *Underlying Themes in Social Media Research*

Six major themes emerge from the analysis of past social media literature (Table 2.2). These are: analysis of a specific SMP to understand its characteristics, understanding the social media users, investigating the relationship between an SMP and its users, examining the brand-consumer relationship via SMP, investigating the inter-consumer relationship on SMP and evaluating SMP as a marketing tool.

Chronological analysis of the various themes further uncovers distinct phases of the evolution of social media research. These phases are however, not mutually exclusive and tend to overlap with each other. The earlier works were primarily focused on analyzing the underlying network structure of different SNS and mining data to explore the potential for application in various fields such as viral marketing.

The second phase involved the investigation of user behavior on SMPs and their segmentation on various parameters such as usage and online activity. This was followed by exploring the relationship between the SMPs and their users and understanding user motivation for participation online. With the proliferation of social media platforms, electronic word of mouth (eWOM) became the key focus of social media research. The significant research questions included how and why consumers share product information online, what are the antecedents to online influence and how

**Table 2.2** Themes in social media research

| *Themes* | *Key focus* | *Key works* |
|---|---|---|
| SMP analysis | Definition; underlying structure; network analysis; information propagation | Domingos and Richardson (2001); Richardson and Domingos (2002); Adamic and Adar (2003); Mori, Sugiyama, and Matsuo (2005); Boyd (2006); Boyd and Ellison (2007) |
| SMP-consumer relationship | Community identification; interpersonal trust; two-way communication; message exchange; perceived community pressure; influence; information quality; system quality | Chen et al. (2008); Shen and Chiou (2009); Rui and Yongsheng(2010);. Wang and Lin (2011) |
| Brand-consumer relationship via SMP | Impact of type of SMP; source credibility; product placement; impact of channel characteristics; satisfaction; commitment; attitude toward SMM; consumer engagement; brand equity | Bickart and Schindler (2001); Cha (2009); Jansen, Zhang, Sobel, and Chowdury (2009); Hsu, Liu, and Lee (2010); Akar and Topcu (2011); Gummerus, Liljander, Weman, and Pihlström (2012); Kim and Ko (2012); Brodie, Ilic, Juric, and Hollebeek (2013); Cvijikj and Michahelles (2013) |
| Consumer-consumer relationship via SMP | Motivation for eWOM; impact of negative eWOM; social influence; value of eWOM; tie strength; homophily; trust | Hennig-Thurau, Gwinner, Walsh, and Gremler (2004); Hung and Li (2007); Smith, Coyle, Lightfoot, and Scott (2007); Lee, Park, and Han (2008); Ermecke, Mayrhofer, and Wagner (2009); Iyengar, Han, and Gupta (2009); Karakaya and Barnes (2010); Phulari et al. (2010); Chu and Kim (2011) |
| SMP user analysis | Motivation for SMP participation; behavior on SMP | Matsuo, Tomobe, Hasida, and Ishizuka (2004); Nardi, Schiano, Gumbrecht, and Swartz (2004); Domingos (2005); Huang et al. (2007); Java et al. (2007); Lerman (2007); Li (2007); Riegner (2007); Bernoff and Anderson (2010) |
| SMP as marketing tool | Impact of media activity on marketing outcomes | Edelman (2007); Jaffe (2007); Landry et al. (2007); Kumar et al. (2009); Mangold and Faulds (2009); Stephen and Galak (2009); Jayanti (2010); Kumar and Bhagwat (2010) |

the online conversations affect consumer attitude and purchase behavior. This phase also involved researchers recognizing the potential of social media as a marketing tool which could boost or dampen the relationship between brand and consumer. Since 2006, considerable work in this area has been presented regarding application of social media in every scope of business. Recent research efforts have been directed toward social media metrics to measure quantitative returns from social media metrics.

Nearly all six themes cover the various aspects of SMM using social networking sites. Researchers have extensively investigated the social media usage of consumers and have proposed various bases for segmentation. Blogs have been the key area for researchers examining the relationship between the consumer and social media platforms and between the consumer and brands. Authors have investigated user motivation for blogging and preferences for using certain blogging platforms. Works related to application of social media are qualitative and discuss most SMPs, looking at how different SMPs can be utilized as a part of the marketers' tool kit.

Virtual communities have been around since the inception of the web, but it is only in the last decade that research in the field, from the marketing perspective, has gained popularity and momentum. Also referred to as knowledge sharing sites (Domingos, 2005; Richardson & Domingos, 2002), or forums (Hung & Li, 2007), consumer opinion platforms are one of the earliest forms of social media to capture the interest of researchers, The work by Bickart and Schindler (2001) was one of the earliest attempts to empirically gauge the impact of online conversations on consumer behavior. Some of the dimensions that were the focus of the earlier works include customer's network value (Domingos & Richardson, 2001), social trust (Matsuo et al., 2004) and social connections (Adamic & Adar, 2003; Mori et al., 2005). With the surge in popularity of MySpace and Facebook, researchers directed their attention toward SNS, focusing on impression management and friendship performance, networks and network structure, online/offline connections, and privacy issues (Boyd & Ellison, 2007).

## Discussion

Marketers clearly need to master social media tools for creating a deeper connection with the consumer. To this end, researchers have explored different facets and attempted to answer questions such as

- Why should companies include social media in their marketing strategy? (Jaffe, 2007; Jayanti, 2010; Landry et al., 2007; Macnamara, 2010)
- How can companies include social media in their marketing strategy? (Edelman, 2007; Jaffe, 2007; Kumar et al., 2009; Precourt, 2010)
- Who are the consumers using social media? (Bernoff & Anderson, 2010; Li, 2007)
- What are the social media being used by the consumers? (Jaffe, 2007)
- What are the motivations of consumers for using social media? (Lerman, 2007)
- What are the implications of social media on eWOM? (Hung & Li, 2007; Smith et al., 2007)

Despite these efforts, the extant social media literature is fragmented and inconclusive regarding the role of social media in consumer behavior. Through our literature review, we identify research areas that, if investigated, can help answer these questions and substantiate the impact of communication through social media and consumer behavior.

### *Consumer Engagement on Social Media*

Researchers have explored the relationship between different dimensions of online communications, eWOM, and consumer behavior. However, most of the research has focused on the consumer-consumer relationship rather than the brand-consumer relationship. In this context, different authors have suggested expanding the number of variables to include factors such as empathy, relevance, credibility (Bickart & Schindler, 2001); SNS features (Cha, 2009); perceived enjoyment, satisfaction, privacy and involvement (Shen & Chiou, 2009); and demographic factors (Karakaya & Barnes, 2010). Despite its ubiquity in social media literature, the conceptualization and applicability of consumer engagement in the online consumer-brand relationship has been largely overlooked. This could possibly be because of the difficulty in conceptualizing this construct in the consumer-brand relationship in general. In the last decade, consumer engagement has become a strategic priority for research (Brodie, Hollebeek, Juric, & Ilic, 2011; Cvijikj & Michahelles, 2013). Researchers such as Calder, Malthouse, and Schaedel (2009), Mollen and Wilson (2010), and Parent, Plangger, and Bal (2011), have attempted to provide a definition for consumer engagement in online settings and specifically in the context of social media but further convergence is required in conceptualizing consumer engagement on SMPs and its role in the consumer-brand relationship. Considering that specific consumer-brand interactive experiences result in different consumer engagement levels dependent on the context, we propose investigating consumer engagement as separate construct in social media research.

There is scarce empirical support for the claims of effectiveness of social media in the marketing context (Huang et al., 2007; Macnamara, 2010). The problem is accentuated by the absence of clear and standardized metrics to measure communication effectiveness through social media (Jaffe, 2007; Landry et al., 2007). Previous works assert the positive consequences of consumer engagement such as enhancing customer satisfaction, loyalty, increasing repurchase intentions and decreasing negative word of mouth (Gummerus et al., 2012), but questions related to the role of consumer engagement on social media in building consumer-brand relationships and influencing the purchase likelihood of the brand remain unanswered. Multiple studies (Akar & Topcu, 2011; Iyengar et al., 2009; Stephen & Galak, 2009) have explored the linkage between social media activity and consumer behavior, but these studies did not consider consumer engagement as a *separate dimension*. Even the traditional response hierarchy models that explain passive communication fail to take active consumer engagement into consideration. Bowden (2009) posits engagement as a distinct entity within the broader engagement process, which is different from other relational constructs such as involvement, commitment, loyalty, and participation, as it takes into account interactive consumer experiences in a comprehensive manner. Calder et al. (2009) argue that most works seem to confuse engagement with the outcomes of engagement, due to the unclear meaning of engagement. Brodie et al. (2011) further state that "involvement" and "participation" are antecedents to consumer engagement. However, given the iterative nature of the engagement process, they need not be strictly antecedents and can coexist or even be engagement consequences. In light of the ambiguity in the academic literature, we suggest future research into consumer engagement on social media, its antecedents and outcomes.

### *Consumer Preferences and Perceptions of Different Social Media Platforms*

Do consumers differentiate in their perception of the various SMPs? If yes, what are the underlying attributes of these differences? Interestingly, the findings of Akar and Topcu (2011) suggest that consumers with higher frequency usage of Facebook and YouTube have a positive influence on the attitude toward marketing with social media. This could indicate that the choice of social media websites is an influencing factor in social media marketing. While it is evident from the typology (Table 2.1) developed earlier that SMPs have different characteristics, the distinguishing attributes from the consumer viewpoint are yet to be researched. By understanding the similarities and dissimilarities between SMPs, researchers can develop insights into the unique positioning of each SMP, which could lead to a targeted and effective SMM strategy design. Therefore, we propose examining the existing SMPs to assess their impact on consumer buying decisions.

### *Profile of Consumers Engaging with Brands on Social Media*

From the literature review, it is evident that many researchers have attempted to categorize Internet users according to different characteristics, such as their purchase behavior (Iyengar et al., 2009; Riegner, 2007) or social media usage (Bernoff & Anderson, 2010; Java et al., 2007; Li, 2007). However, most of the categorization is limited in scope to specific platforms such as microblogging (Java et al., 2007) or social networking (Iyengar et al., 2009). It is important to understand the characteristics of the social media users who are willing to connect and interact with brands on social media platforms. Marketers are still unable to identify the influencers in social networks and online communities (Riegner, 2007; Smith et al., 2007). Therefore, the exploration of social media users must be extended to identifying the social media users who are interacting with brands and companies on social media. Finally, there is also the need to understand the user profile and social media usage patterns of users, especially outside the USA and Europe (Boyd & Ellison, 2007; Macnamara, 2010). There are hardly any studies analyzing and categorizing Indian social media users.

## Concluding Remarks

This study was guided by the need for a holistic view of SMM from the communication perspective. It provides a systematic analysis of the current academic literature on social media and successfully identifies the underlying themes in the existing research. With the retrospective analysis concluded, this study identifies three key research areas that will allow future research to proceed with a firmer footing. The research highlights the potential of using social media for building a brand-consumer relationship and leveraging both online and offline interactions to influence consumer behavior. The research highlights the importance of understanding the profile of social media consumers and their online behavior patterns. The study also suggests evaluating consumer engagement as a key factor in increasing the effectiveness of marketing communication through social media.

## References

Adamic, L. A., & Adar, E. (2003). Friends and Neighbors on the Web. *Social Networks, 25*, 211–230.

Ahlqvist, T., Bäck, A., Heinonen, S., & Halonen, M. (2010). Road-Mapping the Societal Transformation Potential of Social Media. *Foresight, 12*(5), 3–26.

Akar, E., & Topcu, B. (2011). An Examination of the Factors Influencing Consumers' Attitudes Toward Social Media Marketing. *Journal of Internet Commerce, 10*, 35–67.

Bernoff, J., & Anderson, J. (2010). *Social Technographic Redefined*. Retrieved March 6, 2011, from http://www.forrester.com/empowered/ladder2010

Bezjian-Avery, A., Calder, B., & Iacobucci, D. (1998). New Media Interactive Advertising vs. Traditional Advertising. *Journal of Advertising Research, 38*, 23–32.

Bickart, B., & Schindler, R. M. (2001). Internet Forums as Influential Sources of Information. *Journal of Interactive Marketing, 15*(3), 31–40.

Bowden, J. L. H. (2009). The Process of Customer Engagement: A Conceptual Framework. *The Journal of Marketing Theory and Practice, 17*(1), 63–74.

Boyd, D. (2006). A Blogger's Blog: Exploring the Definition of a Medium. *Reconstruction, 6*(4). Retrieved from http://reconstruction.eserver.org/064/boyd.shtml

Boyd, D. M., & Ellison, N. B. (2007). Social Network Sites: Definition, History, and Scholarship. *Journal of Computer-Mediated Communication, 13*(1), 210–230.

Brodie, R. J., Hollebeek, L. D., Juric, B., & Ilic, A. (2011). Customer Engagement: Conceptual Domain, Fundamental Propositions, and Implications for Research. *Journal of Service Research, 14*(3), 252–271.

Brodie, R. J., Ilic, A., Juric, B., & Hollebeek, L. (2013). Consumer Engagement in a Virtual Brand Community: An Exploratory Analysis. *Journal of Business Research, 66*(1), 105–114.

Calder, B. J., & Malthouse, E. C. (2008). Media Engagement and Advertising Effectiveness. In B. J. Calder (Ed.), *Kellogg on Advertising and Media* (pp. 1–36). Hoboken, NJ: Wiley.

Calder, B. J., Malthouse, E. C., & Schaedel, U. (2009). An Experimental Study of the Relationship Between Online Engagement and Advertising Effectiveness. *Journal of Interactive Marketing, 23*, 321–331.

Cha, J. (2009). Shopping on Social Networking Web Sites: Attitudes Toward Real Versus Virtual Items. *Journal of Interactive Advertising, 10*(1), 77–93.

Chen, J. S., Ching, R., Tsai, H. T., & Kuo, Y. J. (2008). Blog Effects on Brand Attitude and Purchase Intention. In *2008 International Conference on Service Systems and Service Management*, pp. 1–6.

Chu, S. C., & Kim, Y. (2011). Determinants of Consumer Engagement in Electronic Word-of-Mouth (eWOM) in Social Networking Sites. *International Journal of Advertising, 30*(1), 47–75.

Cvijikj, I. P., & Michahelles, F. (2013). Online Engagement Factors on Facebook Brand Pages. *Social Network Analysis and Mining, 3*(4), 843–861.

Domingos, P. (2005). Mining Social Networks for Viral Marketing. *IEEE Intelligent Systems, 20*(1), 80–82.

Domingos, P., & Richardson, M. (2001). Mining the Network Value of Customers. In *Proceedings of the Seventh ACM SIGKDD International Conference on Knowledge Discovery and Data Mining in San Francisco, CA, USA*, pp. 57–66.

Drury, G. (2008). Opinion Piece: Social Media: Should Marketers Engage and How Can It Be Done Effectively? *Journal of Direct, Data and Digital Marketing Practice, 9*(3), 274–277.

Edelman, D. C. (2007). From the Periphery to the Core: As Online Strategy Becomes Overall Strategy, Marketing Organizations and Agencies Will Never Be the Same. *Journal of Advertising Research, 47*(2), 130–134.

Ermecke, R., Mayrhofer, P., & Wagner, S. (2009). Agents of Diffusion—Insights from a Survey of Facebook Users. In *HICSS'09, 42nd Hawaii International Conference on System Sciences, 2009*, IEEE, Big Island, HI, pp. 1–10.

Fill, C. (1999). *Marketing Communications:Contexts Contents and Strategies.* Prentice Hall Europe.

Grönroos, C. (1997). Keynote Paper: From Marketing Mix to Relationship Marketing-Towards a Paradigm Shift in Marketing. *Management Decision, 35*(4), 322–339.

Gummerus, J., Liljander, V., Weman, E., & Pihlström, M. (2012). Customer Engagement in a Facebook Brand Community. *Management Research Review, 35*(9), 857–877.

Hennig-Thurau, T., Gwinner, K. P., Walsh, G., & Gremler, D. D. (2004). Electronic Word-of-Mouth via Consumer-Opinion Platforms: What Motivates Consumers to Articulate Themselves on the Internet? *Journal of Interactive Marketing, 18*, 38–52.

Hsu, C. L., Liu, C. C., & Lee, Y. D. (2010). Effect of Commitment and Trust Towards Micro-Blogs on Consumer Behavioral Intention: A Relationship Marketing Perspective. *International Journal of Electronic Business Management, 8*(4), 292–303.

Huang, C. Y., Shen, Y. Z., Lin, H. X., & Chang, S. S. (2007). Bloggers' Motivations and Behaviors: A Model. *Journal of Advertising Research, 47*(4), 472–484.

Hung, K. H., & Li, S. Y. (2007, December). The Influence of eWOM on Virtual Consumer Communities: Social Capital, Consumer Learning, and Behavioral Outcomes. *Journal of Advertising Research, 47*(4), 485–495.

Iyengar, R., Han, S., & Gupta, S. (2009). *Do Friends Influence Purchases in a Social Network?* Working Paper, Harvard Business School. Retrieved from www.hbs.edu/research/pdf/09-123.pdf

Jaffe, J. (2007). *Join the Conversation*. Hoboken, NJ: John Wiley and Sons.

Jansen, B. J., Zhang, M., Sobel, K., & Chowdury, A. (2009). Twitter Power: Tweets as Electronic Word of Mouth. *Journal of the American Society for Information Science and Technology, 60*(11), 2169–2188.

Java, A., Song, X., Finin, T., & Tseng, B. (2007). Why We Twitter: Understanding Microblogging Usage and Communities. In *Proceedings of the 9th WebKDD and 1st SNA-KDD 2007 Workshop on Web Mining and Social Network Analysis*, New York, NY, USA, ACM, pp. 56–65.

Jayanti, R. K. (2010). A Netnographic Exploration: Listening to Online Consumer Conversations. *Journal of Advertising Research, 50*(2), 181–196.

Kaplan, A. M., & Haenlein, M. (2010). Users of the World, Unite! The Challenges and Opportunities of Social Media. *Business Horizons, 53*(1), 59–68.

Karakaya, F., & Barnes, N. G. (2010). Impact of Online Reviews of Customer Care Experience on Brand or Company Selection. *Journal of Consumer Marketing, 27*(5), 447–457.

Kim, A. J., & Ko, E. (2012). Do Social Media Marketing Activities Enhance Customer Equity? An Empirical Study of Luxury Fashion Brand. *Journal of Business Research, 65*(10), 1480–1486.

Kumar, P., Hsiao, M., & Chiu, B. (2009). Generations of Consumers and the Consumer Generated. *Journal of Integrated Marketing Communication*, 20–26.

Kumar, V., & Bhagwat, Y. (2010, Summer). Listen to the Customer. *Marketing Research, 22*(2), 14–19.

Landry, E., Ude, C., & Vollmer, C. (2007). HD Marketing 2010: Sharpening the Conversation. Retrieved January 9, 2011, from http://www.booz.com/global/home/what_we_think/reports_and_white_papers/ic-display/41901826

Lee, J., Park, D. H., & Han, I. (2008). The Effect of Negative Online Consumer Reviews on Product Attitude: An Information Processing View. *Electronic Commerce Research and Applications, 7*(3), 341–352.

Lerman, K. (2007). User Participation in Social Media: Digg Study. In *Proceedings of the WI-IAT Workshop on Social Media Analysis (SMA07)*, Silicon Valley, CA, IEEE Computer Society Conference Publishing Services, pp. 255–258.

Lewis, B. K. (2010). Social Media and Strategic Communication: Attitudes and Perceptions Among College Students. *Public Relations Journal, 4*(3), 1–23.

Li, C. (2007). *Social Technographics.* Retrieved September 8, 2010, from http://www.forrester.com/rb/Research/social_technographics%C2%AE/q/id/42057/t/2

Macnamara, J. (2010). Public Communication Practices in the Web 2.0–3.0 Mediascape: The Case for PRevolution. *PRism, 7*(3), 1–13.

Mangold, W. G., & Faulds, D. J. (2009). Social Media: The New Hybrid Element of the Promotion Mix. *Business Horizons, 52*, 357–365.

Matsuo, Y., Tomobe, H., Hasida, K., & Ishizuka, M. (2004). Finding Social Network for Trust Calculation. In *Proceedings of the 16th European Conference on Artificial Intelligence (ECAI2004)*, pp. 510–514.

Mollen, A., & Wilson, H. (2010). Engagement, Telepresence and Interactivity in Online Consumer Experience: Reconciling Scholastic and Managerial Perspectives. *Journal of Business Research, 63*(9), 919–925.

Mori, J., Sugiyama, T., & Matsuo, Y. (2005). Real-World Oriented Information Sharing Using Social Networks. In *Proceedings of the 2005 International ACM SIGGROUP Conference on Supporting Group Work.* New York, pp. 81–84.

Nardi, B. A., Schiano, D. J., Gumbrecht, M., & Swartz, L. (2004). Why We Blog. *Communications of the ACM, 47*(12), 41–46.

Parent, M., Plangger, K., & Bal, A. (2011). The New WTP: Willingness to Participate. *Business Horizons, 54*, 219–229.

Parr, B. (2008). *It's Time We Defined Social Media. No More Arguing. Here's the Definition.* Retrieved from http://benparr.com/2008/08/its-time-we-defined-social-media-no-more-arguing-heres-the-definition/

Phulari, S. S., Khamitkar, S. D., Deshmukh, N. K., Bhalchandra, P. U., Lokhande, S. N., & Shinde, A. R. (2010, January). Understanding Formulation of Social Capital in Online Social Network Sites (SNS). *IJCSI International Journal of Computer Science Issues, 7*(1), 92–96.

Precourt, G. (2010). Editorial: Is Anybody Listening? *Journal of Advertising Research, 50*(1), 3–4.

Richardson, M., & Domingos, P. (2002). Mining Knowledge-Sharing Sites for Viral Marketing. In *Proceedings of the Eighth ACM SIGKDD International Conference on Knowledge Discovery and Data Mining in Edmonton, Alberta, Canada*, ACM, New York, USA, pp. 61–70.

Riegner, C. (2007). Word of Mouth on the Web: The Impact of Web 2.0 on Consumer Purchase Decisions. *Journal of Advertising Research, 47*(4), 436–447.

Rui, W., & Yongsheng, J. (2010). An Empirical Study on the Relationship Between the Followers' Number and Influence of Microblogging. In *2010 International Conference on E-Business and E-Government (ICEE) in Guangzhou*, pp. 2014–2017.

Shen, C. C., & Chiou, J. S. (2009). The Effect of Community Identification on Attitude and Intention Toward a Blogging Community. *Internet Research, 19*(4), 393–407.

Sheth, J. N., Sisodia, R. S., & Sharma, A. (2000). The Antecedents and Consequences of Customer-Centric Marketing. *Journal of the Academy of Marketing Science, 28*(1), 55–66.

Smith, T., Coyle, J. R., Lightfoot, E., & Scott, A. (2007). Reconsidering Models of Influence: The Relationship Between Consumer Social Networks and Word-of-Mouth Effectiveness. *Journal of Advertising Research, 47*(4), 387–397.

Stephen, A. T., & Galak, J. (2009). The Complementary Roles of Traditional and Social Media in Driving Marketing Performance. *Insead Working Papers Collection*, pp. 1–38.

Wang, S. M., & Lin, J. C. C. (2011). The Effect of Social Influence on Bloggers' Usage Intention. *Online Information Review, 35*(1), 50–65.

CHAPTER 3

# Uniqueness of *Social* in the Overall SMAC Stack

*Easwar Krishna Iyer*

## Introduction

Data has been anointed as the oil of the new millennium. Literature has gone to the extent of elevating data to the status of a fourth factor of modern production after land, labor and capital. Starting from sourcing and ending with storage, the new-age data follows a complex path, a journey that often starts from the amorphous wisdom of the crowd of social media and ends in the nebulous cloud of computing space. Digitization of the world, miniaturization of technology, rapid fall in hardware pricing due to economies of scale production, availability of free space in the cloud for data storage, tendency to create personal space information and uploading the same, and computing machines' rapid advancement in processing intelligence—all these have contributed to the explosion of data. The humongous scaling up of data can be summed up in a single epochal observation: "The smart phones of today have more computing power and storage space than all of what NASA had, when they put man on the moon in 1969" (Frank, 2012).

Some of the largest generators and aggregators of data did not exist a decade back (Iyer et al., 2013). The digital encyclopedia *Wikipedia* was launched at the turn of the millennium in 2001. Netflix, America's largest

E. K. Iyer (✉)
Great Lakes Institute of Management, Chennai, Tamil Nadu, India



G. Heggde, G. Shainesh (eds.), *Social Media Marketing*,
https://doi.org/10.1007/978-981-10-5323-8_3

on-demand Internet streaming media provider, scaled up its operations by coming out with an IPO in 2002. Today it is estimated that the streaming volume of Netflix constitutes about one quarter of the total Internet traffic of the USA. LinkedIn, the business-oriented social networking service was launched in 2003. Today it has a quarter billion user profiles and is the most visited professional networking site. Facebook was launched in 2004. This world's largest (to date) online social media network has in its digital embrace over a billion netizens who indulge in pastimes ranging from sharing to discussing to locating to networking to gaming. Tweets were born, thanks to Twitter, in 2006. Sometimes described as the SMS of Internet, this microblogging service creates small personalized information bursts that are inconsequential at the individual tweet level but insightful at the aggregate level. The first version of iPhone was launched in 2007. iPad hit the market in 2010. Apple, along with the Canadian telecom giant, Blackberry, unleashed the smartphone wave into the market only a few years back. Today, in developed markets, the number of "intelligent" mobile devices exceeds the number of people. The same phenomena would soon be a reality in emerging markets. With this disruptive innovation, data which has hitherto been static and deskbound has suddenly become dynamic and mobile. Meanwhile, cloud computing, as a technology, topped the Gartner hype cycle in 2009. Diverse players such as Amazon, Microsoft, Google, and IBM have helped the cloud to emerge as a substitution offering enabling enterprises to switch from buying computers to buying computing. Each of these players brings a completely different value proposition to the cloud table. With all this new-wave convergence, data has morphed from its original structured form to an amorphous unstructured form. The data collected from such multiple social sources is high in volume, velocity, and variety, yet low in veracity. Unearthing business sense from this data is the prime objective of SMAC.

## What Is the SMAC Stack?

Before looking at SMAC as a stack, let us look at each of the four technology platforms individually. Social, mobile, analytics, and cloud—at an individual stand-alone level—themselves represent a convergence of multiple technologies. The content-context-connection-community framework of social media has been built on the technology pillars of data warehousing, ranking algorithm, search engine optimization, distributed memory caching, map-reduce techniques, and horizontal/vertical scalability for both computation and storage. In a similar vein, the core technologies of pagers, telephones, modems, computers, cameras, music systems, and GPS systems have combined to offer the modern smartphones and tablets. Mixing data with text and moving from static to real-time analysis are two key technology integration steps in the field of analytics. Similarly, cloud offering is a seamless integration of technologies such as virtualization, multitenancy, utilization, idle-time management, dynamic provisioning, and scaling. Each of these four technology platforms can be deployed as a stand-alone and each of them have played a significant role in reshaping the way we run our businesses. Social has changed the way we connect to customers and understand their buying behavior; mobile has enabled the availability of anytime anywhere data; analytics has improved the speed of our decision making, and cloud has eliminated upfront capital investments and converted fixed costs to variable costs in the realm of IT. But the convergence of these technologies has virtualized processes and dematerialized value chains. Let us take a closer look at SMAC through examples.

Take the case of retail industry. Even before stepping into a given store, the customer has gained from social media sites a feel for the available merchandise and its relative pricing. In fact, price comparison is one of the top reasons why online consumers discuss a product, service, company, or brand on social networking sites. The moment the customer steps in, cameras will identify him as a regular shopper and the system will start streaming buying tips to him via his smartphone. The tips, bundling offers, category location, and the like can be customized on a shopper-to-shopper basis, based on CRM analytics of previous buyer behavior. The whole database, application and analytics are architected in a public or private cloud. Thus, a seamless integration of the SMAC variables ensures better customer loyalty and higher customer lifetime value for the retail industry. The best part of the whole game is that both these key performance indicators (KPIs) are measurable on a progressive basis after technology integration.

Another example could be a company such as Netflix (Udhas & Raman, 2013). It scours social media platforms to find out the general likes and dislikes of customers in terms of content. Then, it configures huge cloud server pools on Amazon to create and store the dynamic content. Netflix uses its cloud server farm to stream videos by day and to do data analytics by night. This dual usage of streaming and analytics ensures maximal resource utilization. Finally, the company streams live media to its customers across several devices, some of them being mobile-based devices. Netflix uses SMAC convergence to do microsegmentation to understand individual streaming requirements.

Not all solutions need to incorporate all of the four SMAC elements. Some solutions can be built around fewer elements. Wider data availability, faster data access, unchained business models, dematerialized value chains, knowledge-driven process management and decentralized decision making—these are some of the outcomes of the technology convergence provided by SMAC. It now needs to be seen how one of the four converging spaces—social—is unique and distinct from the remaining three spaces. A finer appreciation of this difference will help in architecting better-integrated solutions.

## Five Core Differences Between *Social* and the Remaining SMAC Stack

The paper now goes on to build the posited argument on how the social space is unique and distinct from the three remaining spaces—mobility, analytics, and cloud (MAC). The differences of the social space are built around five independent vectors, as shown in Table 3.1.

### *Built-In Human Element*

The key differentiator of the social space is that it has a built-in ***human element.*** Because of this human interface, subjective aspects such as sentiments, emotions, needs, and preferences tend to play a significant role in building the social factor. The other three platforms—mobility, analytics, and cloud—are rigor driven and objective in construct. Social focuses on

**Table 3.1** Five core differences of social space with respect to MAC space

| *Social* | *Mobility, analytics, cloud* |
|---|---|
| Built-in human element | No such consideration |
| Absence of a commercial vendor framework | Well defined vendor frameworks |
| Lack of investment intensity | Investment intensive |
| Exogenous elements drive scaling/growth | Endogenous elements drive scaling/growth |
| Data conditioning is key | Data processing is key |

the subtle. The remaining three focus more on the gross. Because of this, intuition and instinct are key considerations in the emerging social picture. Both these "softer" aspects are converted to rigorous mechanical intellect in the subsequent data supply chain. Let us look at an example.

Take the case of data sourced from a microblogging site such as Twitter. The primary content is textual and any measurement that can be done on that content will be driven by lexicon-based judgment. If key words are used for indicating relevance, then the same key word can be used by different tweeters in different contexts. This brings the context element and the associated sentiment element of the individual social media user into the data analysis scenario. Once this data is bound, using a set of criteria, then the gross counting/adding/comparing ways of looking at data is set in motion. The subtle is slowly replaced by the gross.

What normally happens in such a situation is that the steady state behavior of a given ecosystem is mapped and kept as a reference. The system then waits for any deviance from this steady state and as and when such a variance is observed, an intervention and monitoring is planned. The variance that is mapped will tend to be a quantitative one missing the finer aspects. The extract, transform, and load (ETL) frameworks that are used for creating structured data from amorphous inputs will ensure the elimination of the valuable intuitive element. To put it in simpler terms, the conventional row-column database is a suboptimal space for subtle and subjective information.

Whether social media has an intrinsic human angle or has been built in is arguable. Consider this scenario. Social media, in its essence, is a digital transaction devoid of any physical offline interaction. To personalize these transactions, the system has consciously introduced subtle relationship-focused elements that help to bind node-to-node affinity within a mass social network. To enable this one-on-one intimacy, the digital world has borrowed rapport-building terminologies from the real offline world. Friends on Facebook, followers on Twitter, and connections on LinkedIn are examples of tools used for building the natural bonding element into what could otherwise be a dry digital transaction (Kane et al., 2014). The offline terminologies are thus used as cues to modulate anonymous online behavior. It is this relationship nomenclature that augments the key human element in the social part of SMAC.

On a different level, these words indicate proximities (friend), interactions (connections), information directionality (follower), and the like. All these are human behavioral elements. Also, some networks are designed to be symmetric with both the connecting nodes reciprocating identically (Facebook, LinkedIn) while some others are structurally asymmetric (Twitter). This symmetric versus asymmetric structure has also been modeled on natural human behavior: friends tend to be reciprocal and symmetric; followers aren't. None of these human nuances (proximity, interaction, symmetry, flow) can be fully captured by the objective MAC framework. Summing up, it can be concluded that the frequency, depth, and intensity of human engagements remain in the social realm only. The degree of engagement tends to get lost or diluted in further stages of the SMAC stack.

### *Absence of a Commercial Vendor Network*

The second differentiator of the social space is its lack of a *commercial vendor framework*. The situation is not so for the remaining MAC train. In the context of mobility solutions, telecom operators, Internet service providers, payment gateways, telecom solution providers, mobile applications developers, and telecom hardware providers add up to create a vendor landscape that resembles a metamarket. Between these vendors, a slew of mobile solutions can be configured with segregations as diverse as transactional versus nontransactional, synchronous versus asynchronous, informational versus reporting versus interactive, and finally, consumer versus enterprise. As an example, a financial services application via mobile is transactional (money is transferred), synchronous (consumer and bank do the transaction simultaneously), interactive (both parties are involved in closing the transaction) and can be used for both consumers and enterprises. On the other hand, an advertisement delivered to a mobile phone, using a geofencing framework is nontransactional, asynchronous, informational, and, typically, consumer focused. In either of the two extremes, combinations of commercial vendors deliver the billable solution.

From descriptive to diagnostic to predictive to prescriptive, the analytics space is fully vendor driven. This division is based on the depth of analytics. On the width front, we have the market split across domains such as CRM analytics, financial analytics, web analytics and retail analytics. The last space in the MAC train—cloud—is defined by infrastructure providers such as Amazon, platform builders such as Microsoft, solution architects such as IBM, and finally, SaaS providers such as Salesforce.com. Between all of them, cloud represents a well-defined vendor market.

In the context of social, we have an absence of such a billable commercial vendor framework. Social media vendors are more in the social media monitoring space than in the social media offering space. This absence of billability changes the investment perspective of social, which is treated as the next difference.

### *Lack of Investment Intensity*

As a consequence of the lack of a commercial vendor framework, the third factor that differentiates social from the remaining three platforms is its lack of ***investment intensity***. Mobility, analytics and cloud are technology-intensive platforms. Hence, a higher investment in any of these areas will yield a better return. Scale, speed, effectiveness, and efficiency can be enhanced in these three technology platforms by an investment-intensive strategy. The decision to adopt these platforms is ROI driven.

Let's take a few examples demonstrating how high investment intensity will quickly improve the ROI from the MAC part of SMAC. A hosted Hadoop framework such as Amazon's Elastic Mapreduce (EMR) can help to quickly process large amounts of data across parallel servers. Similarly, to deal with unstructured data sources such as blogs, audio/video streaming, and tweets, one can reconfigure databases from the traditional regional database management system (RDBMS) platforms to nonstructured query language (NoSQL). Likewise, private or public cloud environments can be quickly configured, depending upon security requirements, for vast data computation and storage. Complex data visualization techniques can be employed for the graphical outputting of data. All these investment-centric returns will work only on the data processing MAC level.

Their turn from social takes more of behavioral nuances into account. Social media scaling can be achieved only by increasing customer touch points. A higher level of platonic engagement can be enabled by increasing exposure. But a higher exposure need not necessarily guarantee a higher hit rate in terms of garnering genuine touch points. Hence there is an element of wait and watch while engaging with the social media.

Another way of looking at it is that a web-based social media platform is not under the control of any company and it requires no investment, in a sense, to access and use it. Social media can be leveraged for an array of benefits without any ownership per se. Investments at the social stage can be made only at the social media monitoring level and not at the social media origin level. As an example, one can invest in Google AdWords, which is just a social media monitoring tool working on the pay-per-click basis. An investment in AdWords gives no control over either the volume or the velocity of actual clicks, which is the social behavior that needs to be monitored.

Summing up, the social space lacks investment intensity. The remaining three spaces are investment intensive and can be scaled up in terms of capital expenditure (CAPEX) for higher performance as well as productivity.

### *Exogenous Elements Drive Scaling/Growth*

The fourth difference of the social space is its *exogenous element*. A scale-up in mobility, analytics and cloud can be architected internally. All three of these technology spaces are integrative spaces where one can aspire to build value from within. The constraints against not expanding and scaling up in the MAC space are internal. The reasons can be as varied as "not the right time," "untested technology," "does not want to be a pioneer," "unproved solutions," and "investment constraints." The solutions to break free from these constraints—particularly investment constraints—are also internal. But social scaling happens on an interactive external space, dominated by the combined effect of information volatility, scenario uncertainty, systemic complexity, and overall ambiguity: the VUCA effect. Since the constraints are external, growth and scaling cannot be planned and mapped in such an exogenous environment.

### *Data Conditioning Is Key*

The treatment of data is different in social from that of the other three phases. In social, the process that is followed is data conditioning (Kalampokis et al., 2013). This phase ensures transformation of raw and noisy social media data to high-fidelity structured data that can feed the analytics engine. Intermediary data conversion layers such as IBM Info Sphere and SAP Netbase help to convert massive volumes of unstructured social media data into meaningful insights (Kim et al., 2013) by uncovering trends in consumer preferences, emotions, and behavior. These applications help in getting a feel for "gross sentiments" by using sophisticated natural-language-processing engines. High-end data analytics tools are capable of extracting aggregate insights from softer signals such as "likes" and "dislikes" that originate from the social media. This richness of information in the data conditioning stage becomes impaired in the data processing environment of subsequent stages. Subtle gives way to gross and intuition is replaced by intellect.

Let us consider some information nuances that are present in the data conditioning phase. The social media milieu is capable of offering powerful insights into customer intentions and consumer rationalities, based on a wide range of behavioral dimensions. Taking a few examples, some social media behavior is just to enhance ***status***. A large number of connections are sought by people in LinkedIn just to enhance their status; most of these connections are nontransactional. Similarly, Facebook's friend aggregation tendency would be either to enhance ***intimacy*** or to mitigate ***loneliness***. Both of these traits are demonstrated by the millennials, whose device orientation is better than their people orientation. An ***inflated ego*** that manifests itself as a requirement for regular social visibility would be the driver for accumulating Tweet followers. Celebrity tweets come under this category. All these softer interactive aspects of social relationships remain only in the data conditioning phase. Once the predictive analytics phase starts, these nuances tend to get lost. Table 3.2 gives a set of softer differentiators of the social space in relation to the MAC space.

## Implications for Business

The age of building businesses on the generic Porter advantages of cost, differentiation, and focus is passé. The new-age competitive advantage platforms are "competing on data" and "competing on analytics" (Davenport, 2013). Before we look at the implications of technology convergence on business, a literature survey in this area is in order. There is literature that classifies the developing field of business analytics, based on its evolution into versions 1.0, 2.0, and 3.0 (Chen et al., 2012; Dinter & Lorentz, 2012; Davenport, 2013). There are studies that help to integrate

**Table 3.2** A few more soft differentiators of social space

| *Social* | *MAC* |
|---|---|
| Subjective | Objective |
| Subtle | Gross |
| Intuition | Intellect |
| Behavioral | Technological |
| Interactive | Integrative |
| Analogous to analog | Analogous to digital |

mobility perspective into the SMAC stack (Green, 2002; Hurbean & Fotache, 2013; Lee & Cho, 2011; Romanov, 2012). Since this paper focuses on the social perspective, we have looked at articles on social media that range from studies on correlation between public emotions and stock market predictions (Arafat & Habib, 2013) to checking efficacy and credibility of social media information in the case of an emergency (Castillo et al., 2013). A broad classification of social media sites, based on the nature of their activity, is given in Table 3.3.

To fully appreciate the absolute relevance of the social space, the differential relevance of social with respect to the remaining MAC spaces and the overall significance of SMAC in the contemporary business universe, we present the lead versus lag scenario in the context of business analytics and business intelligence (Laursen & Thorlund, 2010). Key lead-lag comparison perspectives are tabulated in Table 3.4.

Modern business analytics and business intelligence (BABI) platforms create breakthrough decision support mechanisms by providing *lead* information. On the other hand, traditional intelligence platforms such as working capital management, customer profitability analysis, accounts receivable management, and the like provide *lag* information, which is useful to measure, monitor, manage, and maximize (4M framework) operational business goals. Lead builds the abstract a priori scenario while lag brings in the concrete a posteriori scenario. Lead helps in proactively getting things started by providing breaking insights. Lag helps in monitoring and maintaining progress on a reactive basis centered on retrospective data. The lead decision support framework is fashioned based on the knowledge that we need. The lag 4M framework sustains the knowledge that we get. In this context, it is worth mentioning that the lead-lag indicators cited here are not the

**Table 3.3** Classification of social media sites

| *Classification of social media sites (SMS)* | | |
|---|---|---|
| *Category* | *Activity* | *Major players* |
| Publishing | Blogging, microblogging, and wikis | Blogs, Twitter, *Wikipedia* |
| Sharing | Content sharing such as music, videos and photos | YouTube, Flickr, SlideShare |
| Discussing | Bulletin boards, comment management systems | bbPress, Disqus |
| Locating | Tracking locations or revealing personal location | Foursquare, Google Places |
| Networking | Professional and personal social networks | LinkedIn, Facebook |
| Gaming | All gaming sites and applications | Pogo, Playfish |

**Table 3.4** Lead versus lag scenario and SMAC

| *Lead* | *Lag* |
|---|---|
| Pre | Post |
| Abstract | Concrete |
| Get things started | Measure/monitor progress |
| Proactive | Reactive |
| Breaking insight | Retrospective |
| Knowledge that we need | Knowledge that we get |

same as those used by economists to understand where the economy is heading. Their only commonality is that in both cases, *lead* is used for prediction.

Let us now look at the relevance of the lead-lag framework as far as this paper is concerned. The proactive, abstract, and insight-giving lead data that businesses need is clearly embedded in the social layer. The predictive and prescriptive power of analytics is driven by the unstructured information provided by social media. If one looks at the subsequent stages in the SMAC stack, mobile is just a collector, analytics a processor, and cloud a storehouse of processed data. But Facebook, with over one billion active users, 4.5 billion "likes" per day, twenty minutes of average log time per day and 50 percent of users religiously visiting the portal at least once per day, is a veritable source for lead signals. These signals will help in building new products, reaching new markets, rationalizing pricing, reducing customers' fears, creating new financial instruments, optimizing supply chains, planning visual merchandizing, refining safety, and improving public health. However, the list is only indicative.

In this context, let us revisit the information that is available in the data conditioning stage vis-à-vis that in the data processing stage. A schematic of the loss of subtle relationship elements when data blocks move from the sourcing layer to the processing layer is shown in Fig. 3.1.

As it can be clearly inferred, unstructured data at the social level includes a lot of tacit information that could help firms in making better business decisions. Within the SMAC stack, such subtle human-angle information resides only in the social space. Current data processing with a focus on identifying the broad predictive elements is killing this vital lead information. This is the single key message that this paper wants to convey. Methods to improve SMAC integration without the erosion of value from the social space is beyond the scope of this work.

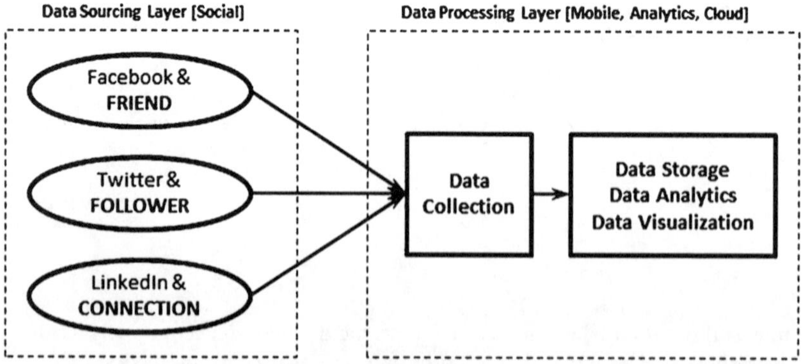


**Fig. 3.1** Loss of subtle relationship elements (such as friend, follower, connection) when data moves from sourcing layer to processing layer in a SMAC stack

## Conclusion

Technology convergence is here to stay. In the convergence stack, social media clearly stands out with a differential behavior. The nuances of this space should be understood in conjunction with the behavior of the occupants of the space. The social space is primarily occupied by the new-age millennial population. Today's consumers and tomorrow's decision makers, this generation (Gen Y) exhibits certain specific behavioral characteristics. Some of them are instant gratification, sense of entitlement bordering on narcissism, higher community feeling compared to the previous generations, high teamwork skills, higher usage of technology, device affinity, texting affinity, multitasking skills, and finally, social networking skills. Understanding this population and its requirements from a social scientist point of view and combining that knowledge with the technology backend of mobility, analytics and cloud will be the right combo in architecting great SMAC solutions.

## References

Arafat, J., & Habib, M. A. (2013, May). Analyzing Public Mood and Emotion Using Social Media. *International Journal of Computer Applications (0975–8887)*, *72*(2).

Castillo, C., Mendoza, M., & Poblete, B. (2013). Predicting Information Credibility in Time-Sensitive Social Media. *Internet Research*, *23*(5), 560–588.

Chen, H., Chiang, R. H. L., & Storey, V. C. (2012, December). Business Intelligence and Analytics: From Big Data to Big Impact. *MIS Quarterly, 36*(4), 1165–1188.

Davenport, T. H. (2013, December 1). Analytics 3.0. *Harvard Business Review*.

Dinter, B., & Lorentz, A. (2012). Social Business Intelligence: A Literature Review and Research Agenda. *33rd International Conference on Information Systems (ICIS 2012)*. Proceedings Editor F. George Joey.

Frank, M. (2012). Don't Get SMACked: How Social, Mobile, Analytics and Cloud Technologies Are Reshaping the Enterprise. *A Cognizant White Paper*.

Green, N. (2002). On the Move: Technology, Mobility and the Mediation of Social Time and Space. *The Information Society, 18*, 281–292.

Hurbean, L., & Fotache, D. (2013). Mobile Technology: Binding Social and Cloud into a New Enterprise Applications Platform. *Informatica Economica, 7*(2), 73–83.

Iyer, E. K., et al. (2013, December). What Drives Big Data Analytics to Cloud. *International Journal of Consumer and Business Analytics, 2*(1).

Kalampokis, E., Tambouris, E., & Tarabanis, K. (2013). Understanding the Predictive Power of Social Media. *Internet Research, 23*(5), 544–559.

Kane, G. C., Alavi, M., Borgatti, S. P., & Labianca, G. (2014, March). What Is Different About Social Media Networks?—A Framework and Research Agenda. *MIS Quarterly, 38*(1), 275–304.

Kim, H. J., et al. (2013, April). Experiencing Big Data Analytics: Analyzing Social Media Data in Financial Sector as a Case Study. *Northeast Decision Sciences Institute Annual Meeting Proceedings*. New York, NY.

Laursen, G. H. N., & Thorlund, J. (2010). *Business Analytics for Managers: Taking Business Intelligence Beyond Reporting*. Hoboken, NJ: John Wiley & Sons.

Lee, S., & Cho, M. (2011, Winter). Social Media Use in a Mobile Broadband Environment: Examination of Determinants of Twitter and Facebook Use. Mobile Marketing Association, *IJMM, 6*(2).

Romanov, A. (2012, Summer). The Near and Far of Proximity Marketing: The Future of Marketing Exists at the Nexus of Digital Signage and Mobility. Mobile Marketing Association, *IJMM Canada Issue, 7*(1).

Udhas, P., & Raman, K. K. (2013). The SMAC Code—Embracing New Technologies for Future Business. *A KPMG Report 2013 (kpmg.com/in)*.

CHAPTER 4

# Lifecycle of Information on the Web: Implications for Aggregator Sites

*H. V. Satyanarayana, T. M. Prasanna, and G. Shainesh*

## Introduction

We are witnessing an exponential growth in user-generated online content. The explosion of information on the web is being revolutionized by the multitude of ways in which information is created, distributed, and consumed. The advent of Web 2.0 tools such as blog sites, wikis, and social networks are enabling new ways of communicating across multiple geographies and different cultures.

Media aggregator sites are connectors in the supernetwork of the Internet that depend on providers such as ABC and Reuters for news, Vevo, Rovi, and Rhapsody for Media, and so on, for most of their content. In addition, they leverage the user-developed content, which is very dynamic. These technology Internet sites are very popular and have their dominant presence across myriad subnetworks. In addition to their presence in multiple networks, they have very close access to user behavior in

H. V. Satyanarayana
Flipkart, Bangalore, India

T. M. Prasanna
Juniper Networks, Sunnyvale, CA, USA

G. Shainesh (✉)
Indian Institute of Management Bangalore, Bangalore, India





G. Heggde, G. Shainesh (eds.), *Social Media Marketing*,
https://doi.org/10.1007/978-981-10-5323-8_4

each of the subnetworks. Owing to their reputation, they can be great at selling (Gladwell, 2006) in each of the subnetworks. Today, most players fall short when it comes to their presence on third-party sites frequented by their users. This paper explores how such aggregator sites can devise their strategies to leverage their connector status on the Internet, study how they can be present in all places where their users are, and bridge the gap between the mavens and interested adapters of the web community more effectively. We also explore how these companies can design their content such that it has a very high adoption index.

We start with a discussion on the context of a social network and a few key concepts including nodes, ties, triadic closure, bridge, strength of a tie, and diffusion. Then we highlight the findings of data analysis on *Wikipedia* dump for select, popular, wiki topics covering one-time, sudden events and anticipated recurring events. We also report the findings of a small-sample consumer survey focusing on users' preferences for, and perceptions of, different websites. Finally, we conclude with implications and recommendations for aggregator websites.

## *Context and Concepts*

A social network is defined by a set of actors (also called nodes) and the relationships (also called ties) between them (Goldenberg, Han, Lehmann, & Hong, 2009). The study of networks involves analysis at two levels: one at the level of individuals (microlevel) and the other as an aggregation of the multitude of such individual interactions (macrolevel). These two together outline the large-scale phenomenon of how information propagates across networks. Networks play an important role in bridging the local and global by highlighting how simple interactions at the level of individual nodes and links can have ripple effects through a population as a whole (Easley & Kleinberg, 2010). Social networks of today are extremely dynamic and this flux in them adds to the complexity of social network analysis.

One of the basic principles that explain the dynamic nature of networks and their constant expansion is the principle of triadic closure. Triadic closure means that "If two people in a social network have a friend in common, then there is an increased likelihood that they will become friends themselves at some point in the future" (Easley & Kleinberg, 2010). The principle of triadic closure relates largely to the transitive property that if A is related to B and B is related to C, then A is also related to C. Another important concept in the literature of social networks is the concept of the bridge. An edge is defined as a bridge if deleting that edge will result in the two subnetworks becoming separate subnetworks. An edge joining two nodes in a network, in a social graph, is called a local bridge if the end-points of the bridge have no friends in common. A major implication of the deletion of an edge between two nodes that do not have any friends in common is that the distance between those two nodes will increase to a value more than two. The span of a local bridge is the distance between the two nodes when the edge between them is deleted.

Another important concept that is found in the literature of social networks is the strength of a tie. The strength of a tie (or a link in a network) is represented by the interactions and kind of relationship between the nodes (actors in the social networks). Thus, the stronger links represent closer friendship and high frequency of interaction, whereas the weaker links represents acquaintances and infrequent interaction. The ties in any social network can be classified as strong or weak depending on the type of relationship between the actors and frequency of interaction between them. The relationship between the strength of ties and the triadic closure of ties can be qualitatively assumed thus: "If a node A has edges to nodes B and C, then the B-C edge is more likely to form if A's edges to nodes B and C are both strong ties." This assumption is known as the strong triadic closure property (Easley & Kleinberg, 2010). The claim established by the research based on the above properties is that if a node A in a social network satisfies the strong triadic closure property and if that node is an end-point with a minimum of two weak ties, then any local bridge involving the node must be a weak tie.

Diffusion of innovation is key to understanding this phenomenon as it focuses on diffusion as well as adoption. The adoption part categorizes users as innovators, early adopters, early majority, late majority, and laggards. The role of social systems is a key element of diffusion research and is relevant for information aggregator sites. Extant literature highlights the role of opinion leaders in forming or changing an opinion of a large number of people who may speed up or slow down the adoption of innovation. In the context of social networks, such opinion leaders with large powers of influence are called hubs, influence leaders, or mavens (Goldenberg et al., 2009). Markets are not homogeneous and one of the reasons for this heterogeneity is that different people can exert different degrees of influence on others, based on how many people they are connected to and whether they have significant influence by way of their expertise or large following. Gladwell (2006) uses the term *mavens* to refer to people who have large social capital and can wield a large influence on others with their expertise and an intense desire to help by spreading it. The other set of people who have exceptionally large social networks and are passionately part of many diverse networks are called connectors. These concepts of social networks—including strength of ties and social capital—play an important role if marketing actions e.g. promotion can provide big business opportunities for Internet aggregators.

So what are some of the characteristics of content that go viral? Hughes (2008) identified the key attributes as six "buttons" that make people talk and share with others. They include

1. Taboo: labeled by a society as improper, unacceptable, prohibited, or profane
2. Unusual: not usual, common, or ordinary; uncommon in amount or degree; exceptional
3. Outrageous: passing reasonable bounds, shocking, unconventional, and extravagant
4. Hilarious: arousing great merriment; funny
5. Remarkable: notable, extraordinary, worthy of notice or attention
6. Secrets: kept from the knowledge of any but the initiated or privileged

In the next two sections, we discuss the findings based on trend analysis of wiki pages and a consumer survey.

*Wikipedia* trend analysis—*Wikipedia* records all page visits publicly and publishes it as a dump. These dumps contain information on the number of page views for each of the wiki topics on an hourly basis. It is an extremely useful public dataset for a preliminary analysis. We classified events as one-time/sudden events (e.g., Asiana air crash in San Francisco in July 2013; Boston Marathon bombing; birth of Queen Elizabeth's great grandson; and anticipated/recurring events such as the USA's Independence Day, India's Independence Day, etc.)

One-time/sudden events cannot be anticipated and so cannot generate buzz before the actual event (expected or unexpected) occurs. But when the event occurs, people seek out this news in a frenzy. Such news items peak very soon and wane away equally quickly. Mapping the wiki data shows that the San Francisco International Airport crash trended for fourteen days while the birth of the royal baby trended for seventeen days continuously.

Anticipated/recurring events are, typically, annual celebrations or anniversaries of interest. We selected the USA's Independence Day, India's Independence Day, and John F. Kennedy's assassination day for trend analysis. The traffic pattern on all of these pages on *Wikipedia* followed precisely the same pattern. The buzz starts, typically, around seventeen days before the marked day of the event. JFK assassination buzz started nineteen days prior. More than 70 percent of the traffic is attracted three days prior to the event and on the day of the event.

We also analysed the trends for a few popular movies (*Man of Steel* and *Wolverine*) and music videos (*What Does the Fox Say?* and the *Harlem Shake*). We found that for all managed marketing campaigns, the jump of the page views to the peak is very abrupt and occurs around the date of release. The peaks for managed marketing campaigns last for around five days, after which they taper off. The starts for the viral information are always small, and it takes more time than managed marketing campaigns do to reach its peak. However, virally spread content peaks multiple times through its lifecycle. The graphs show many crests and troughs till it dies down.

Consumer Survey: We conducted a consumer survey to understand users' preferences for different kinds of website and their perceptions of what these websites offer consumers. We focused on three categories of website, namely:

1. User generated social media sites such as Twitter, YouTube, Tumblr, Facebook.
2. Media aggregator sites such as Yahoo, MSN, Rediff.
3. News websites such as CNN, ABC, BBC.
4. *Wikipedia*.

The objective was to find what users expect to see on each of these sites, study what each of them are offering right now, see if there are any gaps from the perspective of media aggregator sites. and identify ways to bridge that gap to improve the product offering for the target consumers.

We received 153 completed responses through a convenience sampling process. The key findings are:

1. Across all age segments, the majority believes that news sites such as CNN and BBC are better than social media and media aggregation sites when it comes to breaking important news on the web.

2. Of respondents between eighteen and twenty-seven years of age, 26.67 percent also trust social media sites for news information. However, the share of respondents who cited social media sites as news sources is lower in other age groups.
3. Media sites are the least trusted news sources for respondents between eighteen and twenty-seven years of age.
4. Respondents between twenty-eight and thirty-five years of age, and between thirty-six and fifty years of age trust media sites more than social media sites as sources of information.
5. Across all age groups, news channel sites fare well compared to any other news sites.
6. The share of media sites doubles from 13.6 to 27.2 percent when the news is a few days old.
7. The share of *Wikipedia* increases from 6.1 to 19.73 percent when the news is a few days old.
8. The share of social media sites decreases from 12.24 to 4.08 percent when the news is a few days old.
9. The share of news websites decreases from 68.03 to 56.46 percent when the news is a few days old.

The key insight is that as the news gets older (in days), the relevance of media sites and *Wikipedia,* as sources, increases almost equally. The findings also underscore the fact that media sites have different competitors at different points in the lifecycle of a news topic.

Forty-six percent of the respondents prefer news websites as their first source of information followed by 24 percent of respondents preferring *Wikipedia*. Sixteen percent prefer sources such as Twitter and 14 percent prefer sites such as Yahoo/Rediff/MSN. This finding is surprising from the perspective of aggregator sites such as Rediff/Yahoo/MSN, as across all age groups, respondents have the lowest preference for aggregator sites as their first source of information. Thus these aggregator sites need to rethink their strategies for persuading people across all age groups to view their sites as the first source of information.

## *Recommendations*

### *Mavens, Connectors and Salesmen on the Internet*

If one views the Internet as a network where each site represents a person, we could build some parallels to the concept of mavens, connectors, and salesmen. Sites such as news sites where the news originates in the physical world and transits into the virtual world can be termed *information mavens*. There is one startling difference in the attributes of the maven sites on the web and the mavens discussed in literature, which is that the sites exist for the single most important purpose of making profits. In this paper, we refer to them as corporate mavens, or just mavens.

Network sites such as Twitter, Facebook, and LinkedIn are best positioned to be connectors. However, they may be high on the maven rating too. In this paper, we refer to them as user-mavens because a lot of people use these platforms to publicize something original.

Media companies such as Yahoo! and MSN are great web connectors. They connect thousands of information sources on the web with millions of consumers on the other end. They are a part of many subnetworks (interest groups) and connect both sides with the rest of the world. So, these companies competing in the space of the mavens is confusing. As our survey analysis suggests, this strategy may be counterproductive for them. They have been consistently losing their customer base to the more dedicated mavens on the web. For example, movie subsites on media websites have lost their traffic to IMDb over the years.

Mavens are usually domain specific. Or they will have expertise in a few domains they are passionate about. However, connectors are spread wide in each of the networks. They are not necessarily experts in any of the domains, but they have something to give in each of the domains/categories, which makes them relevant and hence welcome in all the networks.

As most Internet mavens are profit oriented, they are not very credible, unlike mavens in the true sense of that word. Salesmen, on the other hand, persuade people that products they know are great. This makes connectors an invaluable asset in the Internet space. They are neutral; their job is to gather as much information from as many mavens as possible. So, the end-users are more likely to be influenced by them. However, the connector has to be cautious about not flooding everybody in every network, or even in relevant networks, with information.

Implications of being hubs (connectors):

The hubs, or connectors, have the following strategy implications for media sites:

1. Linking up with more corporate mavens: Mavens come in all shapes and sizes. Media sites should have a very effective process to evaluate hundreds of maven sites in different spheres, select the best of them, and build partnerships with them.

2. Being selfless and giving sweet deals to mavens: It is imperative that, in order to thrive, media companies offer generous terms for mavens and help them reach their maximum audience. Potential incentives include guaranteed traffic back to their sites, subscription payments, dedicated site pages for each provider, direct content marketing to interested audiences through active promotion of this content to users.
3. Knowing their customers: One of the key qualities of great connectors is that they know the right set of people for anything. This translates to understanding users' interests, dislikes, usage patterns, and mode of access (mobile/tablet/PCs)
4. Being social: Media sites can connect the user-mavens in social networking sites. They can link them up with the users within the social network, in their own websites, and in third-party sites on the Internet. Examples of such implementations are the Twitter modules coming up on these sites. Integration with social widgets is another example. However, a much deeper integration with these social sites is recommended.
5. Doing no evil: Connectors can recommend the right mavens for their users even if these mavens are not their partners. This improves their service to end-users by unconditionally providing the best sources of information, and they also improve their standing among the corporate maven community.

*Competition During Early Days (in the Information Lifecycle)*
Due to the nature of the offering, media sites compete with different types of competitors in the life-cycle of information. In the early stages, they compete with the maven sites. While media sites are more easily accessible due to their heavy branding, and high SEO value, the quality of the content provided scores lower when compared to that of mavens.

| *Sites* | *Discovery* | *Comprehensiveness* | *User opinion* |
|---|---|---|---|
| Corporate mavens | Low | High | Low |
| Media sites | High | Medium | Medium |
| User mavens | Medium | Low | High |

An ideal strategy for media sites would be to leverage corporate mavens' strengths for comprehensiveness and user-maven sites for public opinions during the early days of a news release. Media sites need to invest in technology that can acquire information almost in real-time and analytics for dynamically creating pages that aggregate content from partnered mavens, nonpartnered mavens, and user-mavens. In this paper, we call such pages dynamic info pages. It would help if these companies were to employ thought leaders and prolific opinion leaders who can comment independently on the news.

The following chart shows competition in the later part of the information lifecycle.

| *Sites* | *Discovery* | *Comprehensiveness* | *User opinion* |
|---|---|---|---|
| *Wikipedia* | High | High | Low |
| Media sites | Medium | Medium | Medium |
| User mavens | Low | Low | Medium |
| Corporate mavens | Low | Low | Low |

In the later part of the information lifecycle, we see that *Wikipedia* clearly emerges as a winner among all other sites. The only dimension in which it scores lower is integration with user opinions. Being connectors, media companies can bridge this gap in multiple ways. The dynamic info pages may aggregate a lot of blogs, and user tweets on the page over the lifecycle.

*Strategic Implication from Survey Analysis*

From the analysis, we saw that 55 percent of the respondents believe media sites to be a good source of information for news, but they still don't use them. Also, 40 percent of the population believes social media sites to be good sources, but they do not use them. Gourville (2006) explains the 9X difference between buyers and sellers in their perception of a new product. New products have to strive for an improvement of 10X or more in product experience to make existing users overcome their resistance to let go of their losses and switch to a new product. It is clear that the younger segment rates friends' and other users' opinions of events more highly than the actual coverage of the events themselves. Media sites, through their dynamic info pages, can merge these elements from multiple sources on the web and generate a very viable offering.

*Strategic Implications on Content Creation Based on the Study of Viral Media*

Media sites need to consider the following while creating content:

*Emotional connect*: Almost all media sites today have a presence on social media sites. However, we notice that they miss the human touch. Pages such as MSN Movies or Yahoo! TV do not have as much impact as a credible person would have. It would be better if these media sites were to mark their presence by having several individuals post their opinion of the content—for example, radio jockeys from several radio stations. Media sites should look for a similar web anchor for each of their properties to develop a more human touch in interaction with end-users.

*Videos*: Most of the viral content on the web has been in the form of videos. Rich media such as videos and images are more engaging than plain news. Media companies should employ their technologies to improve the experience of these kinds of rich media, which would greatly differentiate them from stand-alone social sites and corporate mavens.

*Unusual/secret*: One of the key findings of viral media studies is that content tends to spread more when it has an unusual perspective or embodies some secret about to be disclosed. Media companies should work with prominent opinion leaders and psychologists to build such content.

*Strategic Implications of the Wikipedia Event PageView Analysis*

As discussed earlier, recurring events draw visits every cycle—typically, every year. There is also a great deal of chatter on the social media sites about these events every year. Media sites can choose to build a product page for all these events with all the features implied by the above strategies and integrate with user-interaction modules on the page. Today, many queries are seen to start from a search engine (also owned by Yahoo! and MSN) and these queries lead to *Wikipedia* pages. The product can be positioned to draw that audience, with a well-rounded, 360-degree experience on the topic.

## References

Easley, D., & Kleinberg, J. (2010). *Networks, Crowds, and Markets: Reasoning About a Highly Connected World*. New York, NY: Cambridge University Press.

Gladwell, M. (2006). *The Tipping Point: How Little Things Can Make a Big Difference*. Hachette Digital.

Goldenberg, J., Han, S., Lehmann, D. R., & Hong, J. W. (2009). The Role of Hubs in the Adoption Process. *Journal of Marketing, 73*(2), 1–13.
Gourville, J. T. (2006, June). Eager Sellers and Stony Buyers: Understanding the Psychology of New-Product Adoption. *Harvard Business Review*, 1–10.
Hughes, M. (2008). *Buzzmarketing: Get People to Talk About Your Stuff.* London: Penguin.

CHAPTER 5

# Shadow Side of Social Media Marketing: A User's Perspective

*Anuragini Shirish*

## Introduction

Digital transformation initiatives are forcing organizations to envisage new ways of marketing their products and services (Trapp, 2016). The relatively new phenomenon of social media marketing, accelerated by Web 2.0 broadcasting, promises to have great potential for reaching out to a wider set of social media audiences and establishing engagement within a very short span of time using limited resources (Chen, De, & Hu, 2015). It is expected that the number of social media users will grow to 2.95 billion by 2020 (Statista, 2017). A recent survey indicates that the top two reasons for the use of social media marketing communication are (1) to increase exposure to the organization's business so as to increase traffic, and (2) to generate leads for sales of products and services. Though many small and large firms are making considerable investments in social media initiatives with a view to enhancing their profits, there are many unresolved uncertainties related to the envisaged returns (Dickinson-Delaporte & Kerr, 2014). Notwithstanding the fact that academic research has examined social media marketing and its implications from diverse perspectives such as service science, information systems, psychology, and law, it is still a

A. Shirish (✉)
Telecom Ecole de Management (Institut Mines-Telecom), Evry, France



G. Heggde, G. Shainesh (eds.), *Social Media Marketing*,
https://doi.org/10.1007/978-981-10-5323-8_5

nascent research domain with several unanswered questions (see Alves, Fernandes, & Raposo, 2016; Kao, Yang, Wu, & Cheng, 2016; Mackey & Liang, 2013; Thies, Wessel, & Benlian, 2016; Tushnet, 2010; Xie & Young-Jin, 2015). The current study aims to extend the extant understanding on the subject by addressing a few significant gaps.

The social media environment is characterized by the participation, openness, conversation, community, and connectedness of its users, resulting in a number of advantages. Consequently, most academic research and popular press on the subject focuses on the *affordances* or the bright side of social media marketing. But as with any other technology mediated phenomenon, social media marketing has many intended and unintended constraints that constitute the dark side and have larger ramifications for different stakeholder groups (Majchrzak, Markus, & Wareham, 2016). Such constraints and/or unethical effects of social media marketing can hinder the peaceful coevolution of professional and public good in this digital ecosystem and hence need a deeper examination. In this study, we term these constraints the *shadow effect* of social media marketing. Such shadow effects do not allow us to leverage the full potential of affordances offered by social media ecosystems. Hence, examining the negative side of social media will contribute to both research and practice.

Social media marketing as a phenomenon is not static. In fact, its dynamic nature takes into account the relational interaction of the technology, actors, and the situating environmental factors. The combined effect of all three of these elements contributes to the perception of *affordances* or *constraints* in the given context of a sociotechnical system (Majchrzak et al., 2016). Few recent attempts have been made by researchers to study the negative influences in marketing. Most of these studies deal with the subject in a general way and tend to focus on an organizational rather than a customer/user perspective (Alves et al., 2016; Daunt & Greer, 2017). Examining the constraints that may limit the possibility of leveraging the affordances from social media marketing is thus expected to contribute to this growing body of knowledge.

In this article, taking a technology constraints perspective for social media users, we first explore the current research on the dark side of social media marketing via a systematic literature review. Next, we identify two distinct forms of constraints that apply to this context. Subsequently, we highlight the need for meaningful discourse on the subject and describe the two identified shadow effects of social media marketing. Finally, we conclude by highlighting how this study will contribute to research and practice in this domain.

## Systematic Literature Review: Dark Side of Social Media Marketing

Following past guidelines, we undertook a systematic literature review of the subject with the objective of identifying important biases and research gaps (Okoli & Schabram, 2010). We sought not only to synthesize prior literature on the subject but also propose future research directions (Rowe, 2014). Because social media is a cross-disciplinary domain, to conduct a comprehensive search, no restrictions were introduced for the year and type of publication. The search was conducted in digital libraries using the EBSCOhost (EH) interface, which is a multimotor search engine comprising the databases of 116 providers covering the fields of management, social science, humanities, and pure sciences. Using EH also helped in eliminating duplicate material. Some of the popular databases that were covered using EH were EBSCOhost, JSTOR, Science Direct, PsycINFO, ERIC, and Academic Onefile, to name a few. The search terms *social media* and *marketing* as keywords were chosen as the first step. Although the dark side of social media *usage* per se has received a fair share of attention in literature, we preferred to limit the exploration to marketing related papers in order to remain within the chosen context. The search resulted in 2194 papers out of which 2053 were written in English. We further refined this list by choosing papers that squarely dealt with social media marketing as the primary subject matter. We ended up with a total of 117 papers. After manually screening the abstracts of all 117 papers, we found only a handful of the papers discussed the shadow effect of social media marketing (Gainsbury et al., 2016; Hoffman, Pinkleton, Austin, & Reyes-Velázquez, 2014; Mackey et al., 2015). Additional papers that covered ethical aspects of social media marketing in their abstracts were included in this search, which led to three additional papers out of seventeen total papers in this category (Dickinson-Delaporte & Kerr, 2014; Kadić-Maglajlić, Arslanagić-Kalajdžić, Micevski, Michaelidou, & Nemkova, 2017).

Cross-searches through public search engines and cross-citations led to identification of a few other potential articles that were not captured in the initial online library search. We leveraged these research papers to develop a conceptual framework of constraints for social media marketing from the user perspective. Notwithstanding the limitations of this search method, from a purely exploratory stance, we conclude that the current literature on social media marketing is swayed toward the brighter side of this phenomenon and little research has delved deep into the shadow side from a user/consumer/customer perspective.

## Actors in the Social Media Marketing Ecosystem

In addition to other findings, a systematic literature review of the subject helped unearth certain core actors (stakeholders) that are interdependent within the sociotechnical system. Using the stakeholder lens will help examine the phenomenon holistically from a user perspective. Figure 5.1 provides a pictorial depiction of the actors derived from the review. The topmost category relates to *regulatory bodies and public policy bodies* including governments that are trying to enforce social media regulations with a view to providing affordances for businesses and individuals. Actors also include trade regulation bodies that control antispam and antitrust

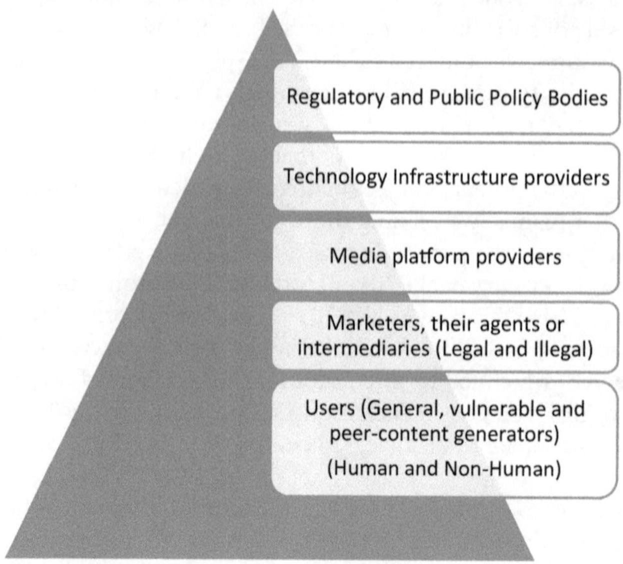


**Fig. 5.1** Key stakeholders' groups in social media

violations, and take care of consumer interests. Additionally, included within this review's ambit are larger bodies such as the European Trade Commission (issuing regulations and guidelines for trade and privacy protection) and other supranational bodies such as the United Nations and regulatory bodies tasked with setting technological standards. The objective of these regulators is to ensure an appropriate balance between private and public good in social media. Other categories depicted in Fig. 5.1 are referred to in the sections that follow.

## Typology of Constraints

Based on the results of the systematic literature review, we divide the dark side of social media marketing into two broad typologies of constraints that are distinct in terms of the factors that cause them. The two distinct categories of causes are *structural* and *behavioral*, and they lead to most of the constraints for different stakeholder groups. Figure 5.2 summarizes the key aspects of the two delineated typologies, listing the relevant details.

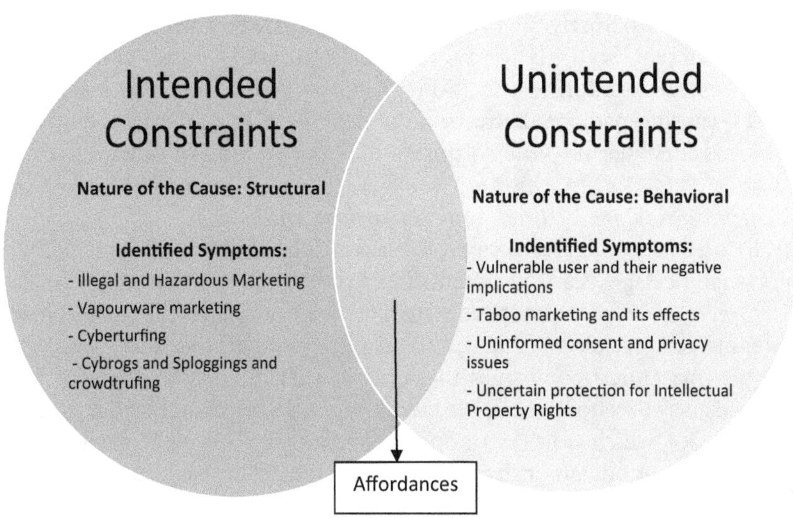


**Fig. 5.2** Typology of constraints from the users of social media marketing

## Intended Constraints

Intended constraints for our purpose are those constraints that can be attributed to an identifiable source or an actor in the social media marketing ecosystem. In other words, the causality of the symptoms can be clearly attributed. These constraints can therefore be mitigated in order to promote the peaceful coexistence of private and public good in market place.

### *Identified Structural Cause: Lack of Transparency and Legitimacy*

One of the factors leading to the perception of intended constraints identified from the literature review is user uncertainty of how to deal with the lack of transparency, and legitimacy issues in social media marketing. The users, including existing customers and potential customers, are often exposed to different kinds of advertisements and promotional campaigns, but they may be unsure about the authenticity of the information source and the legitimacy of the information disseminated through social media. Often, social media marketing relies upon user-generated or peer-produced content as its marketing strategy (Tushnet, 2010). Some users blindly follow the herd and pursue the preferred tendencies promoted by the groups they associate themselves with. This approach may be harmful for the user and is different from that of a traditional "rational" consumer (Tushnet, 2010). Such uninformed-decision practices lead to inappropriate purchases, causing personal harm to individual users and, in effect, may lead to professional harm to the corporations, over a period of time.

#### *Identified Symptom 1: Illegal and Hazardous Marketing*

As discussed above, in some cases, the lack of legitimacy in social media promotional messages leads to potential health hazards if the products or services were sourced from rogue marketers in social media that remain unregulated. Mackey and Liang (2013) demonstrated that there were several pharmaceutical companies that operated illicitly on social media platforms such as Facebook, Myspace, and Twitter, selling outdated drugs and/or drugs for which no prescription was required. The study done in the 2012–2014 period demonstrates that such rogue sellers have been attracting thousands of unsuspecting global users. The paper highlights the need to regulate illicit pharmaceutical companies selling potentially harmful drugs to social media users by taking advantage of the lack of entry barriers and the potential reach in such marketing platforms and practices. Some legal studies have raised the pertinent issue of monitoring the authenticity of user-generated content as it could have widespread harmful effects. Answers to these basic questions are particularly challenging for policy makers in the current digital age (Elliot, 2014; Tushnet, 2010).

*Identified Symptom 2: Cyberturfing*

Cyberturfing is a form of astroturfing mediated by technology (Leiser, 2016). It is used as means to obtain market intelligence and *manage* reputation (Berkman, 2008). Jacobs (2012) defines cyberturfing as the "artificial advocacy of a product, service or political viewpoint, to give the appearance of a 'grassroots' movement" (p. 567). It is a popular organizational malpractice afforded by the viral and anonymous nature of communication through social media platforms. Such a communication is deceptive and inauthentic because it is intended to give an impression that the origin of the information is from the grassroots supporters (i.e., flowing bottom-up and not top-down), whereas in reality such fake support movements of user-generated content are controlled by the sponsoring corporation (Sisson, 2017). Such malpractices are also referred to as green marketing. Well-known corporations have perpetrated such deceptive practices to sway public opinion or to defame their rivals, using a smear campaign. Some studies report a growing service industry of microtask workers who are accomplices to such practices (Conner, 2013; Sisson, 2017), which are prohibited by regulatory bodies in many countries. It was reported in the press that Samsung had to pay a huge fine of 350 million USD to Taiwan's trade regulatory body for having paid people to write negative reviews about HTC, a rival mobile phone company, on social media platforms (Elmer-DeWitt, 2013). Goldschein (2011) lists out a few alleged attempts of such cyberturfing undertaken by companies for profit motives. Walmart was allegedly behind a fake YouTube video post undertaken for the sake of publicity by one of its employees. It was also alleged that Walmart developed a fake blog called *Our Community. Our Choice* in order to gain publicity for new store openings (Ciarallo, 2010). In another case, Ask.com tried to start an information revolution against Google on the London Underground, using cyberturfing strategies (Aaron, 2007). Some of these advertisements were intended to promote vaporware around a new product or service.

*Identified Symptom 3: Cyborgs, Splogging, and Crowdturfing*
In the current age of social media there is growing evidence of automated, self-tweeting accounts that directly communicate with organic accounts with a view to manipulating the users (Li, Mukherjee, Liu, Kornfield, & Emery, 2014). These automated manipulations can pass for authentic, electronic, word-of-mouth exchanges, thereby misleading consumers (Dellarocas, 2006). Such promotional messages are generated using human-assisted computer-bot accounts called cyborgs. A data mining study of e-cigarettes tweets was undertaken in 2013–2015 on the Twitter platform. The study showed the growth of cyberturfing using cyborgs as a vaporware marketing strategy and this has significant regulatory and societal implications (Clark et al., 2016). As a new medical phenomenon that is scientifically unproven and thus risky, the study raised the concern of adolescents on social media platforms becoming addicted to nicotine due to such practices. The study also highlights the need to regulate practices of vaporware promotional tactics to protect public health and safety.

The other phenomenon of interest is flogging, which is cyberturfing using a blog, or splogging, a combination of spamming and cyberturfing. One of the earliest alleged cases of flogging reported in the popular press was that of a Sony executive who set up a fake blog called *All I Want for Christmas Is a PSP* in order to attract PlayStation Portable (PSP) sales, which was later removed (Kohler, 2006). All of these practices are abundant in the marketing industry. Users are uninformed about the perils of such practices and rely very much on such inauthentic referrals and fabricated peer-shared information. Wang and his colleagues (Wang, Wilson, Zhao, Zhu, & Mohanlal, 2012) coined the term *crowdturfing* to describe the practice whereby a company recruits financially compensated users to initiate false campaigns that often violate fair practice social media policies. Hardly any researchers have been interested in uncovering this apparently nontraceable phenomenon. A recent news article reported that Amazon, in an attempt to ensure product reviews were legitimate and reliable, sued 1114 users in 2015 for writing fakes reviews. Because the current security measures do not take into account attacks by humans (Wang et al., 2012), there is a growing need to provide fact-checking sites and authenticity-tracking technology products. More attention needs to be given to tools/regulations that can allay concerns about fabricated computer-mediated and human-perpetrated content to ensure transparency and legitimacy in the social media environment. Educating social media users on such deceptive practices and providing a means of recourse for those victimized by such activities is the key to having some order in this rather noisy market place.

## Unintended Constraints

Unintended constraints, for our purpose, are those constraints that cannot be attributed to a particular source/actor in the social media marketing ecosystem and may be linked to several aspects of the ecosystem and have idiosyncratic characteristics. Such constraints can be considered as the spillover effects of social media marketing.

### *Identified Behavioral Cause: Development of Negative Affect, Cognition and Behavior Among Users*

From our systematic literature review, we found that what can lead to the perception of unintended constraints is the impact of social media marketing on users' affective, cognitive, and behavioral outcomes. These behavioral concerns may be specific to an individual or a group of individuals, but at the same time, can have larger societal implications that need to be resolved. The user groups identified in this category are those that are vulnerable and powerless in nature and those that willingly collaborate with marketers for personal gains. Another set of users comprises those who do not know that they been targeted by other actors of social media ecosystems.

#### *Symptom 1: Powerless and Vulnerable Users*

The literature review reveals that social media marketing can make vulnerable users more prone to risky behavior. Users who already suffer from vulnerabilities such as addiction to alcohol and gambling (Gainsbury et al., 2016; Hoffman et al., 2014; McCreanor et al., 2013) are known to undertake risky, abusive, or illegal behaviors (Nicholls, 2012). These vulnerable users are easy targets of social media marketing, which has rapidly made advances in certain controversial markets such as alcohol and cigarettes. Social media affords pervasive and personalized marketing. Furthermore, that ubiquity of such tools helps marketers gain access to and the attention of vulnerable users, who are often not self-regulated in their behaviors but are driven by endorsements from virtual peers and easily subscribe to unreal social status concerns (Sherman, Payton, Hernandez, Greenfield,

& Dapretto, 2016). In their experiment, Sherman et al. (2016) found that the adolescent population in a simulated Instagram environment favored pictures that had more "likes"—those of their peers undertaking risky behaviors—as opposed to nonpeers' pictures that had fewer "likes" and were mundane in nature. This appetite for enticing promotional messages endorsed by peers is known to reduce the cognitive control of the users, who are driven by a need for instant gratification in order to fit in with their peer groups. There is high risk that such users would indulge in compulsive buying, paving the way to more serious health disorders and addiction due to their reduced self-control. Thus, it is important to consider the broader societal, cultural, and cognitive influences of marketing strategies upon the "vulnerable users" of social media, who would suffer a greater harm than discerning self-regulated users.

*Symptom 2: Controversial and Taboo Advertising*

Encouraging ethical marketing strategies as opposed to relying on controversial advertising is the key. It is common knowledge that many corporations, in a race to get an ounce of user's attention, resort to promotional tactics that can cut through all the available advertising clutter (Kadić-Maglajlić et al., 2017). They play upon the notion of taboo to sensitize promotional messages to social media users (Fam, Waller, Ong, & Yang, 2008). Prior research has shown that taboo advertising and exposure to unwanted offensive content can generate irritation and negative cognition, with consequential spiraling losses to the corporate bottom line (Kadić-Maglajlić et al., 2017). Research has also shown that the effects of such controversial advertising are more pronounced among mobile social media users because of the pervasive and ubiquitous nature of the device (Truong & Simmons, 2010). An integrated policy and regulatory change in social media marketing may be the most suitable way to tackle its behavioral impact among users.

*Symptom 3: Uninformed Consent and User Privacy*

Prolific growth and adoption of social media networks by global users led us to believe that social media communication is one of the primary modes for interpersonal communication in today's world (Nunan & Yenicioglu, 2013). According to one survey, approximately 70 percent of the US population has one or more social media accounts (Pick, 2017). The data-driven marketplace is thriving in a system of uninformed consent that is seen to be in alignment with the rhizomatic nature of such network communications touted to be conducive to marketing models based on peer-based cocreation (Nunan & Yenicioglu, 2013). However, the peril lies in ignoring the essential concept of any data-driven research in the offline world (i.e., informed consent of the users before a data collection process). User's data privacy and even spatial privacy that involves intrusions into one's psychological space/integrity can be grossly violated by social media market research (Cohen, 2008; Shirish, Chandra, & Srivastava, 2017). Social media networks are known to capture the minutiae of individuals' everyday lives (Hanna, Rohm, & Crittenden, 2011; Parent, Plangger, & Bal, 2011). Since there is no legal or technical requirement for informed consent from those targeted in the diverse methods of commercial data gathering made possible by social media, no single actor can be considered responsible for this issue. However, nonalignment of social and commercial interests raises the ethical dilemma of how best to promote the use social media for the benefit of all.

All actions and inactions can be monitored in social media, be it a public or private conversation. Location-based information is also transmitted to others. Legally speaking, the concept of what is sensitive personal information is not very clear in many legal contexts. Cookies collected from the use of social media may be viewed as personally identifiable information implying the need to respect privacy rights. The phenomenon of the privacy paradox looms heavily on social media use (Nunan & Yenicioglu, 2013). Many users are unaware that they are subjects of market research and the structural make-up of the social media networks favors entities with the technical skill to undertake such searches, be they corporations or individuals. Our online interaction creates a digital exhaust and such data can be used for research at later stages. Thus far there is not much clarity on how to regulate the umpteen ways to collect data without violating the privacy rights of the users (Nunan & Yenicioglu, 2013). The European Commission has proposed a general data protection regulation that enforces broader protection for the personal data and privacy rights of consumers in terms of how data can be collected and used. Businesses will be required to report express consent (as opposed to a sweeping privacy policy) in order to operate in the European Union, including in the digital spheres. This regulation is meant to take effect in May 2018 (European Union, 2016). Thus far, social media users are better described as victims of privacy breaches despite structural measures taken to enhance privacy protection and awareness by social media platform owners.

### *Symptom 4: Intellectual Property Rights Concerns*

Intellectual property rights (IPR) protections are again areas that lack clarity and are often ignored in mainstream literature. Users of social media may be infringing proprietary rights over intangible assets such as copyright, trademark, corporate trade secrets, or individuals' trade secrets as they share writings, music, film, photography, or art work that may be proprietary in nature. These infringements, referred to as unknown infringements, can be liable for violation of IPR laws (Verbauwhed, 2014). Several employees/users have faced criminal charges for tarnishing the brand image of corporations negligently. Reportedly, an employee of a famous pizza company was charged with felony for posting a video prank that supposedly tarnished the image of the brand (Clifford, 2009). Further, the coproduction model of marketing does not always provide clarity on how to protect the intellectual inputs of social media users. Therefore, an individual may infringe someone else's intellectual property rights unknowingly or his rightful intellectual property protection may be undervalued. Calls for protection guaranteeing a rule of law in social media platforms have been made in recent research but have, so far, not been empirically demonstrated (Risch, 2009; Shirish, Chandra, & Srivastava, 2013).

Thus, unintended constraints can hinder both the growth of social media marketing and also violate personal and property rights of individual social media users. However, the answers to these questions require a systemic approach where the notion of public good is prime.

## Conclusion

Recent years have seen an exponential growth of social media tools by businesses and individuals for multifarious purposes. Currently, social media is considered a useful marketing tool. A systematic literature review on the subject of social media marketing revealed that the bulk of research on the subject talks about the positives or the bright side of social media marketing. Owing to its pervasive and ubiquitous nature, social media not only provides affordances to its users but may impose constraints that need to be acknowledged. Surprisingly, prior research is largely reticent about the dark or shadow side of social media marketing. Grounding this work in a systematic literature review, we develop a framework and typology for better understanding the shadow side of social media marketing. Specifically, we classify the dark side of social media marketing into two kinds of constraint: ***intended*** and ***unintended***. Through a rich discourse of literature, we develop and describe the two kinds of constraints. We also elaborate the need to tackle these constraints systematically through policies, practices, and regulations to avoid the negative impact of social media marketing on different user groups.

**Acknowledgment and Dedication** I wish to thank Prof. Shirish Chandra Srivastava, Associate Professor, HEC Paris, for his comments on the final draft of this chapter. I dedicate this work to the loving memory of my mother-in-law, Smt. Padma Srivastava.

## References

Aaron, P. (2007, April 5). Ask.Com's 'Revolt' Risks Costly Clicks. *The Wall Street Journal*. Retrieved April 19, 2009, from http://online.wsj.com/article/SB117572581285960181.html?mod=googlewsj

Alves, H., Fernandes, C., & Raposo, M. (2016). Social Media Marketing: A Literature Review and Implications. *Psychology & Marketing, 33*(12), 1029–1038.

Berkman, R. I. (Ed.). (2008). *The Art of Strategic Listening: Finding Market Intelligence Through Blogs and Other Social Media*. New York: Paramount Market Publishing.

Chen, H., De, P., & Hu, Y. J. (2015). IT-Enabled Broadcasting in Social Media: An Empirical Study of Artists' Activities and Music Sales. *Information Systems Research, 26*(3), 513–531.

Ciarallo, J. (2010, January 27). Wal-Mart Busted for Astroturfing, Again. *Adweek*.

Clark, E. M., Jones, C. A., Williams, J. R., Kurti, A. N., Norotsky, M. C., Danforth, C. M., et al. (2016). Vaporous Marketing: Uncovering Pervasive Electronic Cigarette Advertisements on Twitter. *PloS One, 11*(7), e0157304.

Clifford, S. (2009). Video Prank at Domino's Taints Brand. *New York Times*. Retrieved from http://www.nytimes.com/2009/04/16/business/media/16dominos.html

Cohen, J. E. (2008). Privacy, Visibility, Transparency, and Exposure. *The University of Chicago Law Review, 75*(1), 181–201.

Conner, C. (2013, October 30). Online Reputation: New Methods Emerge for Quashing Fake, Defamatory Reviews. *Forbes*.

Daunt, K. L., & Greer, D. A. (2017). *The Dark Side of Marketing*. Retrieved from http://www.jmmnews.com/the-dark-side-of-marketing/

Dellarocas, C. (2006). Strategic Manipulation of Internet Opinion Forums: Implications for Consumers and Firms. *Management Science, 52*(10), 1577–1159.

Dickinson-Delaporte, S., & Kerr, G. (2014). Agency-Generated Research of Consumer-Generated Content. *Journal of Advertising Research, 54*(4), 469–478.

Elliot, S. (2014). Social Media Marketing: Who's Responsible for Monitoring User-Generated Content? *Lawtalk (Online), 840*, 4–7.

Elmer-DeWitt, P. (2013). Samsung Fined $340,000 for Astroturfing in Taiwan. *Fortune*. Retrieved from http://fortune.com/2013/10/24/samsung-fined-340000-for-astroturfing-in-taiwan/

European Union. (2016). *Regulation (EU) 2016/679 of the European Parliament and of the Council of 27 April 2016 on the Protection of Natural Persons with Regard to the Processing of Personal Data and on the Free Movement of Such Data, and Repealing Directive 95/46/EC (General Data Protection Regulation)*. Retrieved from http://eur-lex.europa.eu/legal-content/EN/TXT/?uri=uriserv:OJ.L_.2016.119.01.0001.01.ENG&toc=OJ:L:2016:119:TOC

Fam, K. S., Waller, D. S., Ong, F. S., & Yang, Z. (2008). Controversial Product Advertising in China: Perceptions of Three Generational Cohorts. *Journal of Consumer Behaviour, 7*(6), 461–469.

Gainsbury, S. M., King, D. L., Russell, A. M., Delfabbro, P., Derevensk, J., & Hing, N. (2016). Exposure to and Engagement with Gambling Marketing in Social Media: Reported Impacts on Moderate-Risk and Problem Gamblers. *Psychology of Addictive Behaviors, 30*(2), 270–276.

Goldschein, E. (2011, September 30). 10 Fake Grassroots Movements Started by Corporations to Sway Your Opinion. *Business Insider*.

Hanna, R., Rohm, A., & Crittenden, V. L. (2011). We're All Connected: The Power of the Social Media Ecosystem. *Business Horizons, 53*, 265–273.

Hoffman, E. W., Pinkleton, E. B., Austin, E. W., & Reyes-Velázquez, W. (2014). Exploring College Students' Use of General and Alcohol-Related Social Media and Their Associations with Alcohol-Related Behaviors. *Journal of American College Health, 62*(5), 328–335.

Jacobs, J. (2012). Faking It How to Kill a Business Through Astroturfing on Social Media. *Keeping Good Companies, 64*(9), 567.

Jensen, M. L., & Yetgin, E. (2017). Prominence and Interpretation of Online Conflict of Interest Disclosures. *MIS Quarterly, 41*(2), 629–643.

Kadić-Maglajlić, S., Arslanagić-Kalajdžić, M., Micevski, M., Michaelidou, N., & Nemkova, E. (2017). Controversial Advert Perceptions in SNS Advertising:

The Role of Ethical Judgement and Religious Commitment. *Journal of Business Ethics, 141*(2), 249–265.

Kao, T.-Y., Yang, M.-H., Wu, J.-T. B., & Cheng, Y.-Y. (2016). Co-creating Value with Consumers Through Social Media. *Journal of Services Marketing, 30*(2), 141–151.

Kohler, C. (2006). Sony's Failed PSP Viral Marketing Stunt. *Wired.* Retrieved from https://www.wired.com/2006/12/sonys_failed_ps/

Leiser, M. (2016). AstroTurfing, 'CyberTurfing' and Other Online Persuasion Campaigns. *European Journal of Law and Technology, 7*(1), 1–26.

Li, H., Mukherjee, A., Liu, B., Kornfield, R., & Emery, S. (2014). *Detecting Campaign Promoters on Twitter Using Markov Random Fields.* Paper presented at the IEEE International Conference on Data Mining (ICDM).

Mackey, T. K., & Liang, B. A. (2013). Global Reach of Direct-to-Consumer Advertising Using Social Media for Illicit Online Drug Sales. *Journal of Medical Internet Research, 15*(5), e105.

Mackey, T. K., Miner, A., & Cuomo, R. E. (2015). Exploring the E-Cigarette E-Commerce Marketplace: Identifying Internet E-Cigarette Marketing Characteristics and Regulatory Gaps. *Drug and Alcohol Dependence, 156,* 97–103.

Majchrzak, A., Markus, L., & Wareham, J. (2016). Designing for Digital Transformation: Lessons for Information Systems Research from the Study of ICT and Societal Challenges. *MIS Quarterly, 40*(2), 267–277.

McCreanor, T., Lyons, A., Griffin, C., Goodwin, I., Barnes, H. M., & Hutton, F. (2013). Youth Drinking Cultures, Social Networking and Alcohol Marketing: Implications for Public Health. *Critical Public Health, 23*(1), 110–120.

Nicholls, J. (2012). Everyday, Everywhere: Alcohol Marketing and Social Media—Current Trends. *Alcohol, 47,* 486–493.

Nunan, D., & Yenicioglu, B. (2013). Informed, Uninformed and Participative Consent in Social Media Research. *International Journal of Market Research, 55*(6), 791–808.

Okoli, C., & Schabram, K. (2010). A Guide to Conducting a Systematic Literature Review of Information Systems Research. *Sprouts: Working Papers on Information Systems, 10*(6).

Parent, M., Plangger, K., & Bal, A. (2011). The New WTP: Willingness to Participate. *Business Horizons, 54,* 219–229.

Pick, T. (2017). *47 Superb Social Media Marketing Stats and Facts.* Retrieved from http://www.business2community.com/social-media/47-superb-social-media-marketing-stats-facts-01431126#sm2ttcRugkC6yUZw.97

Risch, M. (2009). Virtual Rule of Law. *West Virginia Law Review, 112*, 1–52.

Rowe, F. (2014). What Literature Review Is Not: Diversity, Boundaries and Recommendations. *European Journal of Information Systems, 23*(3), 241–255.

Sherman, L. E., Payton, A. A., Hernandez, L. M., Greenfield, P. M., & Dapretto, M. (2016). The Power of the Like in Adolescence: Effects of Peer Influence on Neural and Behavioral Responses to Social Media. *Psychological Science, 27*(7), 1027–1035.

Shirish, A., Chandra, S., & Srivastava, S. C. (2013). Virtual Worlds as Platforms for Digital Entrepreneurship: The Role of Internal Governance and the Rule of Law. In Y. K. Dwivedi, H. Z. Henriksen, D. Wastell, & R. De (Eds.), *Grand Successes and Failures in IT. Public and Private Sectors* (Vol. 402). Berlin, Heidelberg: Springer.

Shirish, A., Chandra, S., & Srivastava, S. C. (2017). *Watch Out-It's My Private Space! Examining the Influence of Technology Driven Intrusions on Employee Performance.* Paper presented at the Proceedings of the 50th Hawaii International Conference on System Sciences, USA.

Sisson, D. C. (2017). Inauthentic Communication, Organization-Public Relationships, and Trust: A Content Analysis of Online Astroturfing News Coverage. *Public Relations Review* (In Press).

Statista. (2017). *Social Media Statistics & Facts.* Retrieved June 26, 2017, from https://www.statista.com/topics/1164/social-networks/

Thies, F., Wessel, M., & Benlian, A. (2016). Effects of Social Interaction Dynamics on Platforms. *Journal of Management Information Systems, 33*(3), 843–873.

Trapp, R. (2016). Digital Transformation Drives Business for Social Media Managers. Retrieved June 26, 2017, from https://www.forbes.com/sites/rogertrapp/2016/10/12/digital-transformation-drives-business-for-social-media-managers/#3102bc9a3547

Truong, Y., & Simmons, G. (2010). Perceived Intrusiveness in Digital Advertising: Strategic Marketing Implications. *Journal of Strategic Marketing, 18*(3), 239–256.

Tushnet, R. (2010). Attention Must Be Paid: Commercial Speech, User-Generated Ads, and the Challenge of Regulation. *Buffalo Law Review, 58*, 721–793.

Verbauwhed, L. (2014). *Legal Pitfalls in Taking or Using Photographs of Copyright Material, Trademarks and People.* Retrieved from http://www.wipo.int/export/sites/www/sme/en/documents/pdf/ip_photography.pdf

Wang, G., Wilson, C., Zhao, X., Zhu, Y., & Mohanlal, M. (2012). *Serf and Turf: Crowdturfing for Fun and Profit.* Paper presented at the International World

Wide Web Conference Com—with an URL. We perform detailed analysis of tasks trying to start mittee (IW3C2), France.

Xie, K., & Young-Jin, L. (2015). Social Media and Brand Purchase: Quantifying the Effects of Exposures to Earned and Owned Social Media Activities in a Two-Stage Decision Making Model. *Journal of Management Information Systems, 32*(2), 204–238.

PART II

# Understanding Digital Consumers

CHAPTER 6

# Exploring the Relationship Between Perceived Benefits and Social Media Brands Using Discriminant Analysis

*Rajendra Nargundkar and Avinash Mulky*

## Introduction

The major objective of this study was to foster a greater understanding of social media users in India, with an emphasis on younger users. For our age group, we chose respondents mostly between twenty and thirty-five years of age.

> Online technology ... fosters bonding networks of members connected by a common interest by breaking traditional demographic barriers such as ethnicity or national origin. (Hampton & Wellman, 2003)

Two of the most-used social media in India today are LinkedIn and Facebook. But there are likely to be major differences in the way users perceive them and the benefits they provide. For example, Campbell, Anitsal, and Anitsal (2013) found that their respondents found Facebook

R. Nargundkar (✉)
Indian Institute of Management Indore, Indore, India

A. Mulky
Indian Institute of Management Bangalore, Bangalore, India



G. Heggde, G. Shainesh (eds.), *Social Media Marketing*,
https://doi.org/10.1007/978-981-10-5323-8_6

to be personal, and a website to be corporate. We wanted to find out if these kinds of perception extend to perceived benefits as well.

> LinkedIn, for instance, allows users to see how they are linked to others and how many degrees of separation they are from a 'target' member—possibly an employer they would like to meet .... With a focus on relationship building, LinkedIn has a referral system so that these users can be introduced, through a chain of friends-of-friends, to the person they intended to meet so that they can be closer to the people they would like to meet. (Kietzmann, Hermkens, McCarthy, & Silvestre, 2011)

Kwon and Wen (2010) in their study based on the technology acceptance model (TAM) studied three dimensions—social identity, altruism and telepresence—and tried to segment users based on them to discover how these dimensions would impact consumers' use of *social network services*, their term for social media. They also mention that "affective and social factors are more important in explaining the usage of social network services other than task-oriented systems," and that inadequate attention has been paid to such factors.

According to Venkatesh, Thong, and Xu (2012), hedonic motivation is a critical determinant of behavioral intention in an individual's use of technology (they studied mobile Internet technology in Hong Kong). They also found some gender, age, and experience differences in the use of technology. They found that the effect of hedonic motivation was stronger for young men who had relatively less experience of the technology as compared to women. They also suggest that "in the context of social computing, social outcomes such as higher status in the community or being unique in the group may be important additional drivers of IT use," and that these motivations need further study.

In their discussion of first-time use of technology (in their case, it is students' use of Facebook), Cheung and Lee (2010) found that social influence—meaning the influence of family or friends, which some researchers refer to as compliance, is important in their selection of technology. But this influence becomes less important subsequently.

The authors, who studied only Facebook users, caution that there could be differences between them and other types of online social network users, such as professionals using LinkedIn.

According to a study by the Pew Research Center (2013, accessed on the Internet and referenced at the end of this chapter), "while Facebook is popular across a diverse mix of demographic groups, other sites have developed their own unique demographic user profiles. For example, Pinterest holds particular appeal to female users (women are four times as likely as men to be Pinterest users), and LinkedIn is especially popular among college graduates and internet users in higher income households."

Online social networks are deemed to be equally suitable for formal and informal networks, according to Putnam (2000). Therefore, to find out what differences users perceive among them, we decided to investigate user perceptions of one formal and one informal medium. Facebook represents the informal one and LinkedIn the formal one. A post on the blog *Research Junction* suggests that Facebook's original positioning was "a social space online" and now it could be described as "the world's social graph." To explore some of the perceptions of Indian users, we decided to perform this exploratory study.

## Design/Methodology

A sample of 156 students at an Indian business school was chosen. Doctoral and MBA students were a part of the sample. They filled out a structured questionnaire, which included some general statements on social media usage. These were used to perform an exploratory factor analysis to find the factors underlying them. There was also a question about the social media the study respondents used most frequently, which served to divide them into two groups: LinkedIn users and Facebook users. They rated five characteristics/user benefits of the social medium they used on a scale of 1 to 10. These served as independent variables in a discriminant analysis performed using the two media as groups. The five independent variables rated were (1) user friendly, (2) beneficial personally, (3) beneficial professionally, (4) strengthens my existing network, and (5) generates new contacts or common interest groups.

## Findings

### *Discriminant Analysis*

A statistically significant discriminant model resulted that could distinguish between the perceived benefits of LinkedIn and Facebook. Detailed results are in the following tables.

**Table 6.1** Wilks's lambda

| *Test of function(s)* | *Wilks's lambda* | *Chi-square* | *df* | *Sig.* |
|---|---|---|---|---|
| 1 | .833 | 15.579 | 5 | .008 |

**Table 6.2** Standardized canonical discriminant function coefficients

| *Variable* | *Function* |
|---|---|
| | *1* |
| User friendly | −.062 |
| Beneficial personally | 1.309 |
| Beneficial professionally | −.247 |
| Strengthens my existing network | −.657 |
| Generates new contacts | .264 |

The discriminant model with LinkedIn/Facebook as the dependent and five independent variables is significant, according to Table 6.1. The p value of the chi-square test is .008. The model is able to correctly classify close to 70 percent of the cases, which is reasonably good.

From Table 6.2, we conclude that variables 2 (beneficial personally) and 4 (strengthens my existing network) are the most important in differentiating between Facebook and LinkedIn. Table 6.3 gives us the centroids for the two groups. The midpoint of these two (−.61 and .32) can be used to classify (predict) any new case as either a LinkedIn user or a Facebook user, depending on which of the centroids its Y value is closer to. The coefficients of the discriminant model in Table 6.4 are used to calculate the value of Y to be used for classifying a new case. The model would be Y = −2.455 – .023 (user friendly rating) + .612 (beneficial personally rating) – (beneficial professionally rating) – .25 (strengthens my existing network) + .106 (generates new contacts) from the coefficients in Table 6.4.

### *Factor Analysis*

A factor analysis of seventeen statements relating to social media use was also done to understand the factors that might be underlying these variables. Six factors were extracted from the seventeen variables (the variables can be found in Appendix 1 and factors extracted with eigenvalues can be found in Table 6.5), explaining a total of around 65 percent of the variance.

**Table 6.3** Functions at group centroids

| *Most-used social medium* | *Function* |
|---|---|
| | *1* |
| LinkedIn | −.610 |
| Facebook | .320 |

Unstandardized canonical discriminant functions evaluated at group means

**Table 6.4** Canonical (raw) discriminant function coefficients

| | *Function* |
|---|---|
| | *1* |
| | −.023 |
| | .612 |
| | −.105 |
| | −.250 |
| | .106 |
| (Constant) | −2.455 |

Unstandardized coefficients

The criterion used for extraction was that the factor must have an eigenvalue of 1 or more. The principal components method was used to extract factors, and a varimax rotation followed. Table 6.6 shows the rotated component matrix. Based on factor loadings in the matrix, the following descriptions of factors are appropriate:

Factor 1 comprises variables 1, 2, 9, 11, and 12. This factor can be termed "sharing with old and new friends."

Factor 2 includes variables 14, 15, 16 and 17, and can be termed "transformation through social media."

Factor 3 includes variables 8, 9, and 10, indicating that it covers existing relationships, both personal and office related.

Factor 4 consists of variables 5 and 6, and can be termed "family and colleagues" or extended family.

Factor 5 includes variables 3 and 7, and can be termed "professional networking."

Factor 6 includes variables 4 and 13, indicating what can be termed "distinct use of social media."

**Table 6.5** Total variance explained by factors extracted

| *Component* | *Initial eigenvalues* | | | *Extraction sums of squared loadings* | | |
|---|---|---|---|---|---|---|
| | *Total* | *% of variance* | *Cumulative %* | *Total* | *% of variance* | *Cumulative %* |
| 1 | 4.229 | 24.877 | 24.877 | 4.229 | 24.877 | 24.877 |
| 2 | 1.859 | 10.937 | 35.814 | 1.859 | 10.937 | 35.814 |
| 3 | 1.324 | 7.791 | 43.605 | 1.324 | 7.791 | 43.605 |
| 4 | 1.257 | 7.397 | 51.002 | 1.257 | 7.397 | 51.002 |
| 5 | 1.236 | 7.269 | 58.271 | 1.236 | 7.269 | 58.271 |
| 6 | 1.183 | 6.956 | 65.227 | 1.183 | 6.956 | 65.227 |
| 7 | .926 | 5.449 | 70.677 | | | |
| 8 | .784 | 4.610 | 75.287 | | | |
| 9 | .738 | 4.343 | 79.630 | | | |
| 10 | .692 | 4.069 | 83.699 | | | |
| 11 | .557 | 3.277 | 86.976 | | | |
| 12 | .501 | 2.949 | 89.926 | | | |
| 13 | .435 | 2.557 | 92.483 | | | |
| 14 | .401 | 2.360 | 94.843 | | | |
| 15 | .365 | 2.147 | 96.989 | | | |
| 16 | .273 | 1.603 | 98.593 | | | |
| 17 | .239 | 1.407 | 100.000 | | | |

Extraction method: principal component analysis

These six factors together explain a lot about the views and motivations of social media use among a largely student population.

## Contribution/Value of the Study

The perceptions of Indian users (mainly younger users) regarding social media were captured by this study in two important ways. One, we found the two most-used social media were perceived distinctly. Though among the variables studied, personal benefits turned out to be the one that explained the difference between Linkedin and Facebook the best (from the standardized coefficients table), the other variables (professional benefits, strengthening existing contacts and generating new contacts) also contributed significantly. India has been a rapid adopter of mobile and Internet technologies in general, and social media in particular. But there are hardly any studies documenting the perceptions of Indian social media users. For instance, Wetsch

**Table 6.6** Factor analysis Q. 1 to 17; rotated component matrix

| | *Component* | | | | | |
|---|---|---|---|---|---|---|
| | *1* | *2* | *3* | *4* | *5* | *6* |
| Q1 | .792 | .162 | .119 | .127 | −.052 | −.023 |
| Q2 | .661 | .035 | .170 | −.184 | .113 | −.148 |
| Q3 | .021 | .029 | .001 | .053 | .868 | .157 |
| Q4 | .080 | −.099 | .205 | −.178 | .165 | .698 |
| Q5 | −.063 | −.049 | .031 | .856 | .093 | −.057 |
| Q6 | .295 | −.034 | .310 | .634 | −.069 | −.003 |
| Q7 | .267 | .137 | .042 | −.017 | .583 | −.502 |
| Q8 | −.023 | .097 | .770 | .166 | .110 | .033 |
| Q9 | .589 | .125 | .564 | −.035 | −.162 | .048 |
| Q10 | .371 | .074 | .775 | .110 | −.055 | −.016 |
| Q11 | .654 | .162 | .201 | .133 | .139 | .201 |
| Q12 | .792 | .161 | −.092 | .119 | .105 | .143 |
| Q13 | .122 | .250 | −.383 | .165 | −.069 | .584 |
| Q14 | .014 | .779 | .147 | −.035 | .145 | .022 |
| Q15 | .086 | .790 | .121 | −.099 | .107 | .133 |
| Q16 | .358 | .612 | −.128 | .115 | −.089 | −.141 |
| Q17 | .425 | .565 | −.003 | −.033 | −.212 | −.132 |

Extraction method: principal component analysis
Rotation method: varimax with Kaiser normalization

(2012) is of the view that personal branding can be of immense benefit if done in a planned manner, not just on Linkedin but on all social media. This may have relevance in the Indian context in the light of this study's findings.

Second, this study finds that social media are viewed as "relationship builders" but also as having "transformational power" of the kind that has been seen in social and political movements in Africa and Asia over the last three years. Both general uses and distinctive uses have been found by Indian consumers of social media.

Lastly, this study has contributed to a better understanding of social media users of the two most-used media (LinkedIn and Facebook), who also tend to be consumers of other goods and services. This would be useful for managers who wish to use social media to meet some of their communication goals.

## Appendix 1: Questionnaire Items Used in Factor Analysis

Use this scale for your answers (1 = Strongly agree, 2 = Agree 3 = Neither agree nor disagree, 4 = Disagree and 5 = Strongly Disagree).

1. I find social media useful for keeping in touch with friends
2. I think social media are good for sharing photographs.
3. I think social media are good for sharing recipes.
4. Social media are only for socializing.
5. Family members should also be a part of one's social media circle.
6. Colleagues in your workplace should be in your social media circle.
7. Job search can be done by using social media.
8. Existing relationships with family are strengthened by using social media.
9. Existing relationships with friends are strengthened by using social media.
10. Existing relationships with colleagues are strengthened by using social media.
11. One can make new friends through the use of social media.
12. Common interest groups can be found through social media.
13. Professional networking and social networking should not mix.
14. Social media can change the way we think.
15. Social transformation is possible through social media.
16. Political parties can use social media to convert people.
17. Revolutions are helped by social media.

## Select References

Campbell, S. R., Anitsal, I., & Anitsal, M. M. (2013). Social Media's Key Success Factors: An Analysis of Customer Reactions. *Business Studies Journal, 5*(1), 43–56.

Cheung, C. M. K., & Lee, M. K. O. (2010). A Theoretical Model of Intentional Social Action in Online Social Networks. *Decision Support Systems, 49*, 24–30.

Hampton, K. N., & Wellman, B. (2003). Neighboring in Netville: How the Internet Supports Community and Social Capital in a Wired Suburb. *City and Community, 2*, 277–311.

Kietzmann, J. H., Hermkens, K., McCarthy, I. P., & Silvestre, B. S. (2011). Social Media? Get Serious! Understanding the Functional Building Blocks of Social Media. *Business Horizons, 54*, 241–251.

Kwon, O., & Wen, Y. (2010). An Empirical Study of the Factors Affecting Social Network Service Use. *Computers in Human Behavior, 26*, 254–263.
Putnam, R. D. (2000). *Bowling Alone: The Collapse and Revival of American Community*. New York, NY: Simon Schuster.
Venkatesh, V., Thong, J. Y. L., & Xu, X. (2012, March). Consumer Acceptance and Use of Information Technology: Extending the Unified Theory of Acceptance and Use of Technology. *MIS Quarterly, 36*(1), 157–178.
Wetsch, L. R. (2012, Spring). A Personal Branding Assignment Using Social Media. *Journal of Advertising Education, 16*, 30–36.

## Internet References

http://aytm.com/blog/research-junction/brand-positioning-standards-and-practices-part-3/. Accessed on March 3, 2014.
http://www.pewinternet.org/2013/12/30/social-media-update-2013/. Accessed on March 3, 2014.

CHAPTER 7

# The Influence of Trust and Ease of Use of Social Media Platforms on South Africa's Generation Y Social Media Use Intention and Information Sharing

*Nathalie Chinje and Richard Chinomona*

## Introduction

Social media refers to platforms and applications that encompass easily accessible web instruments that allow individuals to create, share, and seek content, as well as to communicate and collaborate with one another (Kim, Jeong, & Lee, 2010; Popoiu, Grosseck, & Holotescu, 2012). These social media platforms provide their users with, among others, a profile, friend list, chat option and ability to send private or public messages, event creation, and comment posting and receiving feedback (Corritore, Kracher, & Wiedenbeck, 2003). Common among the Generation Y community are social media platforms such as Facebook, YouTube, What's Up, Twitter, Skype and MySpace (Talug, 2012). Having been born in the digital environment where the use of various social media platforms have

N. Chinje (✉)
UPbeat Marketing, Johannesburg, South Africa

R. Chinomona
School of Economics and Business Sciences, Wits University, Johannesburg, South Africa



G. Heggde, G. Shainesh (eds.), *Social Media Marketing*,
https://doi.org/10.1007/978-981-10-5323-8_7

proliferated, Generation Y, also known as the digital natives (Prensky, 2001, p. 2) are leveraging the interactive and collaborative aspects of the Internet (Popoiu et al., 2012).

The increased use of social media has positioned it as a powerful source of information (Purcell, Rainie, Mitchell, Rosenstiel, & Olmstead, 2010). As a result, research on social media networks has grown substantially. However, most of these studies have mainly focused on exploring the determinants of knowledge sharing via employee weblogs (Lin, Hung, & Chen, 2009), news sharing in social media, the effects of trust, security, and privacy in social networking (Shin, 2010), intentions to use social media in organizing and taking vacation trips (Parra-López, Bulchand-Gidumal, Gutiérrez-Tano, & Diaz-Armas, 2011), and Generation Y travelers' commitment to online social network websites (Nusair, Bilgihan, Okumus, & Cobanoglu, 2013).

Despite the burgeoning research and the attention that social media has garnered among academicians, there is a scarcity of studies that explore issues of trust and ease of use of social media platforms for information sharing. Moreover, most of the studies that have attempted to investigate the relationships between some of these variables have been conducted in developed countries of Europe and the USA (Parra-López et al., 2011; Purcell et al., 2010) or the newly developed countries of Asia (Lin et al., 2009; Shin, 2010). Therefore, research that investigates the influence of trust and ease of use on social media platforms use intention and information sharing by social community members in the context of emerging markets remains scant.

Therefore, this paper seeks to fulfill three objectives:

- to examine the causal influence of social media trust and ease of use on information sharing among the Generation Y virtual community in South Africa
- to present an empirical investigation of the mediating role of social media use intention in these relationships
- to apply use and gratification theory (UGT) to this research context

## Literature Review

### *Generation Y Virtual Community*

Generation Y, known as the net generation, or digital natives, refers to individuals who were born between 1978 and 1994 (Nusair et al., 2013).

They are technologically savvy and are more involved in such online activities as text messaging, social networks, podcasts, and blogs (Quan-Haase & Young, 2010; Xiang & Gretzel, 2010). In the USA, Generation Y is regarded as an economically robust cohort with $200 billion in annual expenditures (Djamasbi, Siegel, & Tullis, 2010). According to the *Oxygenz Country Report* (2010) on South Africa, Generation Y represents 22.9 percent of South Africa's total population. In recent years, the use of social media platforms by Generation Y has been continuously increasing and social media platforms have emerged as innovative relationship-building tools in both developed and emerging markets (Dateling & Bick, 2013).

Due to the critical role that social media platforms are playing, issues such as trust have become relevant in determining the users' desire to employ them and share information with other users on social media platforms (Fogel & Nehmad, 2009).

### *Social Media Trust*

Papagapitos and Riley (2009) defines trust as an implicit set of beliefs that the other party will refrain from opportunistic behavior and will not take advantage of the situation. In this study, trust refers to social trust, meaning individual internalization of norms of reciprocity, which facilitates collective action by allowing social media platform users to take risks and to trust that fellow participants will not take advantage of them (Güth, Levati, & Ploner, 2008).

In a virtual community where rules do not provide sufficient guarantees that others will behave as they are expected to, trust tends to serve as a subjective substitute for such rules and therefore creates the necessary atmosphere that makes engagement with others more open (Kim, Kavanaugh, & Smith-Jackson, 2007). It is noted that in such a case, trust rules out undesirable, yet possible, opportunistic behavior on the part of others (Al-Natour, Benbasat, & Cenfetelli, 2005; Cyr, Hassanein, Head, & Ivanov, 2007). Thus, trust is important in virtual communities where the absence of workable rules results in reliance on the socially acceptable behavior of others (Güth et al., 2008).

### *Social Media Ease of Use*

The word *ease* is defined as "freedom from difficulty or great effort" (Choi & Totten, 2012). Thus, the term *social media ease of use* refers to how effortless the social media platform is to use (Nielsen, Molich, Snyder, &

Farrell, 2000; Sivo & Pan, 2005). While the Generation Y virtual community may anticipate enjoying using a social media platform, they may at the same time find it too difficult to use thus outweighing the benefits of usage. In such a case, the intention to use that specific social media platform might be minimal (Zhang & Mao, 2008. Thus, in this regard, social media ease of use explains the user's perception of the amount of effort required to utilize the social media platform or the extent to which a user believes that using a social media platform will be effortless (Sivo & Pan, 2005; Teo, Su Luan, & Sing, 2008).

### *Social Media Use Intention*

The extant literature technological acceptance model (TAM) tends to support the rationale that use intention leads to the actual use of technologies (for example, Chau & Hu, 2001; Dasgupta, Granger, & Mcgarry, 2002; Fusilier & Durlabhji, 2005; Wang & Fesenmaier, 2004; Wang, Yu, & Fesenmaier, 2002). Consequently, the validity of this claim has been tested in social media context by Lee and Ma (2012). Following the supporting empirical evidence from Lee and Ma (2012), this study therefore utilizes *social media use intention* as a dependent construct. In addition, Teo et al. (2008) assert that use intention is also a practical measure of actual use.

However, despite the growing research on social media, little is known about the Generation Y virtual community's motivation to use social media in South Africa. Therefore, an investigation of the extent to which the social media use intention actually impacts Generation Y virtual community information sharing in South Africa is warranted.

### *Social Media Information Sharing*

An essential part of involvement in social media is receiving or disseminating information (Wasko & Faraj, 2000). *Receiving information* simply means reading an ongoing conversation in the community, while *disseminating information* means posting conversation, either in direct response to another member's post or by simply starting a new topic of conversation in the community. According to Prahinski and Benton (2004), information sharing is usually influenced by prosocial attitudes and organizational norms.

We define information sharing as the degree to which the Generational Y virtual community members have access to one another's information considered of mutual and beneficial interest (Bonds-Raacke & Raccke, 2010). This information includes sharing each other's profile information such as photos, contact details, and discussions on topical or current issues of interest to the community.

## Conceptual Model and Hypothesis Development

### *Use and Gratification Theory (UGT)*

Use and gratification theory (UGT) is rooted in communications literature and is based on the premise that people tend to search for those media that will help them achieve ultimate gratification (Whiting & Williams, 2013). It explains what social and psychological needs motivate audiences to select particular media channels and content choices, as well as the subsequent attitudinal and behavioral effects (Diddi & LaRose, 2006; Quan-Haase & Young, 2010). Because of its origins in communications, UGT is considered one of the most effective theories for identifying motivations underlying media use in mass communication studies (LaRose & Eastin, 2004; Whiting & Williams, 2013).

The theory argues that people are aware of their social and psychological needs and actively seek the particular media that fulfill their communicational purposes (Armstrong & McAdams, 2009). Current studies on social media platforms have used UGT to better understand the extent to which users expect various needs and desires will be fulfilled by use of Facebook (for example, Bumgarner, 2007; Foregger, 2008; Papacharissi & Mendelson, 2011; Raacke & Bonds-Raacke, 2008).

In this study, we focus on the gratification sought and the consequence of the gratification obtained (Raacke & Bonds-Raacke, 2008). *Gratification sought* refers to the users' expectations of gratification from their use of a social media platform before they have actually used it (Quan-Haase & Young, 2010)—for instance, the ease of use of the social media platform and the trust the users have in it. *Gratification obtained* refers to users' experience of gratification when using a particular social media platform.

Drawing from use and gratification theory and social media literature, we propose a conceptual model that empirically tests the interrelationships between social media trust, ease of use, use intention, and social media

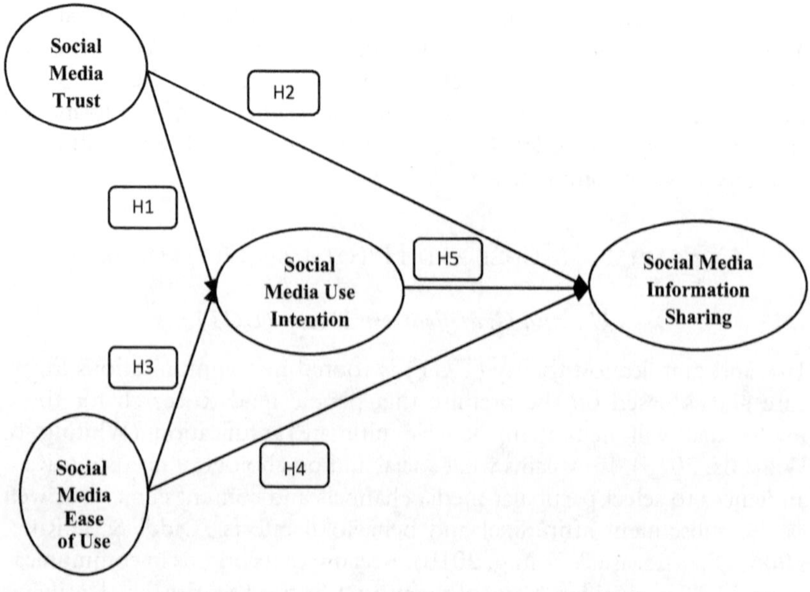


**Fig. 7.1** Conceptual model

information sharing. In this conceptualized model, social media trust and social media ease of use are the predictors, while social media use intention is the mediator. Social media information sharing is the sole outcome variable. Figure 7.1 depicts this conceptualized research model. The hypothesized relationships between the research constructs will be discussed thereafter.

### *Social Media Trust, Use Intention, and Information Sharing*

Trust in social media use and information sharing is widely covered in the literature (Coppola, Hiltz, & Rotter, 2004; Dwyer, Hiltz, & Passerini, 2007; Piccoli & Ives, 2003). When users trust a social media platform, they will exert less effort to scrutinize details or assess the authenticity of the services offered (Gambi, 2009). Because users assume the authenticity of the social media platform, they will not waste time and cognitive effort and thus will experience higher intention to use that on the social media platform. Thus, the higher the degree of trust the Generation Y virtual community places in a social media platform, the more they want to use that social media platform in order to gratify their needs (cf. Joinson, 2008).

Similarly, when trust exists between individuals and within a particular social media platform, users are more willing to participate in shared activity (Kim & Benbasat, 2003). This is because trust helps users reduce their risk perceptions when dealing with other social media platform users (Van der Heijden, Verhagen, & Creemers, 2003), and makes them more comfortable sharing their personal information, which is essential for cooperative information exchange (McKnight & Choudhury, 2006). Therefore, the higher the degree of trust the Generation Y virtual community places in a social media platform, the more they want to share information on that social media platform in order to gratify their needs (McKnight & Choudhury, 2006).

Accordingly, drawing from use and gratification theory and empirical evidence, it can be expected that social media trust fosters social media platform use intention and information sharing among the Generation Y virtual community in South Africa. Therefore, we posit that

H1: trust in a social media platform will be positively associated with users' intention to use it;

H2: trust in a social media platform will be positively associated with users' desire to share information with others on it.

### *Social Media Ease of Use, Use Intention, and Information Sharing*

Perceived ease of use of a particular social media platform is the central driver of attitudes toward, and intentions to use, that social media platform (Lohr, Falro, Hunt, & Johnson, 2007). For instance, the quality of the user-interface design of the social media platform is a critical factor that influences consumers' intention to use a certain social media platform (Martin-Michiellot & Mendelsohn, 2000). Shin and Shin (2011) and Liu, Chen, and Sun (2006) suggest that a user-interface design, which can be determined, for example, by visual feedback, should offer a quick and easy guide to correct usage of the platform.

Thus, the better the social media platform's ease of use, the more likely the users will be to use that platform to share information. Previous studies have also supported a linkage between social media ease of use and intention to use and information sharing (Bonds-Raacke & Raccke, 2010). We hypothesize that

H3: social media platform ease of use will be positively associated with users' intention to use it;

H4: social media platform ease of use will be positively associated with users' desire to share information with others on it.

### *Social Media Use Intention and Information Sharing*

When social media platform use intention leads to actual use, then information sharing may be noteworthy (Liu et al., 2006). Drawing from extant literatures, information sharing has been found to be a motivation for using emergent virtual communities (Wasko & Faraj, 2000). Virtual community members can either receive information or disseminate information on a social media platform (Liu et al., 2006). Prior evidence has indicated that information sharing is influenced by prosocial attitudes and intentions to participate in social media platforms (Constant, Sproull, & Kiesler, 1996; Liu et al., 2006). Therefore, we can postulate that

H5: social media platform use intention will be positively associated with users' desire to share information with others on it.

## Research Methodology

### *Sample and Data Collection*

The data for this research was collected in the Gauteng Province of South Africa from the list of registered students at Vaal University of Technology and North West University Campus in Vanderbijlpark. In order to ascertain the students' status, only research participants with student identification cards were considered for this research. Students from the Vaal University of Technology were recruited to distribute and collect the questionnaires. Of the total of 180 questionnaires distributed, 150 usable questionnaires were retrieved for the final data analysis, representing a response rate of 83.3 percent.

### *Measurement Instrument and Questionnaire Design*

Research scales were operationalized on the basis of previous work. Proper modifications were made in order to fit the current research context and purpose. All the research constructs except social media information sharing (useing a five-item scale) were measured using three-item scales. "Social media ease of use" and "social media trust" measurement instruments were all adapted from Hernández-Ortega (2011) while "social media use intention" measurement instruments were adopted from Lee, Xiong, and Hu (2012). Finally, social media information sharing measurement instruments were adapted from Bock, Zmud, Kim, and Lee (2005).

All the measurement items were measured on a five-point Likert-type scale that was anchored to express the degree of agreement by 1 = strongly disagree to 5 = strongly agree. Individual scale items are listed in Appendix 1.

### *Respondent Profile*

As exhibited in Table 7.1, the profile of the research participants indicates that 56.7 percent of the participating students were female and the remainder were male. 53.5 percent were twenty-five years old, or less than

**Table 7.1** Sample demographic characteristics

| | *Frequency* | *Percentage* |
|---|---|---|
| **Gender** | | |
| Male | 65 | 43.3% |
| Female | 85 | 56.7% |
| **Total** | **150** | **100%** |
| **Age** | | |
| ≦20 | 12 | 0.08% |
| 21–25 | 79 | 52.7% |
| ≧ 25 | 59 | 39.3% |
| **Total** | **150** | **100%** |
| **Academic Level** | | |
| Undergraduate student | 107 | 71.3% |
| Postgraduate student | 43 | 28.7% |
| **Total** | **150** | **100%** |
| **Student University** | | |
| Vaal University of Technology | 113 | 75.3% |
| North West University | 37 | 24.7% |
| **Total** | **150** | **100%** |

twenty-five years old, while the remainder were above twenty-six years of age. Also, 71.3 percent of the respondents were undergraduate students and the remainder were postgraduate students. The students from Vaal University of Technology constituted 75.3 percent of the respondents and the remainder were from North West University, Vanderbijlpark Campus.

## Analysis and Findings

### *Structural Equation Modeling Approach*

In order to statistically analyze the measurement and structural models, this study used Smart PLS software for structural equation modeling (SEM) technique (Ringle, Wende, & Will, 2005). In SEM, the measurement model refers to the linkages between the latent variables and their manifest variables and the structural model captures the hypothesized causal relationships among the research constructs (Chin & Newsted, 1999). Unlike AMOS and LISREL which are covariance-based approaches, Smart PLS is a regression-based technique that originates from path analysis. Smart PLS has emerged as a powerful approach to study causal models involving multiple constructs with multiple indicators (Chinomona & Surujal, 2012). Smart PLS, a component-based method, has an ability to model latent constructs that are uncontaminated by measurement error under conditions of non-normality. It has the ability to handle complex predictive models in small-to-medium sample sizes. Since the current study sample size is relatively small (150), Smart PLS was found more appropriate and befitting the purpose of the current study. In this respect, a bootstrapping resampling method was used to test the statistical significance of the relationships. This procedure entailed generating 200 sub-samples of cases randomly selected, with replacement, from the original data. Below is Table 7.2, presenting evidence on the reliability and validity of the measurement model.

### *Measurement Model*

To ensure convergent validity, the researchers checked whether items loaded on their respective (a priori) constructs had loadings greater than 0.6, while discriminant validity was checked by ensuring that there were no significant inter-research variables cross-loadings (Chin, 1998). As can

**Table 7.2** Accuracy analysis statistics

| *Research construct* | | *LV index value* | *R-squared value* | *Cronbach's α value* | *C.R. value* | *AVE value* | *Communality* | *Factor loading* |
|---|---|---|---|---|---|---|---|---|
| SMT | SMT 1 | | | | | | | 0.833 |
| | SMT 2 | 4.284 | | 0.839 | 0.903 | 0.756 | | 0.914 |
| | SMT 3 | | 0.000 | | | | 0.756 | 0.859 |
| SMEU | SMEU 1 | | | | | | | 0.851 |
| | SMEU 2 | 4.437 | | 0.893 | 0.934 | 0.825 | | 0.956 |
| | SMEU 3 | | 0.000 | | | | 0.825 | 0.915 |
| SMUI | SMUI 1 | | | | | | | 0.902 |
| | SMUI 2 | 4.346 | 0.188 | 0.880 | 0.926 | 0.807 | | 0.929 |
| | SMUI 3 | | | | | | 0.807 | 0.863 |
| SMIS | SMIS 1 | | | | | | | 0.794 |
| | SMIS 2 | | | | | | | 0.836 |
| | SMIS 3 | | 0.538 | | | | | 0.831 |
| | SMIS 4 | 4.479 | | 0.881 | 0.914 | 0.680 | 0.680 | 0.847 |
| | SMIS 5 | | | | | | | 0.868 |

Note: SMT = social media trust; SMEU = social media ease of use; SMUI = social media use intention; SMIS = social media information sharing

be seen (Table 7.2), all items have loadings greater than 0.6 (i.e., ranging from 0.794 to 0.956), with no cross-loadings greater than 0.787, while t-statistics derived from bootstrapping (200 resamples) suggest all loadings are significant at pb0.001. As such, this confirms that all the measurement items converged well on their respective constructs and therefore are acceptable measures.

According to Chin (1998), research variables should have an average variance extracted (AVE) of more than 0.5 and a composite reliability (CR) of more than 0.7 (for establishing convergent validity), and interconstruct correlations should be less than the square root of the Average Variance Extracted (AVE) (for establishing discriminant validity). As can be seen (Table 7.2), all constructs exceed these criteria, with AVE and Composite Reliability (CR) generally equal to, or greater than, 0.6 and 0.9, respectively. Furthermore, as indicated in Table 7.3, the square root of the lowest AVE is 0.82 and is greater than the highest interconstruct correlation value (0.787). All in all, these results confirm the existence of the discriminant validity of the measurement used in this study.

**Table 7.3** Correlations between constructs

| *Research constructs* | *SMT* | *SMEU* | *SMUI* | *SMIS* |
|---|---|---|---|---|
| SMT | 1.000 | | | |
| SMEU | 0.787 | 1.000 | | |
| SMUI | 0.3965 | 0.420 | 1.000 | |
| SMIS | 0.420 | 0.529 | 0.681 | 1.000 |

Note: SMT = social media trust; SMEU = social media ease of use; SMUI = social media use intention; SMIS = social media information sharing

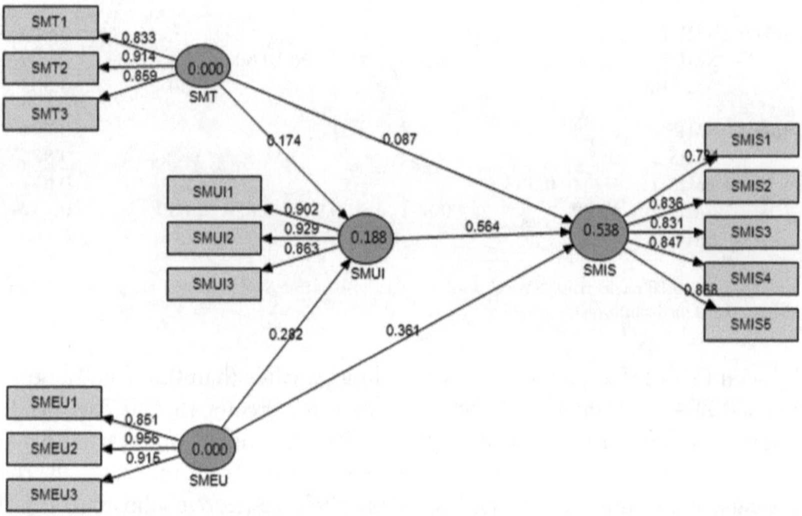


**Fig. 7.2** Measurement and structural model results. Note: SMT = social media trust; SMEU = social media ease of use; SMUI = social media use intention; SMIS = social media information sharing

## *Path Model*

PLS also generates the path coefficients for the relationships modeled among the constructs. The significance of these coefficients was assessed using the bootstrap procedure (with 200 subsamples) that provided the *t*-values for each path estimate. Figure 7.2 and Table 7.4 present the results of the PLS analysis on the structural model along with the path estimates and *t*-values. Support for the study hypotheses, which are labeled

**Table 7.4** Results of structural equation model analysis

| *Proposed hypothesis relationship* | *Hypothesis* | *Path coefficients* | *t-Statistics* | *Rejected/ supported* |
|---|---|---|---|---|
| SMT → SMUI | H1 | 0.087 | 0.681 | Supported |
| SMT → SMIS | H2 | 0.174 | 1.140 | Supported |
| SMEU → SMUI | H3 | 0.282 | 2.002 | Supported |
| SMEU → SMIS | H4 | 0.361 | 2.522 | Supported |
| SMUI → SMIS | H5 | 0.564 | 8.427 | Supported |

Note: SMT = social media trust; SMEU = social media ease of use; SMUI = social media use intention; SMIS = social media information sharing

on their corresponding paths in Fig. 7.2, can be ascertained by examining the directionality (positive or negative) of the path coefficients and the significance of the *t*-values. The standardized path coefficients are expected to be at least 0.2, and preferably greater than 0.3 (Chin, 1998).

The results provide support for the proposed positive relationships between the five relationships (i.e., H1, H2, H3, H4, and H5). However, results in Table 7.4, indicate that only three (i.e., H3, H4, and H5) of the posited relationships are statistically significant (i.e., *t*-statistics value is greater than 2). Figure 7.2 and Table 7.4 provide the path coefficients for H1, H2, H3, H4, and H5 (i.e., 0.087, 0.174, 0.282, 0.361, and 0.564 respectively).

Overall, $R^2$ for SMIS (0.538) in Fig. 7.2 indicates that the research model explains more than 53 percent of the variance in the endogenous variables, while SMUI explains about 19 percent (0.188). The following formulae are provided by Tenenhaus, Vinzi, Chatelin, and Lauro (2005). The global goodness-of-fit (GoF) statistic for the research model was calculated using the following equation:

$$\text{GoF} = \sqrt{\text{AVE}} * R^2$$

The calculated global goodness of fit (GoF) is 0.47, which exceeds the threshold of GoF > 0.36 suggested by Wetzels, Odekerken-Schröder, and Van Oppen (2009). Thus, this study concludes that the research model has a good overall fit.

This study reveals that the social media ease of use has stronger effects on social media use intention (0.282) and social media information sharing (0.361) than social media trust on social media use intention (0.087) and social media information sharing (0.174). However, social media ease of use strongly influences social media information sharing (0.361) more than social media use intention (0.282). It can also be noted that the relationship between social media use intention and social media information is robust (0.564). By implication, this finding indicates that social media ease of use and social media trust have a strong influence on social media information via social media use intention. Perhaps this could be due to the fact that the effects of social media ease of use and trust are likely to be more pronounced in social media information sharing only when Generation Yers have a positive desire to use social media.

## Implications of the Study

The findings of this empirical study provide fruitful implications to both practitioners and academicians.

On the academic side, this study makes a significant contribution to the social media use literature by systematically exploring the impact of social media ease of use and trust on use intention and information sharing in the emerging market context of Generation Y. In particular, the current study findings provide tentative support to the proposition that social media ease of use should be recognized as a significant antecedent to, and tool for, influencing students' desire to use social media for information sharing.

On the practitioners' side, the important influential role of social media ease of use on social media information sharing in South Africa's Generation Y community is highlighted. This study points out that social media platform designers should consider the ease of use aspect when designing social media platforms. When Generation Yers perceive social media platforms to be easy to use, they are likely to desire using them and consequently, they will share more information when using these social media platforms. Similarly, marketers or educators who want to disseminate information on social media platforms to the Generation Y community have to consider those platforms that their targeted audiences find easy to use.

## Limitations and Future Research

The limitations of this research can also be viewed as avenues for future studies. An important limitation is the geographic spread of the study, which only concentrated on a single province (out of the nine South

African provinces). Subsequent research should contemplate replicating this study in other provinces of South Africa or even other African countries for results comparison. Moreover, the study was limited to student perspectives at two universities in South Africa. Future studies should therefore consider expanding data collection to include other virtual community members who utilize social media platforms. Finally, further research could also investigate the effects of other constructs such as *perceived enjoyment* from social media platform use as a possible predictor of the intention to use social media platform and information sharing for education and recreational activities.

## Conclusion

The purpose of this study was to investigate the influence of social media trust and ease of use on South Africa's Generation Y social media use intention and information sharing. In particular, five hypotheses were postulated. To test the proposed hypotheses, data were collected from university students in South Africa. The empirical results supported three out of the five posited research hypotheses in a significant way.

## References

Al-Natour, S., Benbasat, I., & Cenfetelli, R. (2005). *The Role of Similarity in e-Commerce Interactions: The Case of Online Shopping Assistants.* In Proceedings of the Fourth Annual Workshop on HCI Research in MIS, Las Vegas, Nevada, pp. 70–74.

Armstrong, C., & McAdams, M. (2009). Blogs of Information: How Gender Cues and Individual Motivations Influence Perceptions of Credibility. *Journal of Computer Mediated Communication, 14*(3), 435–456.

Bock, G.-W., Zmud, R. W., Kim, Y.-G., & Lee, J.-N. (2005). Behavioral Intention Formation in Knowledge Sharing: Examining the Role of Extrinsic Motivators, Social-Psychological Forces, and Organizational Climate. *MIS Quarterly, 29*(1), 87–111.

Bonds-Raacke, J., & Raccke, J. (2010). My Space and Facebook: Identifying Dimensions of Users and Gratifications for Friend Networking Sites. *Individual Differences Research, 8*(1), 27–33.

Bumgarner, B. A. (2007). You Have Been Poked: The Uses and Gratifications of Facebook Among Emerging Adults. *First Monday, 12*(11) [online]. Retrieved February 5, 2013, from http://firstmonday.org/htbin/cgiwrap/bin/ojs/index.php/fm/article/view/2026/1897

Chau, P. Y. K., & Hu, P. J. H. (2001). Information Technology Acceptance by Individual Professionals: A Model Comparison Approach. *Decision Sciences, 32*(4), 699–719.

Chin, W. W. (1998). Issues and Opinion on Structural Equation Modelling. *MIS Quarterly, 22*(1), 7–16.

Chin, W. W., & Newsted, P. R. (1999). Structural Equation Modeling Analysis with Small Samples Using Partial Least Squares. In R. Hoyle (Ed.), *Statistical Strategies for Small Sample Research, Sage Publications* (pp. 307–341). Thousand Oaks, CA: Sage.

Chinomona, R., & Surujal, B. (2012). The Influence of Student Internship Work Experience on Their Self-Improvement and Professionalism in Sport Management. *African Journal for Physical, Health Education, Recreation and Dance, 18*(4), 885–899.

Choi, Y. K., & Totten, J. W. (2012). Self-Construal's Role in Mobile TV Acceptance: Extension of TAM Across Cultures. *Journal of Business Research, 65*(11), 1525–1533.

Constant, D., Sproull, L., & Kiesler, S. (1996). The Kindness of Strangers: The Usefulness of Electronic Weak Ties for Technical Advice. *Organization Science, 7*(2), 119–135.

Coppola, N., Hiltz, S. R., & Rotter, N. (2004). Building Trust in Virtual Teams. *IEEE Transactions on Professional Communication, 47*(2), 95–104.

Corritore, C. L., Kracher, B., & Wiedenbeck, S. (2003). On-Line Trust: Concepts, Evolving Themes, a Model. *International Journal of Human – Computer Studies, 58*(6), 737–758.

Cyr, D., Hassanein, K., Head, M., & Ivanov, A. (2007). The Role of Social Presence in Establishing Loyalty in e-Service Environments. *Interacting with Computers, 19*, 43–56.

Dasgupta, S., Granger, M., & Mcgarry, N. (2002). User Acceptance of e-Collaboration Technology: An Extension of the Technology Acceptance Model. *Group Decision and Negotiation, 11*, 87–100.

Dateling, M., & Bick, G. (2013). *The Impact of Social Media on the Marketing Strategies of South African Businesses.* Paper presented at the 3rd Annual International Conference on Enterprise Marketing and Globalisation in Singapore. Global Science & Technology Forum.

Diddi, A., & Larose, R. (2006). Getting Hooked on News: Uses and Gratifications and the Formation of News Habits Among College Students in an Internet Environment. *Journal of Broadcasting & Electronic Media, 50*(2), 193–210.

Djamasbi, S., Siegel, M., & Tullis, T. (2010). Generation Y, Web Design, and Eye Tracking. *International Journal of Human-Computer Studies, 68*(5), 307–323.

Dwyer, C., Hiltz, S., & Passerini, K. (2007). *Trust and Privacy Concern Within Social Networking Sites: A Comparison of Facebook and MySpace.* In Proceedings of the Thirteenth Americas Conference on Information Systems, Keystone, Colorado, August 9–12.

Fogel, J., & Nehmad, E. (2009). Internet Social Network Communities: Risk Taking, Trust, and Privacy Concerns. *Computers in Human Behavior, 25*(1), 153–160.

Foregger, S. K. (2008). Uses and Gratifications of Facebook.Com. (Doctoral Dissertation). Retrieved from ProQuest Dissertations & Theses (PQDT).

Fusilier, M., & Durlabhji, S. (2005). An Exploration of Student Internet Use in India. *Campus-Wide Information Systems, 22*(4), 233–246.

Gambi, S. (2009). *The Development of Trust Within Close Relationships Formed Within Social Network Sites.* In Proceedings of the WebSci': Society On-Line, Athens, Greece, March 18–20.

Güth, W., Levati, M. V., & Ploner, M. (2008). On the Social Dimension of Time and Risk Preferences: An Experimental Study. *Economic Inquiry, 46*(2), 261–272.

Hernández-Ortega, B. (2011). The Role of Post-Use Trust in the Acceptance of a Technology: Drivers and Consequences. *Technovation, 31*, 523–538.

Joinson, A. N. (2008). *Looking at, Looking Up or Keeping Up with People? Motives and Use of Facebook.* In Proceedings of the Twenty-Sixth Annual SIGCHI Conference on Human Factors in Computing Systems (pp. 1027–1036). New York: ACM Press.

Kim, D., & Benbasat, I. (2003). Trust-Related Arguments in Internet Stores: A Framework for Evaluation. *Journal of Electronic Commerce Research, 4*(2), 49–64.

Kim, H. N., Kavanaugh, A., & Smith-Jackson, T. (2007). *Implementation of Internet Technology for Local Government Website: Design Guidelines.* In Proceedings of the 40th Annual Hawaii International Conference on System Science (HICSS '07), 93–102.

Kim, W., Jeong, O. R., & Lee, S. W. (2010). On Social Web Sites. *Information Systems, 35*(2), 215–236.

LaRose, R., & Eastin, M. S. (2004). A Social Cognitive Theory of Internet Uses and Gratifications: Toward a New Model of Media Attendance. *Journal of Broadcasting & Electronic Media, 48*(3), 358–377.

Lee, W., Xiong, L., & Hu, C. (2012). The Effect of Facebook Users' Arousal and Valence on Intention to Go to the Festival: Applying an Extension of the Technology Acceptance Model. *International Journal of Hospitality Management, 31*, 819–827.

Lin, M. J., Hung, S., & Chen, C. (2009). Fostering the Determinants of Knowledge Sharing in Professional Virtual Communities. *Computers in Human Behaviour, 25*, 929–939.

Liu, I. F., Chen, M. C., & Sun, Y. (2006). *The Design of a Web-Based Learning Platform: A Case Study in Taiwan.* In Proceedings of the 14th International Conference on Computers in Education (ICCE2006), Beijing, China.

Lohr, L. L., Falro, D. A., Hunt, E., & Johnson, B. (2007). Improving the Usability of Distance Learning Through Template Modification. *Flexible Learning in An Information Society*. Idea Group Inc.

Martin-Michiellot, S., & Mendelsohn, P. (2000). Cognitive Load While Learning with a Graphical Computer Interface. *Journal of Computers & Assisted Learning, 16*, 284–293.

McKnight, D. H., & Choudhury, V. (2006). *Distrust and Trust in B2C Ecommerce: Do They Differ?* In Proceedings of the International Conference on Electronic Commerce (ICEC'06), Fredericton, Canada.

Nielsen, J., Molich, R., Snyder, C., & Farrell, S. (2000). *E-commerce User Experience: Trust*. Nielsen Norman Group, Fremont, CA. Retrieved April 2013, from http://www.nngroup.com/reports/ecommerce/

Nusair, K. K., Bilgihan, A., Okumus, F., & Cobanoglu, C. (2013). Generation Y Travelers' Commitment to Online Social Network Websites. *Tourism Management, 35*(1), 13–22.

Oxygen Country Report. (2010). Generation Y in South Africa: How Would They Like to Work in. [online]. Retrieved Dec 28, 2017, from http://www.gbcsa.org.za/wp-content/uploads/2013/06/NZGBC-Gen-Y-and-The-Workplace-Annual-Report-2010.pdf

Papacharissi, Z., & Mendelson, A. (2011). Toward a New(er) Sociability: Uses, Gratifications and Social Capital on Facebook. In S. Papathanassopoulos (Ed.), *Media Perspectives for the 21st Century* (pp. 212–230). New York: Routledge.

Papagapitos, A., & Riley, R. (2009). Social Trust and Human Capital Formation. *Economics Letters, 102*, 158–160.

Parra-López, E., Bulchand-Gidumal, J., Gutiérrez-Tano, D., & Diaz-Armas, R. (2011). Intentions to Use Social Media in Organizing and Taking Vacation Trips. *Computers in Human Behavior, 27*(2), 640–654.

Piccoli, G., & Ives, B. (2003). Trust and the Unintended Effects of Behavior Control in Virtual Teams. *MIS Quarterly, 27*(3), 365–395.

Popoiu, M. C., Grosseck, G., & Holotescu, C. (2012). What Do We Know About the Use of Social Media in Medical Education. *Procedia – Social and Behavioral Sciences, 46*, 2262–2266.

Prahinski, C., & Benton, W. C. (2004). Supplier Evaluations: Communication Strategies to Improve Supplier Performance. *Journal of Operations Management, 22*(1), 39–62.

Prensky, M. (2001). Digital Natives, Digital Immigrants Part 1. *On the Horizon, 9*(5), 1–6.

Purcell, K., Rainie, L., Mitchell, A., Rosenstiel, T., & Olmstead, K. (2010). *Understanding the Participatory News Consumer*. Pew Internet & American Life Project. Retrieved from http://www.pewinternet.org/Reports/2010/Online-News.aspx

Quan-Haase, A., & Young, A. L. (2010). Uses and Gratifications of Social Media: A Comparison of Facebook and Instant Messaging. *Bulletin of Science, Technology & Society, 30*(5), 350–361.

Raacke, J., & Bonds-Raacke, J. (2008). My Space and Facebook: Applying the Uses and Gratifications Theory to Exploring Friend-Networking Sites. *Cyberpsychology & Behavior, 11*(2), 169–174.

Ringle, C. M., Wende, S., & Will, A. (2005). *SmartPLS 2.0 M3*. Retrieved from http://www.smartpls.de

Shin, D.-H. (2010). The Effects of Trust, Security and Privacy in Social Networking: A Security-Based Approach to Understand the Pattern of Adoption. *Interacting with Computers, 22*(5), 428–438.

Shin, D.-H., & Shin, Y.-J. (2011). Why Do People Play Social Network Games? *Computers in Human Behavior, 7*(2), 852–861.

Sivo, S., & Pan, C. (2005). Undergraduate Engineering and Psychology Students' Use of a Course Management System: A Factorial Invariance Study of User Characteristics and Attitudes. *The Journal of Technology Studies, 31*(2), 94–103.

Talug, D. Y. (2012). Lifelong Learning Through Out Today's Occasions Namely Social Media and Online Games. *Procedia – Social and Behavioral Sciences, 46*, 4431–4435.

Tenenhaus, M., Vinzi, V. E., Chatelin, Y.-M., & Lauro, C. (2005). PLS Path Modeling. *Computational Statistics & Data Analysis, 48*(1), 159–205.

Teo, T., Su Luan, W., & Sing, C. C. (2008). A Cross Cultural Examination of the Intention to Use Technology Between Singaporean and Malaysian Pre-service Teachers: An Application of the Technology Acceptance Model (TAM). *Educational Technology & Society, 11*(4), 265–280.

Van der Heijden, H., Verhagen, T., & Creemers, M. (2003). Understanding Online Purchase Intentions: Contributions from Technology and Trust Perspectives. *European Journal of Information Systems, 12*, 41–48.

Wang, Y., & Fesenmaier, D. R. (2004). Towards Understanding Members' General Participation in and Active Contribution to an Online Travel Community. *Tourism Management, 25*(6), 709–722.

Wang, Y., Yu, Q., & Fesenmaier, D. R. (2002). Defining the Virtual Tourist Community: Implications for Tourism Marketing. *Tourism Management, 23*, 407–417.

Wasko, M. M., & Faraj, S. (2000). It Is What One Does: Why People Participate and Help Others in Electronic Communities of Practice. *Journal of Strategic Information Systems, 9*, 155–173.

Wetzels, M., Odekerken-Schröder, G., & Van Oppen, C. (2009). Using PLS Path Modeling for Assessing Hierarchical Construct Models: Guidelines and Empirical Illustration. *Management Information Systems Quarterly, 33*(1), 177–195.

Whiting, A., & Williams, D. (2013). Why People Use Social Media: A Uses and Gratifications Approach. *Qualitative Market Research: An International Journal, 16*(4), 362–369.

Xiang, Z., & Gretzel, U. (2010). Role of Social Media in Online Travel Information Search. *Tourism Management, 31*(2), 179–188.

Zhang, J., & Mao, E. (2008). Understanding the Acceptance of Mobile SMS Advertising Among Young Chinese Consumers. *Psychology & Marketing, 25*(8), 787–805.

CHAPTER 8

# Decoding Digital Consumer Feedback: Customer Intelligence Insights Through Unstructured Data Mining

*Supriya Tandon and Aswinraj Govindaraj*

## Introduction

The company's Printing and Personal Systems marketing team enlisted the help of the Analytics team to investigate factors driving lower sales results for two key inkjet printer families. This investigation focused on understanding perceived strengths and weaknesses of the company's printers relative to its competitors' offerings by mining consumer opinions and feedback on a major e-commerce website, JD.com. The team conducted text mining and sentiment analysis using an in-house tool. Insights from this analysis helped to identify broad customer themes across different competitor inkjet products, confirm the value proposition of low supply costs for certain printer models, and highlight other key advantages and pain points of company's own inkjet products. The calibration technique employed further by the team helped to identify the key product differentiators and these insights were employed by the Regional Marketing team to redesign their go-to market strategy.

S. Tandon (✉) • A. Govindaraj
Hewlett Packard Enterprise, Bangalore, Karnataka, India



G. Heggde, G. Shainesh (eds.), *Social Media Marketing*,
https://doi.org/10.1007/978-981-10-5323-8_8

## Problem Statement

The printing group within the company had a strategy for developing new business models that targeted price-sensitive customers in emerging markets such as China and India. The technology company's inkjet printer had a value proposition of a relatively high price for hardware but a low price for supply, and vice versa. But in early 2013, in spite of this strategy, the actual sell-thru of key inkjet printer families, (ultra) ink advantage (UIA/IA), was only 50 percent of the target. Hence the Regional Business Unit wanted to understand its advantages and weakness in these printer families compared to those of competitors, based on unstructured data such as real end users' experience, available on social media. Local e-commerce websites such as JD.com were popular purchase avenues and also platforms where several customers shared their user experiences of technology products. The Regional team therefore wanted to drill down inside customer reviews from JD.com to identify specific product attributes and learn how the customers' felt about them. This would not only help to confirm the value proposition that was being offered by the company and understand the advantages and weaknesses vis-à-vis the competition but also redesign/implement the go-to market (GTM) strategy for these printers. The printer families were select models of single-function printers (SFPs) and multifunction printers (MFPs) of key competitor brands where real end-user experience and feedback was available in the public domain.

Thus, the main objective was to understand customers' perceptions of the printers and the features that differentiated one brand from another.

## The Solution

The following data mining approach was adopted (Fig. 8.1):

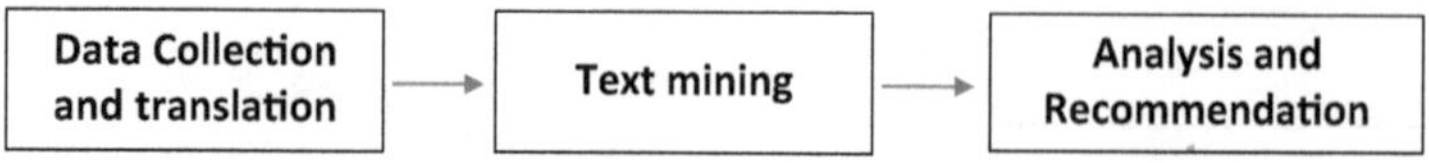


**Fig. 8.1** Data mining approach

## Data Collection and Translations

JD.com is one of the largest e-commerce websites in the Asia-Pacific region, where several users post their experiences of technology products they purchased. A sample comment on JD.com is shown below. The local language of that comment posed a major challenge for further analysis and hence it was essential to translate such comments into English as a first step, using translator tools such as Google. Since such a tool was available from a public source, it was important to check the quality of translations produced by the Google translator kit. A random sample was drawn and sent for validation to the local Regional team. Based on the feedback received, a lexicon was created to clearly define some important regional nomenclature, which was then appended to the translator tool in order to improve the efficiency of the translations. Post final approval, all 70,000 (approximately) customer reviews were then translated into English (Fig. 8.2).

## Text Mining Using the In-House Tool

All the customer reviews obtained from JD.com were essentially unstructured data that necessarily had to be converted into a structured data format. We first converted all the data into a more structured format with these variables to be analyzed: star ratings and advantages, as stated by the customers; inadequacies, also as stated by the customers; and finally, overall experience, which was the user's experience summed up in a few lines.

**Fig. 8.2** Sample of the reviews on JD.com

We then used data-mining and statistical tools to analyze the dataset of customer reviews.

Sentiment analysis technique (Weiss, Indurkhya, Zhang, & Damerau, 2005), which uses statistical modeling and rule-based natural language processing to automatically extract sentiments over a period of time, was adopted for the analysis. A positive opinion word is assigned a semantic orientation score of +1; a negative opinion word is assigned a −1; and a neutral word is assigned a 0. All the scores are then summed up using the following aggregation score function:

$$\text{Score}(e) = \sum wi : wiLi\left(wi\,so / dist(wi,e)\right)$$

where wi = opinion word; Li = opinion lexicon;

s = sentence that contains the attribute *e*;

(dist [wi,e]) = distance between attribute *e* and opinion word *wi* in a sentence *s*;

(wi so) = semantic orientation score of the word *wi*.

Sentiment analysis is an aspect of opinion mining that tries to capture the polarity of comments and opinions (i.e., whether the comment is positive or negative). The in-house tool used for text mining is a social channel analysis platform that taps into what is being said to understand customers' sentiments and also identify the main attribute within the comment.

## Analysis and Recommendation

Sentiment scores derived from the tool formed the basis for the analysis.

### *Attribute Extraction and Clustering*

Identifying the main attribute mentioned by the customer was an important step in the sentiment process—for example, "It is cheap, and is quite good." The main attribute here is price, which is mentioned in a positive way.

Each customer review input into the tool was analyzed and the key word was identified at each ID level. Further, a sentiment value was also assigned, based on the emotion attached to the opinion. As shown below, every time the attribute A1 appeared in a positive context, it was assigned a value of +1 and if it appeared with a negative connotation, it was assigned a value of −1 (Fig. 8.3).

### *Sentiment Score Generation*

Once the algorithm for identifying the key attribute and assigning the sentiment was completed for each customer review, the frequency of its occurrence along with the sentiments (i.e., number of times it occurred in positive, neutral, or negative sentiments) was also calculated. The sentiment score for an attribute was calculated based on the difference between the number of appearances in positive contexts and negative contexts (Fig. 8.4).

$$\text{Sentiment score of attribute A1} = (\text{positive appearances of A1}) - (\text{negative appearances of A1})$$

### *Identifying Key Differential Drivers*

As seen above, sentiment scores were developed for each attribute of the analysis, using the positive, negative and neutral scores for each of the product categories.

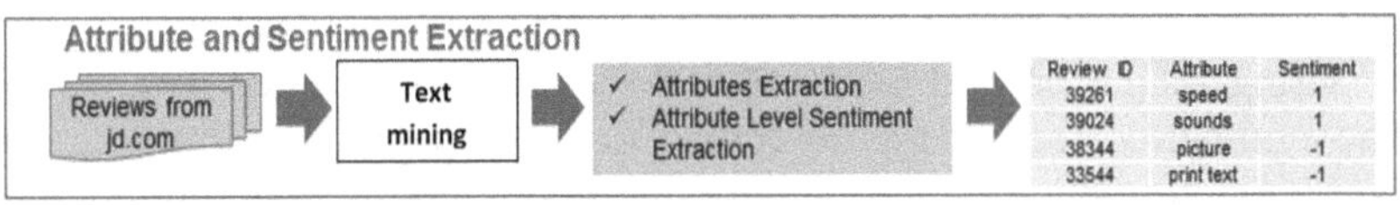


**Fig. 8.3** Attribute and sentiment extraction

**Sentiment Score Generation**

| Attribute | Negative Appearances | Neutral Appearances | Positive Appearances | Difference of +ve and -ve Appearances | Sentiment Score |
|---|---|---|---|---|---|
| speed | 12 | 5 | 26 | 14 | 33% |
| sounds | 7 | 2 | 14 | 7 | 30% |
| picture | 12 | 5 | 6 | -6 | -26% |
| print text | 8 | 13 | 5 | -3 | -12% |

**Fig. 8.4** Example of sentiment score generation

In this phase of the analysis, the key differential drivers/attributes were identified across all product categories from among the various attributes that had emerged as significant for each of the product categories. The sentiment scores generated by the tool were now available. Further, the importance of each attribute (i.e., whether customers cared strongly about it or not) was derived. Thus, importance was indicated by a strong sentiment—either a positive or negative sentiment. Then, the variance metric used to indicate large differences between score and importance was calculated.

Calibration technique was used to identify the differential attribute.

Score: positive or negative sentiment
Importance: strong sentiment (either direction) = (1 −neutral)/total
Variance metric: large differences between score and importance

Let's look at an example below. Print quality was important to customers of all eleven models. However, they felt print quality was similar among all eleven models. Therefore customers couldn't tell the difference among eleven printers by just looking at print quality. On the other hand, supplies were almost equally important to customers. Yet customer's perceptions of supplies varied greatly among all printer models. (The attribute of *supplies* typically refers to the cost and convenience of consumable ink supplies.) Printer D is differentiated with respect to this attribute, while lower-end models from HP and Canon lag (J and E and I) (Fig. 8.5).

Using the calibration mechanism described above helped to quantify the sentiment score and identify the key differential driver attributes across

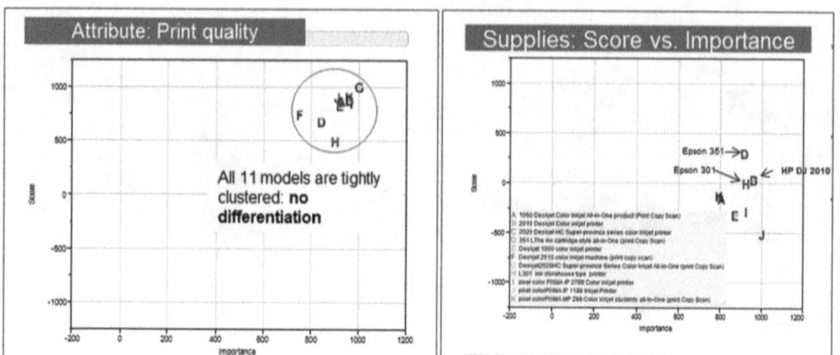


**Fig. 8.5** Key differential drivers

all the product categories, which helped provide the business with actionable insights. Supplies (costs and price), cartridges (function and operation of ink cartridges) and print speed were the top three differentiators that emerged.

## Evidence That the Solution Works

The Regional team concurred with the findings, which were also shared with the global head of printing business. The team considered re-examining the value proposition offered by these printers. The customer sentiment analysis and calibration framework was leveraged for customer intelligence across different business units and across geographies.

## Competitive Approaches

There are several data mining tools available that are helpful in sentiment analysis. But the in-house sentiment analysis tool had a built-in algorithm that analyzed data collected from various social media sources. Further, using the calibration mechanism helped quantify the sentiment score and identify the key differential driver attributes across all the product categories. This was unique to the analysis and was not directly available in any of the data mining tools that were available in the market.

## Current Status and Next Steps

Online opinions represent an invaluable source of information that is now being tapped by several businesses. Providing customer intelligence through the analysis of unstructured data on social media was the first and very important step toward leveraging a plethora of information and providing it to the Regional Business Unit. Going forward, this unstructured data can also be combined with structured customer data such as demographics and transactions, wherever possible, to predict customer purchase behavior and patterns.

**Acknowledgment** We thank Hailing Jiang from the Regional team, who helped us with the translation process by creating a lexicon of some important regional nomenclature, which was then appended to the translator tool in order to improve the efficiency of translations.

## References

Weiss, S. M., Indurkhya, N., Zhang, T., & Damerau, F. (2005). *Text Mining Predictive Methods for Analyzing Unstructured Information* (pp. 163–166). Springer.

PART III

# Integrating Social Media into Marketing

CHAPTER 9

# Social Media Marketing, Corporate Social Responsibility, and Social Change in India

*Sameer Deshpande*

## Introduction

Kaplan and Haenlein (2010) define social media as "a group of Internet-based applications that build on the ideological and technological foundations of Web 2.0, and that allow the creation and exchange of User Generated Content" (p. 61). According to InternetService.net, 2.4 billion people in the world used the Internet in 2013 (Alexander, 2013a). Interestingly, the smartphone penetration is higher, with four billion active smartphones in the world (Alexander, 2013b). If we consider the world population of seven billion, that translates into Internet and smartphone penetration of 34 and 57 per cent respectively. Comparatively, India has a lower Internet penetration of 16 per cent with just over 200 million users (TNN, 2013) and a smartphone penetration of 10 per cent with ninety million devices (Indian Express Tech Desk, 2014). The future for Internet and smartphone penetration looks bright for both India and rest of the world.

With the growth in the use of the Internet and the smartphone, usage of social media has increased substantially (Alexander, 2013c). Facebook had 1.1 billion active users in 2013, up from 845 million in 2012 (30 per cent increase). Twitter, YouTube, Google Plus, and LinkedIn are the other most frequented and fast-growing social media sites. In 2012 the

S. Deshpande (✉)
University of Lethbridge, Lethbridge, AB, Canada



G. Heggde, G. Shainesh (eds.), *Social Media Marketing*,
https://doi.org/10.1007/978-981-10-5323-8_9

social network user penetration was 20 per cent worldwide. It was only 5.7 per cent in India, but both these trends are projected upwards, with an expected penetration of 31.5 per cent worldwide and 17.2 per cent in India by 2017 (eMarketer, 2013).

Given the meteoric rise in social media penetration across the world, it is not surprising that marketers have quickly responded to the changing consumer behaviour scenario and invested a large percentage of their marketing budgets in influencing consumers through social media. This has led to the rise of social media marketing. In India, marketers are quickly embracing social media marketing as a strategy to achieve their marketing objectives (Ernst & Young, 2013). Barker, Barker, Bormann, and Neher (2013) define social media marketing as the "use of social networks, online communities, blogs, wikis or any other online collaborative media for marketing, sales, public relations and customer service" (p. 3). Social media marketing offers unique and enhanced opportunities to marketersincluding the opportunity to communicate in a tailored and timely manner while allowing instant and direct feedback from consumers and other stakeholders and facilitating peer-to-peer and peer-to-expert communication. As a result, the engagement of marketers with their audiences is enhanced substantially, which in turn allows them to achieve their communication objectives.

Previous literature has neglected to discuss the appropriateness of social media marketing strategies and tools for various corporate social responsibility activities and behaviour change activities of the non-profit and the government sector. The current study addresses this gap.

*Appropriateness* is defined as the fit between what the media tool offers (its strengths) and the consumer behaviour objective that the marketer wants to achieve. *Appropriateness of media tools* is an important influencer of the effectiveness of those tools to achieve marketers' media and communication objectives. Usually, quantitative media effectiveness measures include reach and frequency objectives, achieved at the lowest cost. Specifically, these include measures such as effective reach, cost per million (CPM) and cost per rating point (CPRP). Qualitative indicators are also considered. These include measures such as audience engagement (as in how much time consumers spend, on average, with the medium/channel, how involved they are with the content, and so on). These measures are independent measures that are utilized to determine which media and vehicles should be included in the media plan. However, in addition to these criteria, influence of fit or appropriateness of media options, with the relevant marketing strategy for media effectiveness, could also be considered. This relationship has not been investigated in the previous literature. The present study takes the first step in that direction by conceptualizing the appropriateness of media tools for marketing strategy.

In terms of media options, there are several available to a marketer, including television, radio, newspaper, magazine, outdoor, and so on. Online and mobile media are emerging as the most important media options available to marketers these days. The study focuses on new media options. For further discussion on appropriateness and social media options, please refer to the section subtitled, "Classifying Social Media Tools Based on Social Media Strategies."

The focus in this conceptual study is on organizations and activities that relate to positive social change, those efforts that promote behaviours that solve social problems. Two types of organization are examined: corporations that organize CSR activities as well as non-profit organizations and government bodies that are involved in behaviour change activities. Corporate CSR is characterized by do-good activities that benefit society in general, and in return, the corporation manages the influence of external and internal stakeholders including consumers, employees, distributors, investors, and policy makers (Du, Bhattacharya, & Sen, 2010) on achieving corporate objectives and maximizing shareholder value.

On other hand, non-profit and government organizations carry out two kinds of behaviour-change activity: (a) changing behaviour to solve social problems (e.g., promoting condoms to prevent HIV/AIDS or encouraging voting in elections to ensure stronger democracy), and (b) influencing individuals to donate money and volunteer (e.g., donate money to CRY or volunteer to teach one hour every week). This study focuses on the first kind of social change activity undertaken by the government and non-profit organizations. In other words, the study focuses on efforts of non-profit and government organizations to promote behaviours that solve social problems. In both kinds of activity (CSR and behaviour change), social media is emerging as a critical component of a media plan to achieve media and communication objectives.

To address the research gaps, the current study proposes (a) relevant social media strategies for each social media tool, and (b) appropriate social media strategies and tools for each CSR and behaviour change approach. Based on this categorization, the paper (c) reviews past efforts by Indian companies and social change agencies to utilize social media strategies to implement their CSR and behaviour change campaigns, and

(d) identifies gaps and provides recommendations to make future CSR and behaviour change attempts effective.

## Method

The study conducted a review on two fronts. First, the study conducted a qualitative analysis of social media sites in 2014 of fifteen large Indian companies as reported by the Reputation Institute (Charlotte Bang-Moller, personal communication): State Bank of India, Infosys Technologies, Indian Oil, Tata Group, Oil & Natural Gas Corp, NTPC, Bharti Airtel, Wipro Limited, ICICI Bank, Bharat Petroleum, Mahindra & Mahindra, Reliance Group, Hindustan Petroleum, Hindalco Industries, and Chennai Petroleum Corporation.

Second, the study conducted a qualitative analysis in 2013 of social media sites of nine behaviour change campaigns, three of them employing a legal, educational, and marketing approach by either Indian non-profit or state/central government organizations (hereby referred to as social change agencies). The legal approach focused on one initiative for each of anti-smoking, seat belt use, and anti-driving after drinking; the educational approach focused on anti-smoking, anti-drinking, and anti-rape; and the social marketing approach focused on promotion of condoms, iron and folic acid, and green lanterns. All behaviour change efforts included in the review were undertaken by Indian social change agencies.

## Classifying Social Media Tools Based on Social Media Strategies

Based on the classification of Barker et al. (2013) and Nedra Weinreich (personal communication), the study proposes the 7 Cs of social media marketing strategy that are relevant to a CSR/social change campaign. They are explained briefly below.

1. Communicate: To communicate the core message of the business/non-profit/government organization and in particular the CSR/social change campaign. It is the basic function of any communication medium.
2. Converse/connect: To have a dialogue with the consumer so that the message is clear, misperceptions are removed, and communication is improved.

3. Comprehend: To understand consumers and get their feedback on the CSR/social change campaign. This activity is close to conducting consumer research.
4. Collaborate/co-create: To motivate consumers to provide ideas to create the next phase of a CSR/social change strategy.
5. Customize: To provide tailored CSR/social change solutions to consumers
6. Convert: To push consumers from ignorance to awareness to positive beliefs to brand purchase stage.
7. Customer Service: To provide after-sales/behaviour-change service to retain existing consumers.

Several social media tools are available to corporations/social change agencies. The study categorized them in three main groups: corporation/social-change agency, consumer-led or third-party-led, and those groups in which all these parties are involved. Their strengths vary. Corporation-led/social-change-agency-led tools include the organization's own website, blogs, and micro-blogs (such as Twitter), websites where corporations/social change agencies can post videos and photos (such as YouTube and Flickr), and social networking sites (such as Facebook). Similarly, consumers and third parties (such as experts who monitor corporations' actions) post their own blogs, Twitter feeds, YouTube videos, and Facebook posts on corporations/social change agencies, brands, brand communication efforts, and brand experiences. More importantly, visitors' comments posted in response to corporations', peers', and experts' communication efforts on a variety of social media outlets are an important source of information to corporations/social change agencies. Finally, there are couple of platforms where consumers and corporations/social change agencies can interact or collectively post material. These include discussion boards, emails, and collaborative projects (such as *Wikipedia*).

Table 9.1 reflects which tools deliver which benefits to the corporations/social change agencies. Corporation-led/social-change-agency-led activities are appropriate to communicate. They can also evoke visitor comments that can provide useful feedback to the corporations on the quality of CSR/social change strategy. Within these tools, sharing materials can take the persuasion process to more advanced stages. Audience-led communication activities tend to provide important feedback to corporations based on comments, peer conversations, posting of videos and images with brands and brand experiences. Expert comments expressed

**Table 9.1** Ideal usage of social media tools categorized by objectives

| | *Corporation/social change agency-led* | | | | *Consumer/third-party-led* | | | | *Both* | |
|---|---|---|---|---|---|---|---|---|---|---|
| | *Web site* | *Blogs/ micro-blogs* | *Share material* | *Social networks* | *Blogs/ micro-blogs* | *Share material* | *Social networks* | *Consumer comments (relating to communication efforts of peers, marketers, and third parties)* | *Discussion boards/ email* | *Collaborative projects* |
| Communicate | ✓ | ✓ | ✓ | ✓ | | | | | | ✓ |
| Converse/ connect | | | | | | | | ✓ | ✓ | |
| Comprehend | | | | | ✓ | ✓ | ✓ | ✓ | ✓ | |
| Collaborate/ co-create | | | | | | | | ✓ | ✓ | ✓ |
| Customize | | | ✓ | | | | | | ✓ | |
| Convert | ✓ | | ✓ | | | | | ✓ | ✓ | |
| Customer service | | | ✓ | ✓ | | | | | ✓ | |

through blogs, websites, and micro-blogs can also be important influencers for consumers and thus a useful source of information for corporations. Visitor comments posted on a variety of sites go beyond providing feedback; they also allow corporations/social change agencies to converse, collaborate, and convert. Finally, there are couple of social media opportunities such as discussion boards and web emails where consumers and corporations/social change agencies can have a dialogue in real time. These are powerful mechanisms for corporations to influence consumers on numerous points. Collaborative projects such as *Wikipedia* allow any person to add and edit material and are excellent platforms to communicate and collaborate on marketing solutions.

## Classifying Social Media Tools and Social Media Strategies by CSR Strategies

The study next maps social media tools and strategies following CSR strategies. Kotler, Hessekiel, and Lee (2012) propose six ways in which companies can conduct CSR. They are:

1. Cause promotion (funds, in-kind contributions, and other resources to support fundraising and participation in a cause. Examples include Infosys Foundation's A Library for Every School initiative),
2. Cause-related marketing (linking monetary or in-kind donations to the sale of a product or some other consumer action. Examples include Procter and Gamble's Shiksha campaign),
3. Corporate social marketing (changing consumer behaviour. Examples include Tata Tea's *Jaago Re* campaign,
4. Corporate philanthropy (direct donation of cash or in-kind services. Examples include Tata Group's continued donation to the Tata Institute of Social Sciences),
5. Workforce volunteering (encouraging employees and retail partners to volunteer at local community organizations and for various causes. Examples include Tech Mahindra asking its employees to devote 10 per cent of their work hours to causes such as teaching children in municipal schools), and
6. Socially responsible business practices (business practices or investments that improve community well-being and protect the environment. Examples include the adoption of Equator Principles by IDFC).

**Table 9.2** Ideal usage of social media tools by CSR strategy

| | *Cause promotion* | *Cause-related marketing* | *Corporate social marketing* | *Corporate philanthropy* | *Workforce volunteering* | *Social responsible business practices* |
|---|---|---|---|---|---|---|
| Communicate | Presence in all corporation-led efforts | | | | | |
| Converse/connect | | Visitor comments | | | | |
| Comprehend | Monitor all consumer-led efforts | | | | | |
| Collaborate/co-create | | Collaborative projects | | | | |
| Customize | Corporation-led share materials | | | | | |
| Convert | | Corporation-led share materials, visitor comments, discussion boards | | | | |
| Customer service | | | Discussion boards/email | | | |

Referring to Table 9.2, the study proposes appropriate social media tools to achieve positive outcomes for each CSR strategy. Whichever CSR strategy the corporate chooses to employ, it will be imperative to use all kinds of corporation-led social media efforts since they provide a controlled way to communicate to the consumer. Similarly, corporations should monitor all consumer-led efforts to gauge their feedback. However, if corporations are involved in cause-related marketing and corporate social marketing where the success of CSR directly depends on consumer response, they need to be vigilant with visitor comments to connect and involve consumers in collaborative projects to co-create, share materials, and actively participate in discussion boards to customize efforts, convert consumers, and provide adequate and appropriate customer service.

Using these typologies, a review of the CSR efforts of fifteen Indian companies revealed that corporate philanthropy is the most prevalent form, followed by cause promotion and workforce volunteering. Cause-related marketing has recently started to gain traction. Two areas where companies need to pay more attention include corporate social marketing and socially responsible business practices because they have provided positive bottom-line outcomes for corporations in the West (Kotler et al., 2012).

In terms of social media marketing strategy, corporations are primarily "communicating" through their own websites and by sharing resources, but they fail to adequately utilize blogs, micro-blogs, discussion boards, and collaborative projects. There is also a lack of public interaction in the area of visitor comments. This results in corporations failing to converse, collaborate, tailor, and convert, thus failing to exploit the real advantages of a social media tool. This potentially results in poorly conceptualized campaigns that are ineffective and inefficient.

In sum, the study recommends corporations to more frequently employ cause-related marketing, corporate social marketing, and socially responsible business practices. In terms of social media marketing strategy, corporations should focus more on sharing materials, closely monitoring consumer-led communication, closely monitoring visitor comments and discussion board conversations and encouraging more in the future, and most importantly, involving consumers in the co-creation of marketing strategies.

## Classifying Social Media Tools and Social Media Strategies by Behaviour Change Strategies

The study next maps social media tools and strategies along with behaviour change strategies. Michael Rothschild (1999) proposes three ways in which social change organizations can influence individual behaviours. These include education (when organizations employ a communication-only approach. Examples include warning labels on cigarette packets that create awareness of the negative consequences of smoking but don't provide any environmental stimulus); marketing (when organizations provide and promote opportunity in the environment to reduce barriers and enhance benefits. Examples include promotion of green lanterns to motivate environment-friendly behaviours; law (when governments pass laws and make it mandatory for citizens to change behaviour or risk penalties. Examples include the ban on smoking in public places in India).

Referring to Table 9.3, the study proposes appropriate social media tools to achieve positive outcomes for each behaviour change strategy. Whichever strategy the social change manager chooses to employ, it is imperative to use all kinds of social change, manager-led, social media marketing efforts since they provide a controlled way to communicate to the audience. Similarly, social change managers should monitor all audience-led efforts to gauge their feedback. However, if social change organizations are involved in social marketing where success of behaviour change directly depends on audience response, they need to be vigil with

**Table 9.3** Ideal usage of social media tools by behaviour-change strategy

| | *Education* | *Marketing* | *Law* |
|---|---|---|---|
| Communicate | Presence in all social change manager-led efforts | | |
| Converse/connect (when evolving legal policies and less so after they are enacted) | Visitor comments | | |
| Comprehend | Monitor all audience and third-party-led efforts | | |
| Collaborate/co-create | Collaborative projects | | |
| Customize | Social change manager-led sharing of materials | | |
| Convert | Social change manager-led sharing of materials, visitor comments | Social change manager-led sharing of materials, visitor comments, discussion boards | |
| Customer service | | Discussion boards/email | |

visitor comments to connect, involve audience members in collaborative projects to co-create, share materials, and actively participate in discussion boards to customize efforts, convert audiences, and provide adequate and appropriate customer service.

Review of social change efforts reveals that law makers utilize the least of social media tools. They tend to rely mostly on third-party efforts to communicate. They fail to utilize their own social media vehicles. Further, policy makers almost always fail to seek audience input while finalizing the regulations. In educational efforts, the emphasis tends to be on communicating (as in giving wide exposure to the campaign), but very little focus is placed on other aspects that could be easily exploited with social media tools. Some attention is given to gaining audience feedback, but it is mostly focused on measuring audience awareness and very little on actual behavior change. The feedback also tends to be anecdotal and not systematic. When conducting social marketing efforts, the current attempts are again focused on communicating mostly through social change agencies and third-party-led efforts. Less emphasis is placed on connecting and comprehending. Even less emphasis is placed on the remaining aspects such as co-creating, customizing, converting, and offering customer service.

To make future social change attempts using social media more effective, policy makers could utilize these tools to connect with audience members prior to implementing a law. For this purpose, monitoring and encouraging visitor comments as well as monitoring audience-led communication would be useful. For educators, it is critical to focus on co-creating, customizing, and converting, thus requiring an emphasis on collaborative projects, using algorithms to provide customized content, and getting active in monitoring visitor comments and discussion boards. Finally, social marketers need to carry out what educators would do and, additionally, provide customer service with the help of discussion boards and email conversations.

## Conclusion and Future Research

The managerial implication of this study is to analyze how organizations in India use social media tools and to recommend how it could be improved in the future so that they are better able to achieve their organizational objectives and goals.

Organizations can effectively achieve their outcomes with appropriate use of social media tools.

When organizations achieve their objectives and goals, corporations and society benefit.

This is the first study to map social media tools with strategies. This is also the first attempt to map social media tools and strategies with CSR and behaviour change strategies. However, the study also exhibits several limitations, which should be addressed through future research.

First, the review was restricted to social media marketing activities of organizations—commercial, non-commercial- and government—that operate predominantly in India. This was done in order to maintain consistency in the country of origin. The study did not analyze social media marketing activities of multinational organizations, both commercial and non-commercial. Examples include Procter & Gamble in the corporate sector and Population Services International in the non-profit sector. On several occasions in recent years, even the aid units of foreign governments, such as USAID, have started embracing social media marketing strategies. It is likely that the multinational organizations bring social media strategies from their head offices. Future studies should review the social media marketing efforts of multinational organizations and compare them with organizations of Indian origin.

Second, the current framework of matching social media strategies, tools, and CSR, and behaviour change strategies are presented in a conceptual framework, but they have not been empirically tested for their effectiveness. Future studies should empirically test this framework. Specifically, the role of appropriateness should be compared with the impact of popularity, cost, and qualitative measures on social media effectiveness.

Third, the study conceptualized appropriateness of media options and consumer behaviour objective based on social media options. While social media options are emerging as the most important media options, other media tools are still relevant, especially television, newspapers, and magazines. Future studies should investigate how the conceptualization of appropriateness fits with traditional media options.

## References

Alexander, A. (2013a). *Global Internet Usage Statistics* [Infographic]. Retrieved May 13, 2014, from http://ansonalex.com/infographics/global-internet-usage-statistics-2013-infographic/

Alexander, A. (2013b). *Interesting Stats About Smartphones* [Infographic]. Retrieved May 13, 2014, from http://ansonalex.com/infographics/interesting-stats-about-smartphones/

Alexander, A. (2013c). *Social Media Usage Statistics* [Infographic]. Retrieved May 13, 2014, from http://ansonalex.com/infographics/social-media-usage-statistics-2013-infographic/

Barker, M., Barker, D., Bormann, N., & Neher, K. (2013). *Social Media Marketing: A Strategic Approach*. Mason, OH: Cengage Learning.

Du, S., Bhattacharya, C. B., & Sen, S. (2010). Maximizing Business Returns to Corporate Social Responsibility (CSR): The Role of CSR Communication. *International Journal of Management Reviews, 12*(1), 8–19.

eMarketer. (2013). *India Leads Worldwide Social Networking Growth Country Set to Control Largest Facebook Population Worldwide*. Retrieved May 14, 2014, from http://www.emarketer.com/Article/India-Leads-Worldwide-Social-Networking-Growth/1010396

Ernst & Young. (2013). *Social Media Marketing: India Trends Study 2013, Insights from Social Media-Savvy Organizations in India*. Kolkata, India.

Indian Express Tech Desk. (2014, May 9). *Smartphone Penetration to Reach 45% in India by 2020: Ericsson*. Retrieved May 13, 2014, from http://indianexpress.com/article/technology/technology-others/ericsson-identifies-key-elements-of-mobile-broadband-growth-in-india/

Kaplan, A. M., & Haenlein, M. (2010). Users of the World, Unite! The Challenges and Opportunities of Social Media. *Business Horizons, 53*(1), 59–68.

Kotler, P., Hessekiel, D., & Lee, N. (2012). *Good Works!: Marketing and Corporate Initiatives that Build a Better World...and the Bottom Line*. Hoboken, NJ: Wiley.

Rothschild, M. L. (1999, October). Carrots, Sticks, and Promises: A Conceptual Framework for the Management of Public Health and Social Issue Behaviors. *Journal of Marketing, 63*, 24–37.

TNN. (2013, November 14). *With 243 Million Users by 2014, India to Beat US in Internet Reach: Study*. Retrieved May 13, 2014, from http://timesofindia.indiatimes.com/tech/tech-news/With-243-million-users-by-2014-India-to-beat-US-in-internet-reach-Study/articleshow/25719512.cms

CHAPTER 10

# The Future of Social CRM

*Ajay Row*

## Introduction

Social media, we have been told, is a force for good. There are several reasons why: people can easily say what they think, it is easy and it is free! Their voices will be heard by people who know them (in a manner of speaking) and want to hear their views—and eventually through their networks the entire interconnected world if their meme is of enough interest.

From a business perspective, brands, businesses, and organisations can eavesdrop, are 'tagged', and often spoken to directly—and they can of course help monetize social media networks by paying for advertising space. Organisations thus have an opportunity to respond to comments in real-time as the rest of the digital world listens in.

This then is the future of the world, the ultimate democracy, that which will drive us all to that economists' utopia, perfect competition, as everyone will soon know (or at least have access) to every bit of information.

But soon, practical problems get in the way. First, conversations are public and unstructured. This means comments have to be read and understood, and in organisations with access to appropriate data, the customer context understood by a review of his or her history of interaction with the organisation well before the response is thought through and

A. Row (✉)
Mumbai, India



G. Heggde, G. Shainesh (eds.), *Social Media Marketing*,
https://doi.org/10.1007/978-981-10-5323-8_10

sent out. This would be fine if it were a few conversations and data is ready on hand, but too often, and this is the second issue, organisations find themselves dealing with thousands of social comments every single day—and just don't have the resources to manage this scale. Some redeploy contact centre staff but too often discover this is rarely a cost-effective solution.

Naturally, tools have emerged to simplify things, service providers have created sentiment analysis and 'listening tools' and have even delivered response services on behalf of the organisation. These are helpful but, and this is the third issue, not always right. (Not that organisations got it right infallibly before the advent of social media—we are all human.) But this is the new reality and simple errors of judgment now get amplified in real-time as, increasingly, by the very nature of social media, one bad response that goes viral can destroy an organisation's hard-won reputation and even shareholder value in mere hours.

Given the scale of social media, and the reality of human nature, the more successful a brand is, the more folks are interested in it. This is of course good when things go right (or is it, given our utopian dream?) but turns into a double-edged sword when things go wrong. And eventually, for most, something will inevitably go wrong. The question isn't whether; it is when—as with most complex systems. Failure can be one bad tweet away.

## What Has This Got to Do with the Management of Customer Relationships?

Relationships are built in a series of interactions between brands and their customers. Interactions are usually either brand experiences or one-to-one conversations and are usually in the form of a cycle of a number of stimuli and responses (e.g. you speak and I listen; I respond to what you said and you respond to my response, etc.) and over time, multiple cycles build relationships with individual customers, for good or bad. Some of these interactions may be in social media, others at point of experience, still others in communication. Often, interactions are hybrid and omni-channel. For example, a customer has a poor brand experience, calls the contact centre, and winds up with a diatribe via social media.

So it is complex, and made more so as consumers now expect the interaction cycle to be context-appropriate and quick and resolve the issue on hand.

Brands can either manage these cycles (e.g. training front-line staff, creating channels for two-way communication) or leave things to chance. Most are forced to do the latter as practical problems exist. For instance, at the time of writing, most brands do not have a longitudinal view of individual customers deployed at points of interaction. Instead they tend to manage interactions as distinctive work units (so Marketing, typically, creates customer communication; Operations manages the front-line staff; and Training scurries around trying to ensure people know what to do). The customer on the other hand sees his or her interactions with an organisation from a single perspective that evolves over time. What the customer says on social media is often a result of the cumulative effect of those interactions and organisations without the benefit of context can be blind-sided.

Too often, existing channels are broken: calling a telco or bank contact centre usually results in the stuff of nightmares. Social media is routinely ignored by many large organisations, perhaps because of a cynical calculation: being completely unresponsive is better than being inappropriately responsive, and it costs a lot less. Customer data is often a mess, and rarely deployed *appropriately* at the point of customer engagement. The list of CRM shortfalls goes on.

Clearly, doing more of the same won't work. So many smart people trying so hard for so long can't all be incompetent. So perhaps the system, as we now understand CRM, cannot work. The challenge then is to find a new way. Perhaps one possibility is to first create a channel by which brands can cost-effectively manage interactions with all their customers (often numbering in millions and more) and then ensure this channel is the *preferred* source of customer interaction with a brand, the one customers reach out to *before* social media if things go wrong and the one that is their natural choice when things go right. This would be far more manageable by brands, and due to the nature of the channel (appropriate response in real-time) preferable to consumers.

The question, then, is how does one make this happen? Well, in many ways. But one strong possibility is to consider using a device which has become increasingly ubiquitous and omniscient: the mobile (smart) phone. Logical, but how? Well, the phone is already more or less universally established—and often abused—as a mode of one-to-one communication with customers. Companies had become so used to using the short message service (SMS) to 'spam' their customers that it took governmental intervention to bring in some modicum of sense. But SMS has not died. For instance, banks use the 'registered mobile' number in India to send confirmatory messages of transactions.

SMS and other messaging, if used well, can be good, but the real game-changer on the phone is of course the mobile app: folks routinely use apps to hail a taxi (thanks Uber) or find how to get there by other means (Google Maps), respond to emails, chat on social media, play games, figure out the score between meetings, or figure out how to score this evening, plan their leisure time, organise themselves, hear a spiritual leader—the list goes on.

Today, every company worth its salt has either planned, started work on, or launched, a mobile app, sort of like they did with websites a decade or two ago. Often, the challenge—as it was then—is to figure out what the customer will do with the app beyond hearing the advertising spiel, though many apps facilitate transactions, but the belief is undoubtedly that solutions will emerge over time. They have to, or the hard-won space on the consumer's screen will be lost to a 'Delete' soon enough.

Enter the future of social CRM. Here's the real opportunity. With an effective strategy, brands can manage multiple interaction cycles simply, cost-effectively and in real-time, building individual relationships with millions of customers simultaneously.

The way to do this is to create customer interfaces that allow for 'structured conversations'. Market research taught marketers the value of a semantic differential scale decades ago (strongly agree, agree, don't know or care, disagree, strongly disagree). Variations on the theme can now be delivered to customers real-time to find out how things are going. Later, as technology evolves, we are given to understand that sensors will take over to learn how customers are feeling but, for now, this is the best alternative. A start-up called Litmus (disclaimer: I am a co-founder), for instance, has developed several ways to 'talk to customers', asking them how they feel about an experience via what they call a structured conversation. Here are some examples:

The beauty of this simple device is it empowers brands to develop customer relationships simply and effectively, they know what customers want or are thinking/feeling and can respond

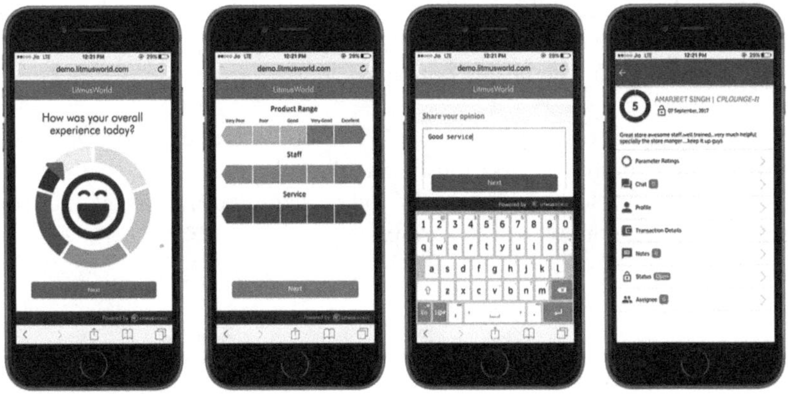


in real-time exceedingly cost-effectively, thus building effective interactions. Since data/insights/conclusions/recommendations can be mirrored to frontline staff at the point of interaction, the

loop between humans and the phone can easily be closed. Since interactions are built on past knowledge, organisations can build increasingly effective relationships with millions of customers, maximising the value of their customer base, their customer asset.

So what is the future of social CRM? Let me make some guesses.

- Social media tools as we know them today will continue to improve but will never be perfect; an organisation or individual will always be one bad judgment call away from being battered on social media
- Cynics will manipulate social media. Actually, sorry, that is already happening, isn't it?

- People at large will get more and more jaded to social media (as they have become to news in general), which will lessen the downside risk but also blunt the upside potential.

And perhaps most importantly, other solutions will emerge. One such will be 'structured conversations' that allow brands and consumers to speak as they should, as friends and good colleagues do: easily, with clarity and immediate, context-sensitive response.

CHAPTER 11

# Sales Professionals' Use of Social Media to Create and Deploy Social Capital in US and Indian Companies

*Rajiv Kashyap, Sudha Mani, Prabakar Kothandaraman, and Raj Agnihotri*

## Introduction

The explosive growth in use of social media by customers has exerted tremendous pressures on companies to respond in kind. Social networks have the potential to transform business on an unprecedented scale. Recent research in marketing has focused upon the process by which organizations can utilize social media to enhance business relationships and facilitate internal processes. Sales professionals are being entrusted with the responsibility for simultaneously implementing strategies to harmonize internal-value-creating functions and enhance the creation and appropriation of value in external customer relationships. In a global context, it has become increasingly important to understand whether social media practices can be standardized across cultures and countries.

R. Kashyap (✉) • S. Mani • P. Kothandaraman
Cotsakos College of Business, William Paterson University, Wayne, NJ, USA

R. Agnihotri
University of Texas-Arlington, Arlington, Texas, USA



G. Heggde, G. Shainesh (eds.), *Social Media Marketing*,
https://doi.org/10.1007/978-981-10-5323-8_11

How can salespeople strategically deploy social media to build social capital? Why and how do salespeople in US and Indian organizations differ in their use of social media? How does a salesperson's social capital affect customer value creation and value appropriation? We focus on these research questions in this paper, and seek to understand the underlying mechanism that makes social media useful to salespeople. We identify *social capital*—the sum of actual and potential resources embedded within, available through, and derived from the network of relationships possessed by an individual or social unit (cf. Nahapiet & Ghoshal, 1998)—as the focal construct that can help us understand this process. We define social capital from the perspective of the sales professional and specify a nomological net to explain links between social media, social capital, and the creation and appropriation of customer value. We elaborate differences in culture and institutional environments to develop a framework for understanding social capital creation and deployment in US and Indian organizations.

## Conceptual Framework

Research on the effects of social media has focused upon the role of influence, specifically, the use of *social contagion* (Christakis & Fowler, 2013) to explain the diffusion of innovations in social networks (Van den Bulte & Lilien, 2000). Social contagion is the process of adopting attitudes or imitating behaviors through social learning (Polansky, Lippitt, & Redl, 1950). Essentially, social contagion theory draws on social influence to explain changes in individual cognitions and behaviors. Social influence has been used to explain changes in awareness, adoption behaviors, and the extent to which individuals choose to associate with one another (Kwon, Stefanone, & Barnett, 2014). Preliminary empirical research to understand the effects of social media use within the supply chain has also utilized social contagion theory (Rapp, Beitelspacher, Grewal, & Hughes, 2013). This research found that significant positive benefits to companies and brands could accrue from the adoption of social media. Social contagion can explain the adoption of social media within organizations as well. However, there is still a gap in our understanding of the process by which the use of social media engenders value creation and value appropriation. Part of this problem is due to the blurring of business and social boundaries that ensues from social media use. Transaction cost and rational utility models are insufficient to explain "the networks of social bonds within which business relationships are embedded" (Husted, 1994). Further, social contagion theories are limited by their reliance on influence as the sole cause of propagation. They ignore homophily effects and, more importantly, are unable to explain why transmissions may be delayed or never occur between members of a social network. To explain these effects, we propose a conceptual framework in which social capital is the central construct that governs and mediates the effects of social media use on customer value (see Fig. 11.1). Social media use enhances the formation of a salesperson's social capital, which can be deployed at will to accomplish individual and organizational goals.

Adopting a social capital theory approach, we derive the boundary conditions under which distinctive components of social capital beget different paths to value creation. Since the concept of social capital is located within the realm of "social" relationships, we draw upon cross-cultural and institutional theories to postulate different paths to the creation of social capital in US and Indian companies.

### *Social Media Use by Salespeople*

According to a recent McKinsey report, social networks have the potential to unlock over a trillion dollars in revenues in just four sectors of the global economy. Buyers' immense interest and use of social media has sales organizations scrambling to understand and evaluate its potential impacts on the selling process. Witnessing the trend, IBM launched a new product line called Smart Commerce to help its partners leverage social media to enhance revenues. This is projected to generate up to $20 billion by 2020. A global survey revealed that over 50 percent of salespeople perceive an

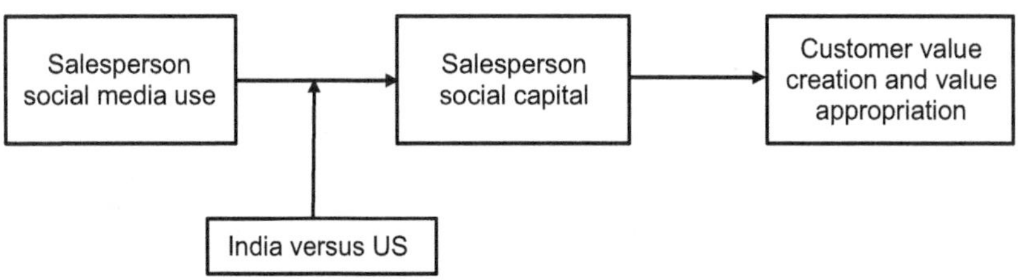


**Fig. 11.1** Conceptual framework linking social media use to the creation and deployment of social capital for value creation and value appropriation

increasing role for social media in the buying process (OgilvyOne global survey, www.B2Bonline.com).

Despite the widespread adoption of social media by customers, companies have been cautious in embracing its use. Most major social media initiatives have emanated from marketing departments seeking to build brand identity and generate conversations around new product launches, event sponsorship, and brand benefits. These programs are aimed at enhancing the brand experience and engaging consumers through meaningful interactions (Gupta, Armstrong, & Clayton, 2011). This effort is largely in the business-to-consumer domain. However, the use of social media by salespeople in the business-to-business (B2B) context remains nascent. This can be attributed to a variety of reasons including lack of ROI metrics, potential liability due to lack of control over communications, discomfort of senior sales managers, and inability to visualize how social media can help accomplish strategic objectives. As a result, social media is generally viewed as just another unit of a salesperson's toolkit. It is often used by salespeople to generate and qualify leads through their traditional networks of referrals. Salespeople have also used social media to clarify points of parity and points of differentiation (Anderson, Narus, & van Rossum, 2006) to create value propositions that resonate with customer needs. These uses represent a managerial mindset that views social media as a tool that assists sales force functions. However, if social media is to help a salesperson and the organization achieve strategic goals, it must play a significant role in salesperson value creation and appropriation efforts. We propose that the effective use of social media by salespeople will lead to the formation of *salesperson social capital*. Salesperson social capital is an asset that can be leveraged in conjunction with, or even instead of, market-based or hierarchical relationships to accomplish strategic goals (Adler & Kwon, 2002). In the next section, we elaborate the concept of salesperson social capital and explain how effective use of social media by salespeople leads to the formation of social capital in US and Indian organizations.

### *Salesperson Social Capital*

Drawing on studies that sought to highlight how members of social communities invested in long-term relationships with cohabitants in order to ensure their own survival, we find that the term *social capital* has been conceived as encompassing the embeddedness of individuals within a community with the attendant benefits of strong interpersonal relationships based on trust, cooperation and collective action (Nahapiet & Ghoshal, 1998). Social capital provides members of a social network access to resources that can enhance the efficacy of their actions. The notion of capital is akin to the classical theory of capital in that it is, essentially, treated as an investment with an expectation of future returns (Lin, 1998). Thus, *social capital* alludes to the investment an individual makes in interpersonal ties so as to benefit at a later date. Burt (2000) argued that social capital was the contextual complement to human capital and noted that "the people who do better are somehow better connected."

"We suggest that social capital should be viewed in terms of the goodwill that resides in the structure and content of a salesperson's social relationships" (Adler & Kwon, 2002). This goodwill is manifested in the form of long-term obligations as a result of gratitude, respect, and friendship or institutionally guaranteed rights derived from the formal structure of the network (e.g., organization, professional association, etc.) within which the relationships are embedded (Bourdieu, 1986). In the following section, we discuss three different components of social capital and develop propositions linking social media use to these dimensions.

### *Structural, Cognitive, and Relational Social Capital*

The *structural*, *cognitive*, and *relational* components of social capital (Nahapiet & Ghoshal, 1998; Tsai & Ghoshal, 1998) provide salespeople with the *information*, *influence*, and *solidarity* to help create and appropriate customer value. Drawing upon theories that provide insight into cross-cultural differences (Hofstede, 1980), we discuss differences in the *motivation*, *opportunity*, and *ability* of salespeople in US and Indian organizations to utilize social media for the formation of social capital (Adler & Kwon, 2002). We argue that such differences will lead to variances in the quantum and rate of social capital formation in US and Indian companies.

*Structural social* capital refers to the nature and extent of ties in a salesperson's social network. The *structure* of a salesperson's network provides *opportunities* to reach new prospects, increase referrals, and maintain relationships (Agnihotri, Kothandaraman, Kashyap, & Singh, 2012). The important characteristics of a salesperson's structural social capital include (1) size, which refers to the number of members in a salesperson's social network, and (2) density which is the degree of interconnectivity among members of the network and structural holes (i.e., brokerage opportunities available to salespeople among otherwise independent networks).

An increased use of social media by the salesperson will motivate customers to connect with the salesperson. For example, a salesperson sharing product expertise on blogs will attract current customers and other prospects to engage with the salesperson using social media. Similarly, a salesperson actively using social media will have ties with intracompany colleagues in an effort to improve customer support. Salespeople seeking to be active on social media will seek out new ties in an effort to build their network and be a center of influence. Thus,

*P1a: Increased use of social media by a salesperson will lead to an increase in the size of the salesperson's social network.*

Even though we expect that the size of the network will increase both for Indian and US salespeople, the nature of ties are expected to be different. Specifically, there is a higher degree of institutional protection in the US business environment vis-à-vis the Indian business environment (Meyer, Estrin, Bhaumik, & Peng, 2009). This additional uncertainty associated with enforcing contracts in India adds a new wrinkle to an Indian salesperson's responsibilities. Indian salespeople are likely to be more concerned about the impacts of network members' behaviors since they may feel incumbent to assume part of the responsibility for the interests of their stakeholders due to weaker institutional safeguards. A salesperson in an Indian company might be encouraged to increase the number of redundant relationships so that effective group norms may emerge due to network closure (Coleman, 1988). Here, the focus is on imbuing trust in the network, so as to build credibility and grow the reputation of the network. The Indian salesperson will focus on creating a cohesive network using social media. In contrast, due to the strong institutional governance available to US businesses, salespeople will try to bridge ties among unconnected members or groups (Burt, 1992; Granovetter, 1973). In a US company a salesperson might be encouraged to exploit structural holes to connect with members separated by a few degrees since the focus is on individual entrepreneurship and innovation. Salespeople are motivated to access unique information by connecting otherwise independent networks. These differences between US and Indian salespeople can be attributed to the degree of interdependence between the members of the salesperson's network—that is, greater emphasis on individualism in the

USA as compared to India. Previous research (see https://www.hofstede-insights.com) has found that individualism is much higher in the USA (Hofstede score 91) than in India (Hofstede score 48). Therefore,

*P1b: Increased use of social media will lead to*

a. *an increase in network density of an Indian salesperson's social network*
b. *an increase in structural holes of an US salesperson's social network*

*Cognitive* social capital refers to the resources that provide the salesperson with the *ability* to create value by combining and exchanging intellectual capital with members of the network. Nahapiet and Ghoshal (1998) refer to this component as "the shared representations, interpretations, and systems of meaning among parties." We suggest that social media provides the platform to create a common vocabulary to share narratives that ground the context for subsequent intellectual discourse. Many salespeople understand the importance of this cognitive aspect of customer interactions and attempt to build cognitive social capital by sharing market information with customers, supporting customers' offerings with blogs, and online discussions, and endorsing products on social media platforms. Salespeople often use social media to share opinions and insights on specific topics such as sales software, best practices, CRM, and so on, or worldviews in order to inculcate a sense of common purpose in their networks.

We expect considerable differences in social media approaches to creating shared meanings and cognitive social capital between US and Indian salespeople simply based upon cultural differences in cognition. Nisbett, Peng, Choi, and Norenzayan (2001) suggest that Western cultures tend to favor a more *analytic* cognitive style whereas Eastern cultures tend to favor *holistic* approaches. This implies that US salespeople would gravitate toward rule-based taxonomies and a narrow focus on visual attention, harbor dispositional biases in causal attribution, and utilize formal logic in reasoning. In contrast, Indian salespeople might use thematic categories, focus on contextual information and relationships in visual attention, emphasize situational causes in attribution, and dialecticism to resolve conflicts (Varnum, Grossmann, Kitayama, & Nisbett, 2010). Practically, this means that US salespeople are more likely to try and disentangle specifics to extrapolate success and failure and place greater value on the diversity of individual opinions. Indian salespeople might be more inclined to focus upon context and relationships to explain success or lack thereof and favor cohesive group sentiment (Chatterjee, 2009; Gabbay &

Leenders, 1999; Lin, 1999). This implies that the social media paths to the development of cognitive social capital are likely to differ widely between US and Indian salespeople. We expect that

*P2a: Increased use of social media will lead to a*

a. *higher emphasis on the general context in communications and decrease in the diversity of opinions in an Indian salesperson's social network*
b. *higher emphasis on specific cases in communications and increase in diversity of opinions in an US salesperson's social network*

We also expect substantive differences between sales people in US and Indian organizations based upon their *social orientation*—that is, independence versus interdependence. In the USA, such independent social orientation would lead to a greater emphasis on self-direction, autonomy, and self-expression. Hence, a salesperson in the USA might accord greater importance to creative approaches and innovation. The goal of symbolically elevating oneself at the expense of others (Kitayama, Ishii, Imada, Takemura, & Ramaswamy, 2006; Kitayama, Mesquita, & Karasawa, 2006) might be met by highlighting individual achievements in social media. In contrast, Indian salespeople are likely to favor harmony, relatedness, and connection. An interdependent social orientation would be more inclined to emphasize similarities and cohesion, and attribute success to relationships and context (Varnum et al., 2010). This has direct implications for salespersons' ability to mobilize the resources embedded within their social networks. In the USA, there is a focus on self-reliance, individualism, and independence (Emerson, 1841; Markus & Kitayama, 1991; Triandis & Gelfand, 2012). Hence, one might expect a greater focus on the ability of the individual salesperson in the USA to mobilize his or her network resources. Accordingly, a salesperson in the USA is likely to prioritize individual goals and manage network resources to achieve them. This is in contrast to India, where the emphasis is on group welfare, collectivism, and interdependence. Here, one would expect salespeople to rely on the competencies and resources of network members. Therefore, we expect that,

*P2b: Increased use of social media will lead to a*

a. *lower emphasis on individual abilities and individual achievements in an Indian salesperson's social network*
b. *higher emphasis on individual abilities and individual achievements in an US salesperson's social network*

A salesperson's *relational* social capital refers to the shared norms and values that bind members of the salesperson's network. Relational social capital reflects the salesperson's *motivation* to be part of a network in which the returns are neither immediate nor certain. It relates to the goodwill and ensuing benefits accruing to a salesperson as a result of social relationships. Repeated social interactions create bonds based on trust, reciprocity, and affect. The strength and quality of these relationships may vary from one salesperson to another, based on the history of interactions (Granovetter, 1992). Such connections bind the members of the network together through a common identity and relational norms (Burt, 1992; Coleman, 1990). They reduce the costs of coordination and transactions. In this regard, as in many Western cultures, US sales organizations tend to emphasize rational utility models or instrumental approaches in which salespeople view creation and utilization of social capital as instrumental in reducing transaction costs and providing a competitive advantage. In these situations, obligations created in a dyadic social exchange are enforceable due to network and institutional norms. In contrast, Eastern cultures such as India tend to emphasize generalized reciprocity norms—for example, *I will do this for you now, knowing that you will help me when I need that help in the future.* These norms are often engendered over time through socialization and a vision of a shared destiny. This implies that salespeople in the USA are likely to utilize dyadic instrumental approaches such as incentives, promises, and reciprocal endorsements in social media. In contrast, one might expect Indian salespeople to focus upon social media approaches such as reputation-building blogs and endorsement of credentials.

*P3a: Increased use of social media use by a salesperson will lead to*

a. *an increase in generalized reciprocity norms in an Indian salesperson's social network*
b. *an increase in specific reciprocity norms in an US salespersons' social network*

Another norm relevant to social media and networks is the norm of solidarity. *Solidarity* implies that salespersons will act as if their success is vested in the fortunes of their network and signals a strong willingness to support network members in the face of adversity. According to Kaufmann and Stern (1988), solidarity implies that people will act in a way that nurtures relationships, often subordinating self-interest to that of the relationship. There are two cultural forces, collectivism and *dharma*, that can lend additional insight into our discussion of differences between the networks of Indian and US sales professionals. As discussed earlier, Indians tend to be much more collectivistic than Americans. Collectivism gives primacy to the interests and welfare of the group as opposed to the individual. The USA has an individualistic culture that places greater importance on self-reliance and individual achievement. Further, the doctrine of *dharma* (Narasimhan, Bhaskar, & Prakhya, 2010), which is highly prevalent and practiced by the majority of Indians, is a well-known antecedent to the formation of individual values and belief systems. Dharma holds that one's actions have consequences not only for one's self but also for others. It recognizes means and ends as equally important and advocates the explicit identification of the consequences of one's actions upon others, as appropriate. Due to these well-documented differences in value systems, we expect that

*P3b: Increased use of social media by a salesperson will lead to*

a. *an increase in solidarity norms in an Indian salesperson's social networks*
b. *a decrease in solidarity norms in an US salesperson's social networks*

The above discussion has highlighted the differences in paths to the formation of social capital in US and Indian sales organizations. In the next section, we discuss how social capital can be deployed for the purpose of creating and appropriating customer value. Consistent with contemporary marketing theory, we limit the scope of our discussion to *value-in-use* (Gronroos & Voima, 2013; Vargo & Lusch, 2004). From a managerial perspective, value appropriation is as important as value creation as it renders the marketing function accountable (e.g., Gronroos & Voima, 2013; Hoyer, Chandy, Dorotic, Krafft, & Singh, 2010; Kashyap, Mir, & Iyer, 2011). We observe a big gap in theory development regarding the relationship between social capital and customer value. Therefore, we focus our efforts on articulating the logic to relate dimensions of salesperson social capital to value creation and value appropriation instead of trying to discern *ex ante* differences between US and Indian salespeople.

### *Creation and Appropriation of Customer Value*

Structural social capital provides three important resources that are fundamental to the creation of customer value. We refer to these drivers as the trinity of *access* (who is reached), *referral* (how they are reached), and *influence* (what they offer). Access refers to the ability of a salesperson to receive and disseminate unique, timely, and accurate information. Highly placed social contacts can provide enhanced access to valuable and high-quality market information due to their authority and access to diverse sources of market intelligence (Seevers, Skinner, & Dahlstrom, 2010). Such information can be critical to salespersons' efforts to create customer value. It can help refine target market strategies, reduce time-to-market, and increase probabilities of new product success.

Referrals are word-of-mouth recommendations arising from a salesperson's social network connections that may yield unique opportunities (e.g., being in the right place at the right time). Referrals solve the problems of legitimacy and logistics (Burt, 1992), and reduce transaction costs associated with adverse selection (Dahlstrom & Ingram, 2003). Referrals help "simplify the selection of business partners by signaling reputation and attractiveness" (Seevers et al., 2010, p. 312). The reputation of highly placed contacts in a salesperson's social network can provide a halo of trust to facilitate new alliances and reduce monitoring costs.

The influence of salespersons resides in their ability to control the flow of resources or access between members of their social network. Salespersons' influence stems from their unique boundary-spanning role that provides opportunities to broker valuable information and resources. New insights into the company's product pipelines, alternate product uses, service innovations, and other market intelligence can help customers realign business strategies, reduce costs, and generate new revenue streams. Further, salespeople can help broker transactions between members of the network to supplement customer competencies and help cocreate value. Therefore, we propose that

*P4: A salesperson's structural social capital*
- a. *increases access to resources and information*
- b. *legitimizes and increases the scope of referrals*
- c. *increases influence over the flow of information and resources*

While social media provides platforms to increase customer engagement, cognitive social capital provides customers with the means and impetus for cocreating value (Hoyer et al., 2010; Vargo & Lusch, 2004). Customers can cocreate value by recombining and integrating (Gronroos & Voima, 2013) available network resources. For instance, Dell's Women's Entrepreneur Network (DWEN), which connects female entrepreneurs across the globe with networks of like-minded women, funding sources, knowledge and technology, boasts of several success stories (see http://www.dell.com/learn/us/en/04/women-powering-business). By focusing on transparency and clarifying company policies on IP, salespeople can offset potential impediments to cocreation that may arise from fears of secrecy and intellectual property rights, and concerns about feasibility (Hoyer et al., 2010). From a positive standpoint, motivations to engage in cocreation may be stimulated by potential social benefits such as social learning and social esteem (Nambisan & Baron, 2009). Drawing upon extensive social knowledge about product use and customers, salespeople have the opportunity to accurately define and elaborate the importance of key product attributes for the purpose of value creation (Agnihotri et al., 2012). Further, the collective intelligence of the network can be effectively used to generate innovative solutions and resolve customer problems. They can also deploy the intellectual capital of the network to increase the comprehensiveness and accuracy of solutions for buyers of complex products with multiple buying criteria. In this way, customers can identify the *locus*, define the *nature*, and expand the *scope* of value creation (Gronroos & Voima, 2013). Therefore, we propose that

*P5a: A salesperson's cognitive social capital influences the*
  a. *locus*
  b. *nature*
  c. *scope of customer value*

A salesperson's relational social capital is key to the success of efforts aimed at appropriating customer value. We focus on two key elements of customer value—namely, customer advocacy and customer lifetime value. Customer advocacy can be defined as an attempt "to build deeper customer relationships by earning new levels of trust and commitment and by developing mutual transparency, dialogue and partnership with customers" (Lawer & Knox, 2006, p. 123). Customer advocacy has been linked to a host of intangible benefits such as amplifying marketing messages (Kozinets, de Valck, Wojnicki, & Wilner, 2010), diffusing barriers to adoption (Van den Bulte & Lilien, 2000), acquisition of new customers, and increases in purchase frequency, volume, and cross-buying (Libai et al., 2010). Salespeople use social media to increase customer interactions and engagement (Agnihotri et al., 2012). One of the major benefits of customer engagement is the positive effect of engaged customers on the attitudes and behaviors of other customers (Libai et al., 2010). Customer engagement is a focal antecedent to the development of long-term relationships that are aimed at converting customers into advocates (Sashi, 2012). In order to form such relationships, it may be necessary at times to transcend self-interest in favor of customer needs. According to Urban (2004, p. 81), "The best salespeople are those who help solve customer problems even when their company's products are not involved." Shared solidarity norms in a salesperson's social network can lead to lower monitoring costs and higher commitment (Adler & Kwon, 2002). Stronger commitment has been found to increase customer advocacy, especially in the B2B context (Lacey & Morgan, 2009).

In a B2B context, customer lifetime value assumes even greater importance due to the smaller number of customers, share-of-wallet, and marketing resource allocation considerations (Kumar, Venkatesan, Bohling, & Beckmann, 2008). Further, it has been found that customers are more likely to increase their perceptions of value and share-of-wallet when they utilize the competitive intelligence provided by salespeople (Hughes, Le Bon, & Rapp, 2013). As companies increase their dependence on revenues from long-term customer relationships (Rust & Huang, 2014), relational assets will continue to grow in importance. To facilitate this process, companies have begun to use social CRM systems (or CRM 2.0) (e.g., Chaffey, 2011; Dutot, 2013), which are aimed at increasing transparency and engendering trust. From a salesperson's standpoint, these systems offer the benefit of formally identifying customer profiles, objectively analyzing customer sentiment, and mapping customer experiences. Regardless of whether social CRM systems or informal social media platforms are employed, trust and commitment remain the most critical determinants of customer decisions to continue business relationships (Mukherjee & Nath, 2007). Therefore, we propose that

*P5b: A salesperson's relational social capital improves*

a. *customer advocacy*
b. *customer lifetime value*

## Summary

This research has enormous significance for both academics and practitioners. First, the appropriate use and benefits of social media for sales professionals are not apparent. Our manuscript helps clarify social media's strategic potential for value creation and value appropriation. Second, we aim to shed light on the accountability of the marketing function by illuminating the pathways from social media to social capital. Third, an appreciation of the differences between social media use by salespeople in US and Indian organizations can provide managers with a finer-grained understanding of the transformative potential of social technologies in global organizations.

## References


Adler, P., & Kwon, S.-W. (2002). Social Capital: Prospects for a New Concept. *Academy of Management Review, 27*(1), 17–40.

Agnihotri, R., Kothandaraman, P., Kashyap, R. K., & Singh, R. (2012, Summer). Bringing "Social" Into Sales: The Impact of Salesperson's Social Media Use on Service Behaviors and Value Creation. *Journal of Personal Selling and Sales Management, XXXII*(3), 335–350.

Anderson, J., Narus, J., & van Rossum, W. (2006). Customer Value Propositions in Business Markets. *Harvard Business Review, 84*, 90–99.

Bourdieu, P. (1986). The Forms of Capital. In J. G. Richardson (Ed.), *Handbook of Theory and Research for the Sociology of Education* (pp. 241–258). New York: Greenwood.

Burt, R. S. (2000). The Network Structure of Social Capital. *Research in Organizational Behavior., 22*, 345–423.

Burt, R. S. (1992). *Structural Holes: The Social Structure of Competition*. Cambridge, MA: Harvard University Press.

Chaffey, D. (2011). *E-business & E-commerce Management, Strategy, Implementation and Practice* (5th ed.). New York: Prentice Hall.

Chatterjee, S. R. (2009). Managerial Ethos of the Indian Tradition: Relevance of a Wisdom Model. *Journal of Indian Business Research, 1*(2), 136–162.

Christakis, N. A., & Fowler, J. H. (2013). Social Contagion Theory: Examining Dynamic Social Networks and HumanBehavior. *Statistics in Medicine, 32*, 556–577. https://doi.org/10.1002/sim.5408

Coleman, J. S. (1988). Social Capital in the Creation of Human Capital. *American Journal of Sociology, 94*(Supplement), 95–120.

Coleman, J. S. (1990). *Foundations of Social Theory*. Cambridge, MA: Belknap Press.

Dahlstrom, R., & Ingram, R. (2003). Social Networks and the Adverse Selection Problem in Agency Relationships. *Journal of Business Research, 56*, 767–775.

Dutot, V. (2013). A New Strategy for Customer Engagement: How Do French Firms Use Social CRM? *International Business Research, 6*(9), 54–67.

Emerson, R. W. (1841). Essay II Self-Reliance. *Essays: First Series*. Retrieved September, 12, 2014.

Gabbay, S. M., & Leenders, R. T. A. J. (1999). CSC: The Structure of Advantage and Disadvantage. In R. T. A. J. Leenders & S. M. Gabbay (Eds.), *Corporate Social Capital and Liability*. Boston, MA: Springer.

Granovetter, M. (1992). Economic Institutions as Social Constructions: A Framework for Analysis. *Acta Sociologica, 35*(1), 3–11.

Granovetter, M. S. (1973). The Strength of Weak Ties. *American Journal of Sociology, 78*(6), 1360–1380. https://doi.org/10.1086/225469

Gronroos, C., & Voima, P. (2013). Critical Service Logic: Making Sense of Value Creation and Co-Creation. *Journal of the Academy of Marketing Science, 41*, 133–150.

Gupta, S., Armstrong, K. A. B., & Clayton, Z. S. (2011). Social Media. Harvard Business School Background Note 510–095, March 2010. (Revised October 2011).

Hofstede, G. (1980). *Culture's Consequences.* Thousand Oaks, CA: Sage.

Hoyer, W. D., Chandy, R., Dorotic, M., Krafft, M., & Singh, S. S. (2010). Consumer Co-creation in New Product Development. *Journal of Service Research, 13*(3), 283–296.

Hughes, D. E., Le Bon, J., & Rapp, A. (2013). Gaining and Leveraging Customer-Based Competitive Intelligence: The Pivotal Role of Social Capital and Salesperson Adaptive Selling Skills. *Journal of the Academy of Marketing Science, 41*(1), 91–110.

Husted, B. W. (1994). Transaction Costs, Norms, and Social Networks: A Preliminary Study of Cooperation in Industrial Buyer-Seller Relationships in the United States and Mexico. *Business & Society, 33*(1), 30–57.

Kashyap, R. K., Mir, R., & Iyer, E. S. (2011). *The Dynamics of Value Creation, Value Capture, and Value Erosion: Towards a Theory of Firm Sustainability.* In Proceedings of 2011 World Marketing Congress, Reims, France.

Kaufmann, P. J., & Stern, L. W. (1988, September). Relational Exchange Norms, Perceptions of Unfairness, and Retained Hostility in Commercial Litigation. *The Journal of Conflict Resolution, 32*, 534–552.

Kitayama, S., Ishii, K., Imada, T., Takemura, K., & Ramaswamy, J. (2006). Voluntary Settlement and the Spirit of Independence: Evidence from Japan's "Northern Frontier". *Journal of Personality and Social Psychology, 91*, 369–384.

Kitayama, S., Mesquita, B., & Karasawa, M. (2006). Cultural Affordances and Emotional Experience: Socially Engaging and Disengaging Emotions in Japan and the United States. *Journal of Personality and Social Psychology, 91*(5), 890–903.

Kozinets, R. V., de Valck, K., Wojnicki, A. C., & Wilner, S. J. S. (2010). Networked Narratives: Understanding Word-of-mouth Marketing in Online Communities. *Journal of Marketing, 74*(2), 71–89.

Kumar, V., Venkatesan, R., Bohling, T., & Beckmann, D. (2008). The Power of CLV: Managing Customer Lifetime Value at IBM. *Marketing Science, 27*(4), 585–599,749,751,753.

Kwon, K. H., Stefanone, M. A., & Barnett, G. A. (2014). Social Network Influence on Online Behavioral Choices: Exploring Group Formation on Social Network Sites. *American Behavioral Scientist, 58*(10), 1345–1360.

Lacey, R., & Morgan, R. M. (2009). Customer Advocacy and the Impact of B2B Loyalty Programs. *The Journal of Business & Industrial Marketing, 24*(1), 3–13.

Lawer, C., & Knox, S. (2006). Customer Advocacy and Brand Development. *The Journal of Product and Brand Management, 15*(2), 121–129.

Libai, B., Bolton, R., Bügel, M. S., de Ruyter, K., Götz, O., Risselada, H., et al. (2010). Customer-to-customer Interactions: Broadening the Scope of Word of Mouth Research. *Journal of Service Research, 13*(3), 267–282.

Lin, N. (1998). Building a Network Theory of Social Capital. *Connections, 22*(1), 28–51.

Lin, N. (1999). Social Networks and Status Attainment. *Annual Review of Sociology, 25*(1), 467–487.

Markus, H., & Kitayama, S. (1991). Culture and Self: Implications for Cognition, Emotion, and Motivation. *Psychological Review, 98*, 225–253.

Meyer, K. E., Estrin, S., Bhaumik, S. K., & Peng, M. W. (2009). Institutions, Resources, and Entry Strategies in Emerging Economies. *Strategic Management Journal, 30*(1), 61–80.

Mukherjee, A., & Nath, P. (2007). Role of Electronic Trust in Online Retailing. *European Journal of Marketing, 41*(9), 1173–1202.

Nahapiet, J., & Ghoshal, S. (1998). Social Capital, Intellectual Capital, and the Organizational Advantage. *Academy of Management Review, 23*(2), 242–266.

Nambisan, S., & Baron, R. A. (2009). Virtual Customer Environments: Testing a Model of Voluntary Participation in Value Co-creation Activities. *The Journal of Product Innovation Management, 26*(4), 388–406.

Narasimhan, N., Bhaskar, K., & Prakhya, S. (2010). Existential Beliefs and Values. *Journal of Business Ethics, 96*(3), 369–382.

Nisbett, R. E., Peng, K., Choi, I., & Norenzayan, A. (2001). Culture and Systems of Thought: Holistic vs. Analytic Cognition. *Psychological Review, 108*, 291–310.

Polansky, N., Lippitt, R., & Redl, F. (1950). An Investigation of Behavioral Contagion in Groups. *Human Relations, 3*, 319–348.

Rapp, A., Beitelspacher, L. S., Grewal, D., & Hughes, D. E. (2013). Understanding Social Media Effects Across Seller, Retailer, and Consumer Interactions. *Academy of Marketing Science Journal, 41*(5), 547–566.

Rust, R, T. & Huang, M. (2014). The Service Revolution and the Transformation of Marketing Science. *Marketing Science, 33*(2), 206–221.

Sashi, C. M. (2012). Customer Engagement, Buyer-seller Relationships, and Social Media. *Management Decision, 50*(2), 253–272.

Seevers, M. T., Skinner, S. J., & Dahlstrom, R. (2010). Performance Implications of a Retail Purchasing Network: The Role of Social Capital. *Journal of Retailing, 86*(4), 356–367.

Triandis, H., & Gelfand, M. (2012). A Theory of Individualism and Collectivism. In P. A. M. Van Lange, A. W. Kruglanski, & E. T. Higgins (Eds.), *Handbook of Theories of Social Psychology*. Thousand Oaks, CA: Sage.

Tsai, W., & Ghoshal, S. (1998). Social Capital and Value Creation: The Role of Intrafirm Networks. *Academy of Management Journal, 41*(4), 464–476.

Urban, G. L. (2004). The Emerging Era of Customer Advocacy. *MIT Sloan Management Review, 45*(2), 77–82.

Van den Bulte, C., & Lilien, G. (2000, March). Social Contagion Versus Marketing Effort. *American Journal of Sociology, 106*(5), 1409–1435.

Vargo, S. L., & Lusch, R. F. (2004, January). Evolving to a New Dominant Logic for Marketing. *Journal of Marketing, 68*, 1–17.

Varnum, M. E. W., Grossmann, I., Kitayama, S., & Nisbett, R. E. (2010). The Origin of Cultural Differences in Cognition: Evidence for the Social Orientation Hypothesis. *Current Directions in Psychological Science, 19*(1), 9–13.

PART IV

# Social Media Applications and Case Studies

CHAPTER 12

# Influence of Social Media Marketing on Health Care and Automobile Sectors in India

*Joyeeta Chatterjee and Ambrish Joshi*

## Introduction

The emergence of social networking sites (SNSs) globally has brought in a paradigm shift in word-of-mouth (WOM) communications, enabling users to observe, interact, and exchange information. Although the Internet has long been flaunted as an effective, inexpensive and a global corridor to make any business grow, there has been a gold-rush-like response from organizations to the recent wave among the web surfers of what are popularly known as social networking sites (SNS)—for example, Facebook, MySpace, LinkedIn and Twitter. This has opened new avenues for businesses to reach their target customer base as never before. In India, although penetration of the Internet continues to remain low, it is estimated that around 180 million people (out of a population of more than 1.2 billion) are active users of online services and various social media and

J. Chatterjee (✉)
Lal Bahadur Shastri Institute of Management, New Delhi, India

A. Joshi
GENPACT LLC, Bengaluru, Karnataka, India



G. Heggde, G. Shainesh (eds.), *Social Media Marketing*,
https://doi.org/10.1007/978-981-10-5323-8_12

e-mail platforms.[1] By 2019 this is expected to increase to 600 million, making India second only to China in the number of citizens using this new medium. Such an explosive figure affords an opportunity for India to transform its Internet profile to expand usage, even ahead of present projections, and boost GDP sustainability. One of the important benefits of the Internet has been its usage in marketing communication. SNSs are growing rapidly all over the world and India is one of the biggest growing markets for social networks. Indian businesses too are jumping onto the social networking bandwagon, catering to their "most-sought-after clientele" and collecting valuable information about them for a minimal investment. Marketing, which is conceived as the process of identifying and meeting customer needs and wants over time, tends to view technology as the new moment of truth describing the interface of a product, service or brand with customers, consumers or even noncustomers. In the millennium generation, the conventional mode of communication is increasingly being replaced by the social media or SNSs. Promotion on the digital platform is growing enormously popular. Marketing communication is becoming precise, personal, interactive, interesting and social. From Facebook to Twitter, LinkedIn to Pinterest, and so on, there has been an increasing trend by the businesses in India to use the different formats of SNS platforms to reach out to their customers, partners and their employees as well.

## Literature Review

Today social networking sites are reckoned to be the most popular technologies on the World Wide Web, with millions of users across the globe. Research is still being conducted to discover how people are using this powerful medium, for what purposes, and in what settings, and to explore how these SNSs are shaping the way people think, work and communicate. Social networking is a new phenomenon made possible on a global scale with Web 2 technology. The revolution in the form of the Internet has transformed the way we interact through informal online networks of friends. Word of mouth (WOM) has become a strategy element of social media marketing and interactive integrative marketing communications (IMC) (Fogel, 2010). A significant share of word of mouth has shifted from small groups and communities to large-scale online networks of consumers (Avery, Resnick, & Zeckhauser, 1999), such as those facilitated by social networking sites (SNSs). This trend has important implications for marketers as social networking sites present a one-of-its-kind opportunity to achieve unparalleled depth and reach in marketing efforts. This new medium provides marketers with an opportunity to explicitly influence word-of-mouth (WOM) communications in a manner that is quite impossible with conventional IMC tools, such as mass advertising or personal selling. SNSs are extraordinary and powerful not simply because they allow marketers to communicate with customers but because they allow consumers to communicate with one another (Mangold & Faulds, 2009). Moreover, for the younger generation, SNSs play a crucial role in information and communication consumption behavior (Sago, 2010). Success of IMC strategies depends on choosing the correct mix of IMC. Hence businesses and marketers have realized these inimitable capabilities of social media and very strategically started to make use of this platform as one of the IMC tools. With the growth of user-friendly and attractive sites and the ever-increasing demand for smart phones over the last few years, SNSs have become more trendy, making them a highly popular medium for businesses wanting to get the word out about products and services (Ahuja, 2013).

In 2010 *Harvard Business Review* (*HBR*) observed from one of its studies that the major benefit of using social media enjoyed by businesses was "increased awareness of their brands" (*Harvard Business Review*, 2010). Even today this stands to be one of the prime reasons for social media adoption, but the topmost reason for business organizations to go social is "to build communities". A community provides a platform for brands to reach out to various customers at one go for promotional initiatives. It also facilitates the bonding of customers, shores up brand experience stories and creates strong WOM. In the long run, it assists in generating leads, enhances customer loyalty, provides faster resolution of customer queries, reduces the cost of marketing and servicing, and encourages innovative ideas. Many of us do web search before we pay money for a product or a service. For example, organizations in the hospitality sector are highly vulnerable to consumer assessment as guests check web pages prior to deciding on a particular hotel or resort. Thus, it has become all the more important to develop social media outreach to answer customers' queries. Although, at present, the actual number of users of social media might be low, their influence is far reaching and it is difficult to predict how many users will be there tomorrow. This new media has become much more than just a means to communicate with family and friends or to exhibit pictures or share first-hand experience of the latest movies or the eateries in town. With thousands glued to their smart phones or laptops for several hours a day, several companies are "smarting up" to join the race in offering consumers the latest ways of buying products and experiencing services. Emergence of new media has brought new models of interactive user-to-user messages (Liu & Shrum, 2002; Mitra, 2009). Customers in emerging economies are embracing social media at a unusual rate of growth. The few top countries among them are India, Indonesia, Mexico, and Brazil. India and Indonesia are increasingly witnessing a major increase in Facebook usage with many users actively posting videos, messages, pictures, and so on. Social media is making interaction between end users and service providers possible by providing a simple and easy-to-access platform for all to share feedback. Increasingly driven by regulatory pressures, the need to "get it right the first time and minimize costs" always remains a concern for businesses. New media facilitates a platform for user-generated content that comes in the form of peer reviews of products or services. Such reviews, or feedback, improve business and help business leaders to better understand customers' requirements as well as identify the failure points of the products or serviced they offer. Indian organizations' use of social media is much higher than the global average and those of their counterparts in emerging economies. Of the social media savvy organizations in India, 95.7 percent use social media to build communities while 76.1 percent use social media as a platform to highlight brand news. Approximately 16 percent of user organizations employ the social platform to resolve customer grievances, generate leads, and conduct research, indicating high social maturity and a trend toward acquiring business from engagements.

### *Objectives/Purpose*

The purpose of this study was to carry out a comparative analysis of the use of social networking sites as a marketing communication tool across two sectors in the country: health care and automobile. Comprehensive analysis was carried out to study the presence of the various social media platforms and understand how the health care and automobile sectors are leveraging them for their own benefit. The study also attempts to understand the nature and level of usage of social media by both the health-care sector and the automobile sector.

### *Methodology*

A comprehensive literature research was carried out, initially, to build the hypothesis that formed the basic framework for conducting this research. In both sectors, input from a diverse respondent group was analyzed using interviews. There were approximately 115 respondents from each sector. They were randomly selected within their respective sector to represent the target market population and their responses were analyzed.

## Health-Care Sector

Over the past decade, India has been undertaking the transformation of its health-care system. The government introduced important structural reforms and has re-emphasized its vision of creating access to a minimum set of health-care services for the entire population. The private sector experienced unprecedented growth during this period. In addition to medical advancements and technological developments, the Internet revolution also took the sector by storm. Just as happened in every other sector, there was an expectation that the health-care sector would also jump onto the social media bandwagon. A surprising number of health-care centers started using social media in their marketing programs/campaigns. Therefore, it is essential to understand how the Internet and the social media world have influenced the health-care sector. To unearth more insights into the influence of social media on health-care sector, we have analyzed forty hospitals across India. Although sufficient information related to health and medicine is available on the web, the authors of this paper were keen to determine the degree of difference between information hospitals acquired from the web and information hospitals acquired from sharing information on various social platforms. Table 12.1 shows the presence of forty leading Indian hospitals on various social media platforms.

Of those hospitals, approximately twenty-two have a more active social media presence on more than one platform. We conducted a detailed exploration to ascertain the top five hospitals/hospital groups, based on their presence on various social media platforms, their approach, engagement ratio, and so on. They are (a) Apollo Hospitals, (b) Fortis Healthcare, (c) Kokilaben Hospital, (d) NU Hospitals, and (e) Wockhardt Hospitals. The authors were eager to understand the objectives of these hospitals. Hence their activities were followed on different platforms. It has been

**Table 12.1** Select list of hospitals having a presence on various social media platforms

| *Name of the hospital (city/state)* | *Facebook* | *Twitter* | *LinkedIn* | *Google+* | *Youtube* | *Slide Share* | *Social icon on websites* |
|---|---|---|---|---|---|---|---|
| Apollo Hospitals, Multispecialty (Group) | ✓ | ✓ | ✓ | ✓ | ✓ | ✓ | ✓ |
| Fortis Healthcare, Multispecialty (Group) | ✓ | ✓ | ✓ | ✓ | ✓ | ✓ | ✓ |
| Max Healthcare, Multispecialty (Group) | ✓ | ✓ | | | ✓ | | ✓ (Also have their presence on Pinterest) |
| Sankara Nethralaya Hospitals, Superspecialty, (Group) | ✓ | | | | ✓ | | ✓ |
| Manipal Hospitals, Multispecialty (Group) | ✓ | ✓ | | | | | ✓ |
| Wockhardt Hospitals, Superspecialty (Mumbai) (Group) | ✓ | ✓ | ✓ | ✓ | ✓ | ✓ | ✓ |
| Vasan Eye Care Hospitals, Superspecialty (Group) | ✓ | ✓ | | | | | ✓ |
| AIIMS (Delhi) | ✓✓ | – | – | – | – | – | – |
| Fortis Heart Inst. & Research Centre (Delhi) | ✓ | ✓ | ✓ | | | – | ✓ |
| Rajiv Gandhi Cancer Inst. & Research Centre (Delhi) | ✓ | – | – | – | – | – | – |

(*continued*)

**Table 12.1** (continued)

| *Name of the hospital (city/state)* | *Facebook* | *Twitter* | *LinkedIn* | *Google+* | *Youtube* | *Slide Share* | *Social icon on websites* |
|---|---|---|---|---|---|---|---|
| Breach Candy Hospital (Mumbai) | ✓ | | | | | | |
| Lilavati Hospital (Mumbai) | ✓ | | | | | | |
| Kokilaben Hospital (Mumbai) | ✓ | ✓ | ✓ | ✓ | ✓ | ✓ | ✓ |
| Nanavati Hospital (Mumbai) | ✓ | ✓ | | | | | ✓ |
| Bombay Hospital (Mumbai) | ✓ | | | | | | |
| Chittaranjan National Cancer Research Centre | | | | | | | |
| B. M. Birla Heart Research Inst. Kolkatta | ✓ | | | ✓ | | | |
| Vijaya Hospital, Multispecialty (Chennai) (Private Trust) | ✓ | ✓ | | | | | ✓ |
| Sri Ramchandra Medical College & Reseach Inst. (Shri Ramchandra University) (Chennai) | ✓ | ✓ | | | | | ✓ |
| Billroth Hospital, Multispecialty (Chennai) | | | | | | | |
| Cancer Inst., Superspecialty (Adyar-Chennai) | | | | | | | |
| Kalyani Hospitals, Superspecialty (Gurgaon) | ✓ | | | | ✓ | | ✓ |

(*continued*)

**Table 12.1** (continued)

| *Name of the hospital (city/state)* | *Facebook* | *Twitter* | *LinkedIn* | *Google+* | *Youtube* | *Slide Share* | *Social icon on websites* |
|---|---|---|---|---|---|---|---|
| St.John's Medical College & Hospital, Specialty, Superspecialty (Bangalore) | | | | | | | |
| Sanjay Gandhi Hospital, Govt. Hospital (Delhi) | ✓ | | | | ✓ | | |
| Shanti Mukund Hospital, Diagnostic and General Medical Care (Delhi) | | | | | | | |
| Vivekananda Hospital, Multispecialty (Durgapur, WB) | | | | | | | |
| Christian Medical College (Vellore) | | | | | | | |
| TATA Memorial Hospitals, Superspecialty (Mumbai) | | | | | | | |
| Hinduja Hospitals, Multispecialty (Mumbai) | ✓ | ✓ | ✓ | | ✓ | | |
| Post Graduate Hospital of Medical Education & Research (Kolkata) | | | | | | | |
| NU Hospitals Superspecialty (Bangalore) | ✓ | ✓ | ✓ | ✓ | ✓ | ✓ | ✓(Hospital's own blogs) |
| Jaslok Hospital (Mumbai) | ✓ | ✓ | ✓ | | ✓ | | |

(*continued*)

**Table 12.1** (continued)

| *Name of the hospital (city/ state)* | *Facebook* | *Twitter* | *LinkedIn* | *Google+* | *Youtube* | *Slide Share* | *Social icon on websites* |
|---|---|---|---|---|---|---|---|
| Global Hospitals, Multisuper-specialty (Group) | ✓ | ✓ | ✓ | ✓ | | | ✓ |
| B. L. K Superspecialty (Delhi) | ✓ | ✓ | | | | | ✓ |
| Delhi Heart & Lung Institute | ✓ | ✓ | ✓ | ✓ | | | ✓ |
| R. G. Stone Urological Research Institute (Delhi) | ✓ | | | | | | ✓ |
| Indian Spinal Injuries Centre (Delhi) | ✓ | ✓ | | | | | ✓ |
| Institute of Liver & Biliary Science (Delhi) | ✓ | ✓ | | | | | |

observed that Facebook is the most popular of all social networking sites (47 percent), followed by Twitter (15 percent) and LinkedIn (14 percent). Hospitals prefer to promote themselves on Facebook. Table 12.1 suggests that Facebook is a huge hit among all types of hospital.

### *Hospitals on Facebook*

With the majority of the hospitals promoting their services on Facebook, the authors sought to ascertain whether they were highly active or dormant on Facebook and other social media platforms. Surprisingly, only 35 percent of the hospitals were highly active on Facebook (with Apollo Hospitals updating on a daily basis), followed by Twitter and YouTube, which had just 9 percent of the activity share. With a plethora of visual information on social platforms, hospitals have taken the initiative to share medical facts and tips and help patients resolve concerns. Pictures, videos and applications are used at length to make information more appealing.

### *Strategy*

- Daily health tips, easy-to-follow advice, and facts that most people need to know are provided.
- Live chats with specialized doctors on Facebook are smart ways that hospitals have adapted to keep their followers active.
- Few hospitals are creating awareness of healthy food habits and exercise on these platforms.
- Lifeline numbers, testimonials, value-added services, and so on, are among the most prevalent information provided.

### *Highlights and Unique Selling Propositions (USP)*

- Apollo's campaigns, such as those conducted on The Blood Connection, which is a social platform for blood donations, and Ask the Doctor deal with FAQs related to health and medicine. Surprisingly, this hospital has minimal promotional activity on its Facebook page.
  - Apollo Hospitals also host live chats on Facebook that allow people to post questions on a particular topic that is announced as a status update.
- Fortis enjoys amazing goodwill among all its patients. It responds quickly to any feedback or query posted on its page. Its campaign to help victims of acid attacks greatly boosted its reputation among followers.
- With its unique updates, Wockhardt aims at broad coverage of health and fitness issues to keep its followers engaged. The hospital also has self-explanatory apps for a back specialist, a knee specialist, and so on.
- NU Hospitals are among India's leading nephro-urology health-are group and their Facebook page provides medical facts, brain teasers, and important days to celebrate.
- Established in 2009, Kokilaben Hospital also has a very different approach to educating the population on health and fitness. Its updates focus on creating awareness of healthy food habits and exercise.

– Most of the page gives advice on maintaining a healthy lifestyle and avoiding diseases.

### *Hospitals on Twitter*

Twitter has changed how some people connect and communicate. Unlike other virtual worlds, its system is amazingly rapid with low time investment. Thus hospitals attempt to provide brief and prompt updates. Listening to, and responding to, patient queries is how hospitals, basically, use Twitter.

#### *Strategy*

- On average, these hospitals put up three to four tweets a day that can be more or less categorized as tips, advice, information, and broadcasting.
- Most hospitals duplicate content on Facebook and Twitter to ease the administrative burden.
- Hashtag campaigns on common health issues broaden followers' perspective and provide valuable information.
- Fortis took the initiative on Twitter and Facebook to create "#monsoonmantra," which has developed into a bundle of amazing health tips for dealing with monsoons. Along with this, Fortis provides a few updates on organ donation and undertakes a few self-promotional activities. Fortis is enjoying a huge fan following on Twitter with such campaigns.
- Apollo Hospitals, on the other hand, are very active in listening to their tweeple and respond promptly to their patients' questions and grievances. For example, they search for tweets that have keywords such as headache, cold, body ache, and so on, and respond with advice on home remedies.
- Kokilaben Hospital's simple policy is to complement tweets with pictures. The famous "#didyouknow" campaign is well executed by them.
- NU Hospital's activity on Twitter is much like an awareness portal for kidney-related problems. Regular tweets provide all the necessary information.

### *Hospitals on LinkedIn*

LinkedIn offers a strong network base. The health-care sector has yet to exploit this service effectively but has shown an active presence so far.

- The quality of a LinkedIn page is judged by its overall recommendations, listings, or services, and career section. Of all the study respondents, Apollo Hospitals, with more than 10,286 followers, have the best LinkedIn presence. LinkedIn also helps showcase the number of employees listed on the hospital's page. For example, Apollo's profile showcases 3000+ employees, which, in itself, boosts credibility. Hospitals with a presence on LinkedIn offer customary corporate communications, preferring to talk about corporate growth and finance.
- Fortis and NU Hospitals do not yet have a customized page on LinkedIn.

### *Hospitals on YouTube*

YouTube is the second largest search engine after Google. Ideas conveyed through YouTube videos have revolutionized learning and teaching. The health-care sector also takes the advantage of this network to deliver services and testimonials. Videos relate to hospital services, patients' comments, testimonials, doctors' advice, health media, and so on.

- Apollo has created approximately 150 videos with more than 162,000 views. Fortis has around 126 videos with more than 169,000 video views. These two hospital groups top the social media presence on YouTube. Apollo has taken a further step in uploading educational videos of medical emergencies on topics such as first aid for burns, choking, and heart attacks.
- Health-care organizations are increasingly learning the importance showcasing their infrastructure. Few videos showcase the infrastructure they have built.

### *Hospitals on Google+*

Google+ is very unpopular, +but there are some +organizations that provide updates on Google+ pages. The health-care sector is no exception.

Apollo Hospitals once again lead in having a presence on this channel too. However, in general, the top five hospitals/hospital groups do not have a very active presence on Google+.

- Apollo and Escorts / Fortis hospitals top the chart with their mere presence. Apollo Hospitals engage with their audience while Escorts does the same by posting facts, tips, health problem solutions, and the like. However, these hospitals mostly post content they have also posted on Facebook.

The marketing of health-care services and related promotional activities on the social media platform are a fairly new concept, but this study's top-rated five hospitals have proven otherwise to the authors of this study by their simple yet smart ways of social media marketing and they have particularly excelled on all the platforms. The most active hospital group on all social media platforms is Apollo Hospitals, but all five hospitals have already taken the social media world by storm and are most likely to thrive through their innovative strategies and style of engagement. They have revolutionized the health-care sector by effectively reaching out to their audiences and engaging with them through updates on topics such as health tips, situations requiring first aid, listening to their audiences, and responding accordingly without resorting to broadcasting. The difference between the other hospitals and these five hospitals is that they haven't limited their marketing strategies to broadcasting but have continued to engage and thus build their follower base. They haven't just set up accounts which they then abandoned on platforms such as Google+ because of they had no audience but have continued to post updates and engage with their audience.

The authors also conducted a survey of 112 respondents to determine social media habits with reference to buying health-care services. The sample comprised of 36 percent males and 64 percent females. The brief demographic profile of the respondents is illustrated in Fig. 12.1.

- Among the surveyed respondents, 78 percent are active on social media, 16 percent are not active and 7 percent do not possess a social media account.

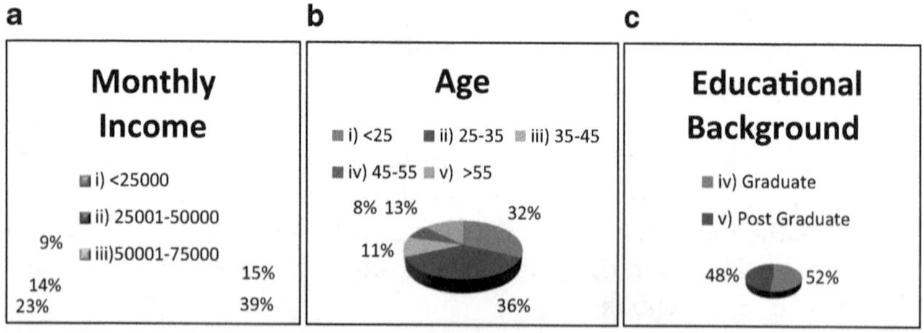


Fig. 12.1 Demographic profile of respondents

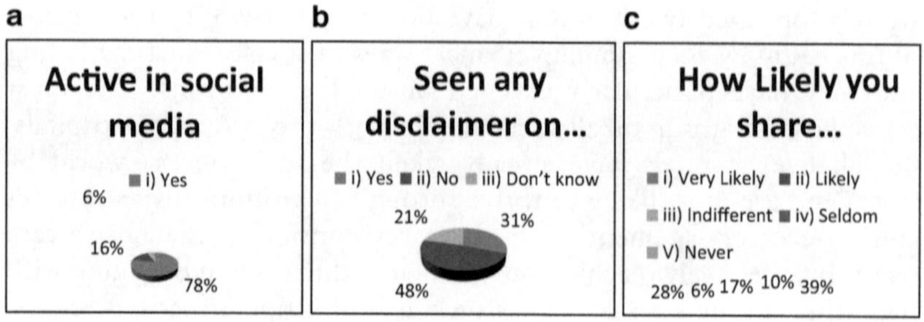


Fig. 12.2 Percentage of the surveyed respondents with respect to social media. Source: Authors' compiled data

- Regarding social media site disclaimers about the information on their sites, 48 percent of the respondents reported seeing none, 31 percent reported seeing some disclaimers, and 21 percent reported not being aware that disclaimers existed.
- Of the total number of respondents, 39 percent reported having an interest in discussing their health issues on social media platforms while 17 percent reported that they had no interest in sharing health-related information on a social media platform (see Fig. 12.2).

The authors of this study also sought to learn why respondents preferred using a social networking platform for health-care services.

- Of the surveyed respondents, 56 percent were satisfied with their health-care experiences on social media.

- Fifty-seven percent were interested in the comments on health-care services, 14 percent were interested in posted reviews of medication, 47 percent shared health-related videos or images, 16 percent wanted to share as well as understand health-related symptoms, and so on, and 15 percent wanted to join and support a health-related cause.
- Interestingly, among the surveyed respondents, Facebook topped the list. Ninety percent of the respondents were active Facebook users, followed closely by YouTube (55 percent) and Twitter (44 percent).
- However, there were a few who have no interest in using social media for health care. Their reasons are explained in Fig. 12.3.

### *Automobile Sector*

The automobile sector is encountering a period of marketing disruption. Traditional advertising models and budgets are withering. Today's consumers have quickly transitioned to social and digital platforms, which have given birth to brand advocates and detractors who share their purchase and ownership experiences by posting comments, or sharing photos or videos on their personal networks. This process alone exercises significant influence on purchase decisions. The major change agents that are shaping the digital landscape and redefining information in order to connect with consumers are Apple, Amazon, Facebook, Twitter, and Google. This change is largely driven by affluent customers and millennial buyers,

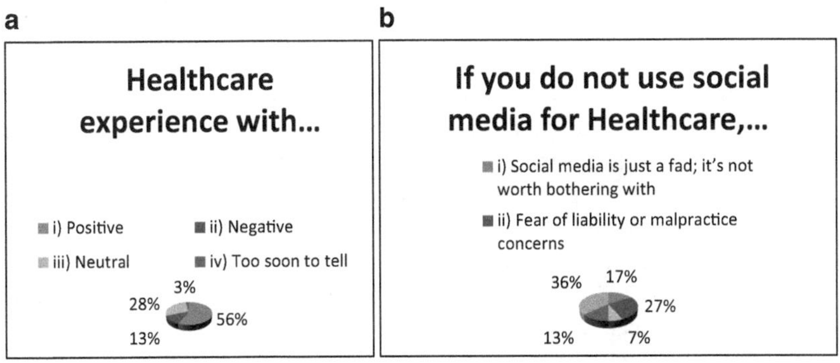


**Fig. 12.3** Percentage of the surveyed respondents for the healthcare services. Source: Authors' compiled data

known popularly as Generation Y. For these customers, online personal experiences are important as continuous conversations in the social news feeds their lives. Engagement has become part of the communication process. Brands are increasingly expected to participate in social channel information sharing. "Always-on" communication is the buzz these days. It is an era of infinite communication possibilities.

For automobile companies, cars will function as digital hubs with their own ecosystems that share data between owner and dealer, owner and original equipment manufacturer (OEM), and owner and OEM partners in real time. The challenge for the automakers is to provide car owners with a platform to integrate their four-wheeled digital hub into their social networks to freely share data and updates similar to sharing experiences of exotic locales or other product experiences. Automobile manufacturers can gamify the ownership experience so that customers share details of trips, fuel consumption, vacation destinations, and so on, on their personal networks, thus adding more data and awareness to social news feeds. The reality is that people are increasingly introduced to the car they ultimately purchase by family and friends via social media updates. The sum of connected experiences shared online and how they influence transactions have given birth to the concept of social selling. As organizations' use of social media increases, they should start looking at identifying and measuring these benefits. Some organizations from among those we reached out to are already on the way to doing this. Organizations influenced by social networking sites (SNSs) in India are moving toward utilizing the medium beyond simply connecting with customers and prospects; they are leveraging business meanings from those engagements. Organizations need to ask themselves if they are providing value to their fans in their channels or communities.

The authors of this study seek answers to some pertinent questions about marketing through SNSs among social-media-savvy automobile organizations in India such as Tata Motors, Maruti Suzuki, BMW India, Ford India, Honda Cars India, and Harley-Davidson India. Most of these automakers are already using popular social platforms such as Twitter, Facebook, and LinkedIn, and also emerging platforms such as Pinterest, Google+, and so on. All these organizations reported conducting campaigns where social media was the leading component. The authors attempted to gauge how automobile manufacturers engaged their social communities. The following are the popular practices identified:

1. *Nature of content*: the majority of the automakers preferred to post generic updates rather than brand specific updates.
2. *Frequency of updates*: Social-media-savvy automobile manufacturers post multiple updates each day. The majority of these respond to fan queries within thirty to sixty minutes on Twitter and within thirty minutes to a couple of hours on Facebook.
3. *Tools used*: many of the Indian automakers use tools for online monitoring, response management, and managing social media platforms
4. *Promotions*: Picture contests are the most popular contests among social-media-savvy organizations in the country, and they are organized almost every month. The majority of the auto manufacturers surveyed pointed out that they have used social media ads, the majority of which were designed to promote a contest or promotion for brand awareness.
5. *Mobile*: Several Indian business organizations including automobile companies have installed mobile phone apps.
6. *Social Media Research*: Approximately 60–65 percent of the automobile manufacturers in India conduct research using social media tools to obtain customer feedback and gain a better understanding of customers' behavior.

In most of these organizations, the marketing department handles the social media and the rest is taken care of by a cross-functional team or by the PR team. Other than marketing, they use social media for thought leadership and CSR. In addition, these organizations have an in-house social media expert in middle management. Around 2–5 percent of their marketing budget is spent on social media.

The authors also attempted to gauge the influence of social networking sites by collecting the customers' responses. Among the 112 respondents interviewed, 45 percent were male and 55 percent were female; 37 percent were graduates, and 63 percent were post graduates. Income and age details are explained in the Fig. 12.4a, b.

- Around 62 percent of the customers used SNSs to collect opinions from friends, peers, and so on, while considering purchasing a car.
- Before purchasing a car, 96 percent of customers use manufacturers' websites, while 86 percent use review sites, and 36 percent use social media platforms to help them make their purchase decision.

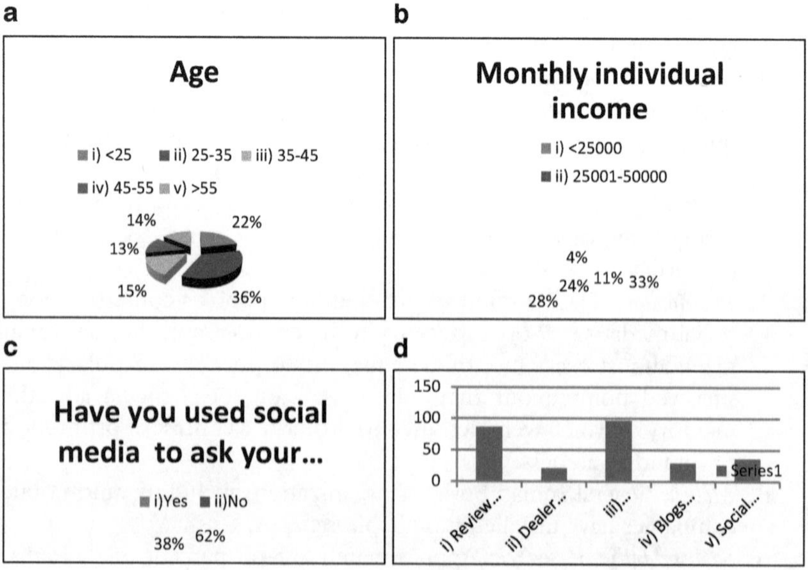


**Fig. 12.4** (**a, b**) Income and age details. (**c, d**) Percentage analysis of the customers who used SNSs. Source: Authors' compiled data

- Seventy-one percent of our study respondents agreed that an automaker's or auto-dealers' social media presence offers information that helps them in making their purchase decision.
- Seventy-eight percent reiterated that autodealers' presence on social media platforms brings transparency. They not only build a community of car owners but also take customers' complaints seriously, and they offer customer services.
- Approximately 63 percent of the surveyed respondents agreed that they used their smartphones to compare car features and prices while they were inside an automobile showroom.
- Only 24 percent of the surveyed respondents reported that they did not depend on online sources for information gathering, whereas 76 percent of the respondents were hooked on the web to search for the latest updates on their brand of car or the brand they aspired to buy. For these respondents, negative online reviews had a marked negative impact on their purchase decision (see Fig. 12.5).

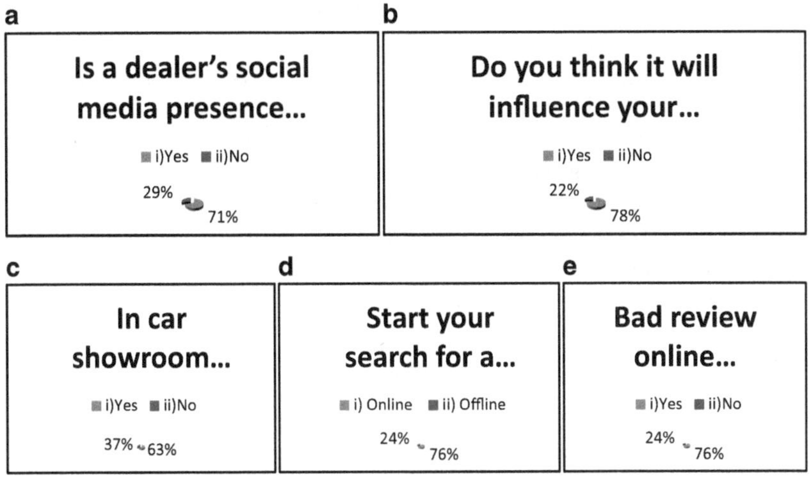


**Fig. 12.5** Percentage analysis of surveyed respondents of automobile sector. Source: Authors' compiled data

## Conclusion

The respondents are very positive about social media. Though sales and leads are not easily measurable for any business using social media, Indian businesses realize that social media plays a crucial role in generating insights and engaging with customers on a continual basis. Social media has helped businesses to create their own communities of fans, customers, and prospects. In the future, Indian businesses hope to place greater focus on social media and look forward to its increasing adoption within their organizations.

### *Recommendation*

Social media needs the attention and commitment of top management. There has to be a clear understanding of the relevance of this medium to the brand in question and a process to leverage it. With the advent of social media, consumer conversations about, and with, a brand have become more measurable. Marketers should continuously try to improve their understanding of this new form of engagement with their brand. The authors of this study recommend that health-care service providers should also think of hosting a hangout with doctors on generic topics for which they can create public awareness, and should make their presence felt on LinkedIn to target professionals and reach out to corporate members to enhance their brand image.

With the tremendous growth in the use of social media, brands have been working hard on how to best capitalize on it. This new medium, as a marketing communication tool, in our country, is still in its incipient form, and marketers are currently devising new objectives and metrics for the use and evaluation of social media on the basis of changing market dynamics.

## Notes

1. http://www.dw.de/indias-political-parties-embrace-social-media/a-17410388

## References

Ahuja, R. (2013). *Top 5 Emerging Markets in Social Media.* Retrieved from http://offervault.com/ top-5-emerging-markets/

Avery, C., Resnick, P., & Zeckhauser, R. (1999). The Market for Evaluations. *American Economic Review, 89*(3), 564–584.

Fogel, S. (2010). Issues in Measurement of Word of Mouth in Social Media Marketing. *International Journal of Integrated Marketing Communications, 2*(2), 54–60.

Harvard Business Review. (2010). *The New Conversation: Taking Social Media from Talk to Action, Harvard Business Review Analytic Services.* Retrieved February 28, 2013, from http://hbr.org/hbrg-main/resources/ pdfs/comm/sas/16203-hbr-sas-report-r3.pdf

Liu, Y., & Shrum, L. J. (2002). What Is Interactivity and Is It Always Such a Good Thing? Implications of Definition, Person, and Situation for the Influence of Interactivity on Advertising Effectiveness. *Journal of Advertising, 31*(4), 53–64.

Mangold, W., & Faulds, D. (2009). Social Media: The New Hybrid Element of the Promotion Mix. *Business Horizons, 52*(4), 357–365.

Mitra, K. (2009, June). *India Inc. Wakes Up to Social Media.* Business Today.

Sago, B. (2010). The Influence of Social Media Message Sources on Millennial Generation Consumers. *International Journal of Integrated Marketing Communications, 2*(2), 7–18.

CHAPTER 13

# A Critical Analysis of Consumer Protection in Social Media Selling with Reference to Information Disclosures

*Pratima Narayan and Githa Heggde*

## Introduction

*The future belongs to social media. It is egalitarian and inclusive. Social media is not about any country, any language, any colour, any community but it is about human values and that is the underlying link binding humanity.*
—Prime Minister Narendra Modi at the launch of Digital India.

Technology advancements in digitization have revolutionized the business model from a mere marketplace to market space. Electronic commerce through online shops, mobile apps and social media has almost been an inevitable tool for businesses to market their goods and services. The architecture of electronic commerce provides a dynamic and collaborative platform to business and consumers. Consumers get to choose from a whole range of goods and services across the world, from anywhere and at any time. Businesses are constantly innovating new technologies in order to adapt to new and evolving challenges in the area of e-commerce.

P. Narayan (✉) • G. Heggde
National Law School of India University, Bangalore, Karnataka, India

IFIM Business School, Bangalore, Karnataka, India



G. Heggde, G. Shainesh (eds.), *Social Media Marketing*,
https://doi.org/10.1007/978-981-10-5323-8_13

The Internet is a bustling industry connecting more than two billion people worldwide. In the context of the Indian Internet landscape, a December 2012 McKinsey report offers seven key findings concerning the impact of and outlook for the Internet in India. According to the report, India's base of about 120 million Internet users is currently the third largest in the world. India is likely to develop into the second-largest user base in the world, and the largest in terms of incremental growth, with 600 million Internet users in 2019. The report also shows that India has the potential to double its economic contribution from the Internet from 1.6 percent of GDP at present to 2.8 to 3.3 percent by 2015 (Chandra, Anu et al., 2012).

A recent eMarketer report shows a consistent rise in the digital penetration in business (www.emarketer.com).

Digital buyers worldwide, by country, 2011–2016 (in millions)

| | *2011* | *2012* | *2013* | *2014* | *2015* | *2016* |
|---|---|---|---|---|---|---|
| **Asia Pacific** | 334.8 | 391.1 | 457.6 | 523.1 | 591.7 | 653.5 |
| China | 178.4 | 219.8 | 270.9 | 322.1 | 374.9 | 423.4 |
| Japan | 70.2 | 73.3 | 75.6 | 77.0 | 78.2 | 79.2 |
| India | 14.5 | 19.2 | 24.6 | 30.0 | 36.2 | 41.8 |
| South Korea | 22.2 | 23.3 | 24.4 | 25.4 | 26.3 | 26.9 |
| Australia | 9.8 | 10.2 | 10.6 | 10.9 | 11.2 | 11.5 |
| Indonesia | 2.0 | 3.1 | 4.6 | 5.9 | 7.4 | 8.7 |
| Other | 37.6 | 42.2 | 47.0 | 51.8 | 57.3 | 62.1 |
| **Western Europe** | **156.8** | **168.6** | **178.8** | **186.1** | **192.1** | **197.3** |
| Germany | 38.2 | 41.2 | 43.3 | 44.4 | 45.2 | 45.9 |
| UK | 33.0 | 34.8 | 36.5 | 37.5 | 38.2 | 38.9 |
| France | 24.5 | 26.5 | 28.1 | 29.2 | 29.8 | 30.4 |
| Spain | 13.4 | 14.5 | 15.9 | 17.2 | 18.6 | 19.5 |
| Italy | 10.5 | 11.7 | 13.0 | 14.2 | 15.4 | 16.6 |
| Netherlands | 7.3 | 7.8 | 8.1 | 8.3 | 8.5 | 8.6 |
| Sweden | 4.1 | 4.3 | 4.5 | 4.6 | 4.7 | 4.8 |
| Denmark | 2.5 | 2.7 | 2.9 | 3.0 | 3.0 | 3.1 |
| Finland | 2.3 | 2.4 | 2.5 | 2.6 | 2.7 | 2.8 |
| Norway | 2.2 | 2.3 | 2.4 | 2.5 | 2.6 | 2.7 |
| Other | 18.8 | 20.3 | 21.6 | 22.6 | 23.4 | 24.1 |
| **North America** | **156.7** | **164.2** | **171.3** | **178.8** | **185.8** | **192.6** |
| USA | 143.4 | 149.8 | 156.1 | 162.6 | 168.7 | 175.0 |
| Canada | 13.3 | 14.4 | 15.2 | 16.2 | 17.1 | 17.6 |
| **Eastern Europe** | **63.9** | **75.2** | **85.2** | **95.2** | **102.5** | **107.4** |
| Russia | 19.6 | 23.1 | 26.2 | 29.3 | 31.4 | 32.7 |
| Other | 44.3 | 52.1 | 59.0 | 65.9 | 71.1 | 74.7 |

(*continued*)

(continued)

| | *2011* | *2012* | *2013* | *2014* | *2015* | *2016* |
|---|---|---|---|---|---|---|
| **Latin America** | **50.3** | **63.6** | **73.0** | **82.5** | **90.6** | **97.5** |
| Brazil | 19.1 | 23.7 | 26.7 | 29.7 | 31.9 | 33.9 |
| Argentina | 6.4 | 8.1 | 9.2 | 10.4 | 11.3 | 11.8 |
| Mexico | 5.8 | 7.2 | 8.4 | 9.6 | 10.9 | 12.1 |
| Other | 19.1 | 24.7 | 28.8 | 32.8 | 36.5 | 39.7 |
| **Middle East & Africa** | **30.0** | **40.9** | **49.8** | **58.6** | **65.8** | **73.1** |
| **Worldwide** | **792.6** | **903.6** | **1015.8** | **1124.3** | **1228.5** | **1321.4** |

Note: For Internet users aged 14+ who have made at least one purchase via any digital channel within the past year, including online, mobile and tablet purchases, the numbers may not add up to the total due to rounding

Source: eMarketer, Jan 2013

Recent years have seen the use of social media as a pertinent tool to the retail industry. Anyone hoping to start a retail business or even improve their online sales success sees social media as a component to building customer relationships as part of the sales process. Since the process of sales take place through the use of social media such as Facebook, Twitter and Pintrest, it is also coined *social selling*.

However, the virtual aspect of the Internet and social media throws up newer obstacles to consumer trust and confidence. When a dispute arises in a face-to-face transaction, consumers have a wide variety of options available to help them resolve the issue. The buyer usually takes the item back to the store where he purchased it, demonstrates the problem and rectifies it directly with the seller. If the seller does not respond well, the buyer may report the problem to the conventional law enforcement body or approach the consumer court to sue the seller. Societies around the world have developed these institutions for speedy redress. But it is not as easy as this for online purchases. Buyers cannot walk back to the store where they purchased the item to get a refund. Moreover, if the seller is not responsive to the buyer's problem, it is very difficult for a consumer to rely upon local law enforcement to handle the matter. Social selling gets even more complicated where sellers provide little or no information about their physical presence, terms and conditions, and transaction policies on their social media page. While some businesses use social media as a supplement to their online shopping portals (such as Amazon and Flipkart), other retailers use social media exclusively to sell their products and services. In such cases, it is often difficult for the consumer to find adequate and relevant information about the business and its policies, which, in turn, creates difficulty for customers seeking a resolution of their product or service complaint..

This paper attempts to examine industry trends in the exercise of due diligence by online retailers using social media platforms to sell their products and services. The paper also attempts to examine the existing Indian legal framework with respect to information provided by online portals to their customers. Inference is also drawn from some of the international best practices of upholding consumer trust and confidence in electronic commerce in general, including social selling.

This paper begins with an introduction to online shopping and its development in the Indian scenario. The second part of the paper briefly outlines existing laws in India pertaining to e-commerce and consumer protection. The third part assesses information about online consumer contracts. The fourth part analyses international standards and guidelines on the adequacy and integrity of information in online consumer transactions. Drawing inferences from the above study, the paper's conclusion attempts to understand if there is a need to upgrade regulation on information standards through state machinery.

## Literature Review

Consumerism as an ideology has come to stay in business literature. Consumers deserve to get what they pay for in real quantity and true quality. In every society, consumers remain the centre of gravity of all business and industrial activity. The need to ensure basic rights to consumer welfare has long been recognized by legislations the world over. The 1985 adoption of the United Nations General Assembly's guidelines on consumer protection, (United Nations Guidelines for Consumer Protection 1985, expanded in 1999) brought about a vibrant consumer movement leading to the enactment of special laws and the establishment of separate machinery to redress consumers' grievances in various countries around the world. Modern legislation has initiated an era that clearly identifies, with a formal system of enforcement, consumers' rights and their protection.

The Consumer Protection Act of 1986 marked the beginning of an active consumer protection movement in India. The Act protects a consumer against defective goods, deficient services and unfair trade practices. The Act also provides for three-tier, quasi-judicial machinery to provide simple, speedier and inexpensive redress of consumers' grievances.

Consumer law was established at a time when the use of information technology in business-to-consumer (B2C) transactions was an unknown phenomenon.

The Internet, born and first used as means to exchange knowledge and information between institutions and research centres, or between cultural and research centres, has now metamorphosed into a powerful business media. The advent of social media has afforded limitless sales opportunities to manufacturers of goods and services. At the receiving end of this media blitz is the poor consumer!

The Internet has raised a variety of legal issues since it first became widely used in the mid-1990s, mostly in the area of consumer rights and protection. Legislation affecting consumer and business rights in areas such as privacy, cyber squatting, and electronic signatures have been passed. These laws are only the first attempts to regulate the Internet marketplace. Since the Internet continues to evolve, these new laws are certainly not the last in terms of Internet regulation (Cristina, 2005).

Some of the recent developments in the existing legal framework pertaining to e-consumer protection in India are:

1. The Consumer Protection Bill, 2015 has introduced a section on 'deficiency in service' (Section 2(12)) to include any act of omission or commission on the part of a service provider in withholding 'relevant information', which may cause damage to the consumer.
2. Failure on the part of a business to allocate a thirty-day cooling-off period after the purchase of goods or services is also being considered for inclusion as 'unfair trade practice' under Section 2(41) of the 2015 Consumer Protection Bill. The same provision also attempts to provide data security for consumers' personal information disseminated on online shopping portals.
3. Online marketplaces are included in the definition of 'intermediaries' under Section 2(14)(w) of the Information Technology Act, 2000 (amended in 2008). The Act also provides for immunity to online market intermediaries from certain liabilities, provided the intermediary observes due diligence and such other guidelines as the Central Government may prescribe (Section 79).
4. Under the Information Technology (Intermediaries Guidelines) Rules of 2011, the intermediary is required to publish rules and regulations, privacy policy and a user agreement for consumers' access to, or usage of, the intermediary's online resources. When

any information is discovered to be grossly harmful, harassing, defamatory, obscene or unlawful in any manner or violative of any currently enforced law, the Guidelines require intermediaries to act within thirty-six hours to remove such information from their online portals. They are also required to retain that information and associated records for at least ninety days for investigative purposes. The Rules also require intermediaries to publish on their websites the name and contact details of their grievance officer so that users who suffer as a result of exposure to that harmful online resource can notify the grievance officer of their complaints.

## Statement of Problem

Lack of information disclosure standards undermine consumers' trust and confidence in social selling.

## Hypothesis

A regulatory framework for clear and comprehensible information from online businesses, prior to the conclusion of a consumer contract, has an impact on consumer protection in India.

## Research Questions

1. To what extent are the conventional consumer laws adequate in providing sufficient and reliable information to consumers of goods and services available online?
2. What are the international guidelines and standards relating to information deficiencies in such consumer contracts?
3. Is there a need to upgrade the legal/regulatory framework governing consumer protection in the context of information in online shopping?
4. Research methodology: This research study involves a doctrinal approach to solving the research problem. The primary sources include an analysis of the information disclosures made by businesses adopting an active social media page to sell their products/services. Secondary resources include articles, books, commentaries, recommendations of international bodies on e-commerce, and case laws. The limitation of this study is that only businesses directly

selling goods and/or services through social media are considered for the purpose of analysis, not those businesses that adopt social media as a tool for promoting their online business (such as Flipkart and Amazon).

## Disclosure of Information in Online Consumer Contracts: An Appraisal

In general, an online consumer contract involves the following stages as shown graphically:

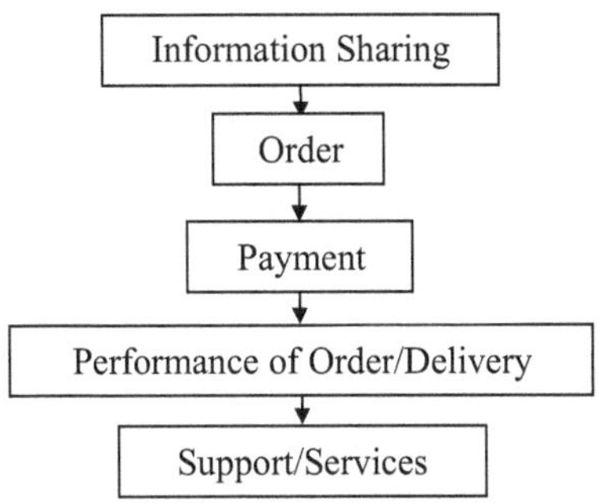


Some of the concerns of consumers purchasing through social media are:

1. Is the company doing business through the social media a legitimate one and where is it located?
2. Are the selling conditions clear and accessible? Does the social media page of the seller provide adequate information about the business and transactions taking place through the page?
3. Is the business committed to customer satisfaction? What recourse is available for the quick and fair resolution of a consumer dispute?

Given that the architecture of e-commerce is virtual, adequate and reliable information is key to consumer trust and confidence. This requires the 'information society' consumer to be better informed and more emancipated than the offline consumer. In the consumer sphere, dispute avoidance is as important as, if not more important than, dispute resolution. Consumer complaints often arise on the grounds of misunderstandings rather than as a result of a breach of contract by the supplier. A predominant feature of consumer law is to promote good business practices such that the consumer is well informed about the transaction. The anonymous character of the online market in its many forms demands a greater need for clear information at every technical step of the way to the conclusion of the contract, and it also requires an effective means to identify and correct input errors prior to the completion of the contract. Cross-border shopping presents the additional risk of having to seek redress against traders established in another country (Hill, 2008).

The Consumer Protection law recognises several unfair trade practices such as false and misleading representation of goods and services in terms of standard, quality, grade, and so on, materially misleading the public as regards the price at which the goods are ordinarily sold, disparaging of goods, misrepresentations as to warranty or guarantee, and so on. However, the law does not deal with failure on the part of the business to provide adequate disclosure of information regarding the address of the supplier, characteristics of goods and services, availability of product or service, delivery costs, pricing, withdrawal, and so on, in the case of distance selling. In other words, lack of information or low product/service quality or obscure information provided by the seller are other challenges which remain unanswered in traditional consumer law.

In the online consumer context, most complaints relate to allegations of non-performance or defective performance of the supplier's product/service, and rarely raise complex questions of law. Information is generally poor on a significant proportion of social selling pages and the number of fully compliant social media pages in terms of information is also very low. A legal framework for unfair trade practice/deficiency in service will be costly to administer and require a decision maker to exercise discretion to determine whether such conduct falls within the ambit of the framework (Iain, 2007).

While the use of social media in commerce is sweeping across the country, there appears to be inadequate supervision and a dearth of laws dealing with quality control of such companies, and this is what makes the rapid growth alarming. As a result, it is unlikely that social selling will deal effectively with the issue of consumer welfare and sovereignty of consumers. Most businesses adopting social selling hide behind the social media platform and provide very little or no information about their physical location, area-wise availability of product/services, cancellation and return policies, and refund and modes of refund, and so on.

## International Standards and Guidelines with Respect to Information Disclosure Standards

The need to regulate consumers' right to information in the cyber space has long been felt by several international bodies. The initiative to create a regulatory framework for adequate information in distance selling was taken by the European Union (EU) in its directive on the protection of consumers with respect to distance contracts (EU Directive 97/7/EC). The Directive applies to *distance contracts* between professionals and consumers for provision of goods or service. The Directive emphasises the need for businesses adopting distance selling to furnish clear and comprehensible information prior to conclusion of consumer contracts. Such information includes, as a minimum:

- Identity and possibly the address of the supplier;
- Characteristics of the goods or services and their price including all taxes;
- Delivery costs;
- Arrangements for payment, delivery or performance of the contract;
- Existence of a right of withdrawal;
- Period for which the offer or the price remains valid and possibly the minimum duration of the contract;
- Cost of using the means of distance communication, where it is calculated other than at the base rate.

The Directive also provides adequately for consumers' right of withdrawal and performance of such distance selling contracts. The new directive on consumer rights (2011/83/EC),[1] adopted on 13 June 2014 lists in detail the consumer information to be provided by off-premise or distance sellers including the main characteristics of the goods or services, identity of the trader, geographical address and contact information, the total price of the goods or services inclusive of taxes, cost of using the means of distance communication for the conclusion of the contract where that cost is calculated other than at the basic rate, arrangements for payment, delivery, performance, the date by which the trader undertakes to deliver the goods or to perform the services, conditions, time limit and procedures for exercising the right of withdrawal, circumstances under which the consumer will have to bear the cost of returning the goods in the case of withdrawal, the existence and conditions of after-sale customer assistance and guarantee, duration of the contract where applicable, the possibility of having recourse to an out-of-court complaint and redress mechanism to which the trader is subject, and the methods for having access to it.

The OECD Council's Guidelines for Consumer Protection in the Context of Electronic Commerce, 1999, provide a clear guidance to the core characteristics of information disclosure and fair business practices that businesses should provide and consumers should expect in the context of electronic commerce. The Council lays emphasis on accurate, clear and easily accessible information by e-commerce businesses on the following grounds:

- Identification/location of business
- Information about the goods/service
- Information about the *terms, conditions and costs associated with a transaction*
- Confirmation process
- Payment
- Dispute resolution mechanism
- Privacy
- Education and awareness

The United Nations is now looking at upgrading its 1985 Guidelines on Consumer Protection—which are about a quarter century old—in tune with the digital paradigm and with special emphasis on information disclosure guidelines in online transactions. In 2013 Consumer International, the world federation on consumer rights, together with the United Nations Conference on Trade and Development (UNCTAD) proposed certain changes to these guidelines. Consumers' right to information in the digital age has been highlighted in the proposal. The Recommendation emphasises, among other things, the importance of information regarding identification of the business, effective channels of communication with consumers, effective resolution of disputes, and clear information about terms, conditions and costs of a transaction, so as to enable the consumer to make an informed decision on whether to undertake a transaction or not.

Likewise, self-regulating schemes have developed tools that enable consumers to check on the reliability of these online businesses. For instance, the Better Business Bureau (BBB) established in 2000, developed a Code of Online Business Practices designed to guide ethical B2C conduct in e-commerce. Within the EU, Euro Label involves the co-operation of national suppliers of Internet trust marks to assure electronic consumers of the reliability of e-retailers' products and services. Likewise, TrustSg is a nation-wide trust mark initiative of the National Trust Council to boost the electronic commerce environment in Singapore. These self-regulating bodies act as neutral third parties in assessing whether the e-commerce business complies with information standards set by the respective country's legal and regulatory system.

## Conclusion

The recent growth of social selling has been rapid. Most entrepreneurs find social media a cost-effective and viable tool for selling their products/services. Consumers also benefit from such social selling where they get to choose from a wide variety of goods and services at competitive prices.

However, in light of the inadequacies of information standards in social selling and taking into consideration the rapid growth of this industry, it is important that disclosure of information is taken seriously and guidelines created to make shopping on the Internet a safe experience. Firms doing business over the Internet should incorporate extensive information about their offerings and customize information to consumers' needs. Once consumers have the information they are looking for, they will feel more confident about transacting with the e-tailers. Lack of regulation on information disclosures can only result in the rise of more 'cons' than '.coms' in social selling in the future.

The technological and cross-border features of the Internet call for regulatory innovation in the following areas:

1. *Standards in information disclosure and cooling-off period*: Nothing on social media business pages indicates the authenticity of their contents and physical space. The website domains and e-mail addresses of e-tailers are inadequate and potentially misleading in determining the location of the seller (Reich, 2000). There is an immediate need of a regulatory framework for adequate disclosures with respect to the geographical location of the supplier/intermediary, pricing details (whether the price is inclusive of tax, hidden costs), description of goods/services offered for sale, delivery costs, duration of contract, cancellation rights, return and refund policy, availability of after-sales service/warranty, and so on.

2. *Consumer redress and harnessing market gatekeepers*: Redress for an unsatisfactory Internet transaction may pose problems for consumers, particularly since it may often raise cross-border issues. This is an important pre-requisite for consumer welfare and sovereignty. Social selling, especially involving cross-border sales, should provide alternative means of dispute resolution. Enhancing consumer protection agencies' power to block 'rogue traders' from conducting online transactions would make consumers less likely to find themselves in such disputes.
3. *Enhancing reputational devices through trust marks:* Trust marks such as the Better Business Bureau, Trusted shops, TrustSg, and so on, are neutral third parties that ensure that commitment to regulatory standards are met by the online businesses in form and substance. These trust marks conduct audits of e-tailers' commercial communications and fair market practices, payment and security, data protection, grievance handling and alternative dispute resolutions. Establishment of such trademarks at the national level should be initiated by state machinery. It should also be mandated that e-businesses registering themselves with such trust marks display their certificate of registration on their web portals. This would enhance consumer trust and confidence in online consumer contracts.

## Notes

1. DIRECTIVE 2011/83/EU OF THE EUROPEAN PARLIAMENT AND OF THE COUNCIL of 25 October 2011 on consumer rights, amending Council Directive 93/13/EEC and Directive 1999/44/EC of the European Parliament and of the Council and repealing Council Directive 85/577/EEC and Directive 97/7/EC of the European Parliament and of the Council, Official Journal L 304, Vol. 54, 22 November 2011, available at http://eur-lex.europa.eu/legal-content/EN/TXT/PDF/?uri=CELEX:32011L0083&rid=1 (last visited July 28, 2014).

## References

### Books

Cristina, C. (2005). *Cyber Consumer Law and Unfair Trading Practices* (pp. 116–117). Ashgate Publishing Company.

Hill, J. (2008). *Cross Border Consumer Contracts* (pp. 6–7). Oxford: OUP. In Z. S. Tang. (2009). *Electronic Consumer Contracts in the Conflict of Laws* (p. 51). Oxford and Portland, Oregon: Hart Publishing.

Iain, R. (2007). *Consumer Law and Policy: Text and Materials on Regulating Consumer Markets* (p. 127). Oxford and Portland, Oregon: Hart Publishing.

Reich, N. (2000). Consumerism and Citizenship in the Information Society. In T. Wilhelmsson, S. Tuominen, & H. Tuomola (Eds.), *Consumer Law in the Information Society* (p. 168). The Hague/London/Boston: Kluwer Law International.

## Websites

*1 Million Retailers Sell Online.* Retrieved May 7, 2014., from http://www.iamai.in/PRelease_detail.aspx?nid=3313&NMonth=3&NYear=2014

Chandra, G. et al. (2012, December). *Online and Upcoming: The Internet's Impact on India.* Retrieved May 10, 2014, from www.mckinsey.com

Directive 97/7/EC of The European Parliament and of the Council of 20 May 1997 on the Protection of Consumers in Respect to Distance Contracts. Retrieved May 7, 2014, from http://eur-lex.europa.eu/LexUriServ/LexUriServ.do?uri=OJ:L:1997:144:0019:0027:EN:PDF

http://www.emarketer.com/Article/Ecommerce-Sales-Topped-1-Trillion-First-Time 2012/1009649#W72ph2WLuIkQBAoE.99. Retrieved May 11, 2014a.

*India's e-commerce industry may reach $70 billion by 2020.* Retrieved April 20, 2014., from http://articles.economictimes.indiatimes.com/2014-02-10/news/47201050_1_binny-bansal-sachin-bansal-online-shopping

OECD. (2012). *Report on Consumer Protection in Online and Mobile Payments.* OECD Digital Economy Papers, No. 204, OECD Publishing. Retrieved May 30, 2014, from https://doi.org/10.1787/5k9490gwp7f3-en

United Nations Guidelines for Consumer Protection 1985 (as expanded in 1999). Retrieved May 20, 2014, from http://www.un.org/esa/sustdev/publications/consumption_en.pdf

*Updating the United Nations Guidelines for Consumer Protection for the Digital Age.* Retrieved May 30, 2014., from http://www.consumersinternational.org/

www.core.nic.in. Retrieved May 28, 2014b.

CHAPTER 14

# Portea: Social Media Applications

*K. Ganesh*

## Introduction

From what can be seen, trends in mature Internet markets tend to gradually make their way into maturing markets. Some quick India-specific Internet stats for the curious reader are:

- India is the third country in the world to have over five Internet companies valued at over US$ 1 billion.
- India constitutes the second largest market in the world for Facebook and LinkedIn with only 19 percent Internet penetration as compared to 50 percent in China and 61 percent in Brazil.
- By 2020 the Internet is estimated to grow to over 4 per cent of India's GDP.

I'm sharing these figures because they make me, an entrepreneur from India, smile. When Internet connectivity increases, it's only natural that more users will join various social media channels. Over the past few years, the emergence and adoption of social media has been nothing short of spectacular. From creating billion-dollar companies overnight, toppling governments and affecting consumer behavior, social media in all its diversity has given people around the world the power of "oneness."

K. Ganesh (✉)
Bangalore, Karnataka, India



G. Heggde, G. Shainesh (eds.), *Social Media Marketing*,
https://doi.org/10.1007/978-981-10-5323-8_14

As the Internet penetrates deeper into developing economies such as India, social media will integrate itself into the daily lives of people from diverse backgrounds and industries. The opportunities social media will bring for aspiring entrepreneurs are staggering beyond belief and I'm sure we'll see even more billion-dollar brands emerge from India in the near future.

Evolution of social media is now at a tipping point where brands do not have a choice: they must either be onboard or miss the chance to connect with global audiences on a platform that is bound to be the most significant factor to affect consumer decision making in modern times.

For a business, being on social media is like having a corner store on a very busy street. Even when customers are not directly buying, they are watching and listening to the interaction between brands and other customers, which creates a perception of the brand. A good or bad review posted by existing customers will influence other customers' future purchasing decisions and hence it is important for brands to be alive and interact with their audience.

## Social Media Marketing: What's in It for Me?

Before I get into the nitty-gritty of social media marketing, I want to introduce to you a company on GrowthStory, my entrepreneurship platform. This company, Portea, is performing exceptionally well with social media marketing. Portea is a health-care company that provides hospital-quality medical care for patients at home. It has a consistent record of growing leads, engaging audiences and building brand awareness through social media, primarily Facebook.

The health-care industry is not known for stand-out marketing campaigns and, moreover, the audience is not as responsive to marketing campaigns as audiences of other industries are, as for instance, FMCG. But health-care customers, especially the younger generation, are information hungry. They rely on social media for research and making important decisions, especially those concerning their family's health. These decisions include selection of doctors, reviewing hospitals, information about courses of treatment and anything else they need to know.

Social media communities with members who have undergone medical treatment are ready to share their experiences (good or bad), so it was vital for Portea to include social media as part of the long-term marketing strategy.

Social media is all about relationships and so are brands. For brands, it is essential to cultivate meaningful relationships with customers (also potential customers) and most companies associated with GrowthStory will vouch that social media is a powerful tool that can forge strong, loyalty-evoking relationships with minimal time and effort.

Different brands in partnership with GrowthStory use different strategies to build relationships via social media. Though not as "personal" as traditional business relationships, the social media relationship between a brand and a consumer is just as effective. With other people watching the interaction and developing a perception of the brand, it's important that brands get it right—from the start.

While we are on the subject, here are some pointers on how you can build long-lasting social media relationships:

### *Stay True to Your Brand Personality*

Every brand has a unique personality. For brands that are active on social media, it is important to maintain the same brand personality throughout, in every form of interaction with customers. This includes content sharing, responding to customers or competitors, and even ads that reach out to new audiences. While staying true to your brand personality, you should maintain a level of intimacy within the communication. Portea deeply cares for its customers, and understands their pain, so the conversation aims to be of help—and it works.

### *Understand the Customer*

The target audience of a brand is a congregation of individuals. For a brand to understand its target audience, it needs to first understand the individual customer. Customers of several brands associated with GrowthStory have very different needs and it's challenging to understand and seamlessly deliver value to all of them.

### *Build Trust, Don't Censor*

In any business, there are bound to be unsatisfied customers. Social media provides these customers with a platform to express their dislike for the brand to the world. For brands to create meaningful relationships on social media, it is important that customers are given the freedom to express their opinions without fear of censorship (unless of course absolutely necessary).

In this way, followers who are watching the conversation will trust the brand and know that the brand is trying to improve its service. In the future, when potential customers need a product/service that you offer, their first preference will be your brand.

For Portea, Facebook is the largest source of feedback, complaints, and appreciation. Portea uses feedback to improve services, and I know from experience that it is better to listen to customers' honest feedback and improve than pretend everything is fine.

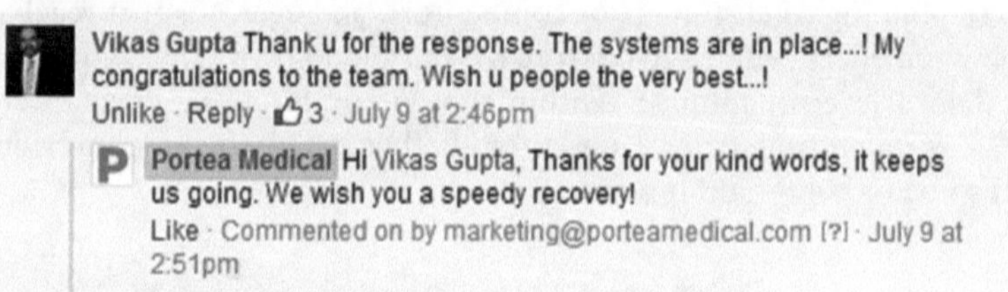


### *Be Passionate When Helping Followers*

Passion for helping followers goes a long way. For any brand, most followers will expect help from the brand when needed. For the health-care industry, this passion is not an option but an absolute necessity. My wife, Meena, who is the CEO of Portea, often gets encouragement from customers about how the company's services helped them take care of their parents in their last days. The passion with which you interact and offer help spreads the word and before you know it, more people start following your brand.

### *Learning Never Ends*

Lastly, be open to learning. There are times when a customer can show you something you've missed. Your brand might be offering the best product/service, but there will always be scope for improvement and when someone points this out, take it as a learning experience. Be thankful and show your appreciation. It will do wonders for the relationship!

Portea and other companies in our portfolio used these techniques to establish relationships with their audience on social media. These are not hard and fast rules for building social media relationships, but they lay a solid ground to get started.

## Social Media Success Strategies

As I mentioned earlier, there is no single strategic key that unlocks all social media platforms (How I wish there were one!). Different social media platforms have different advertising options but marketing success depends on some common attributes, such as the use of the right platform, creativity, accurate targeting, and optimization. Let me tell you what I know about them.

### *Be Where Your Audience Is*

Depending on the type of product or service, it is important to choose the right platform so that you'll be present where your audience is likely to be. Then again, as with any rule, there are some exceptions. For instance, I now know that Facebook is the right platform for Portea even though the company is in the health-care domain. Before Facebook became Portea's primary platform for social media marketing, I had my doubts. Mainly because

- Facebook is considered to be used by the young (and restless) for socializing, sharing pics and keeping in touch, whereas Portea's audience were forty-five to eighty years of age.
- The domain of health care didn't seem in tune with the kind of people generally using Facebook.

- No other business (in health care) had used Facebook as its primary mode of customer acquisition. We were venturing into uncharted waters.
- And lastly, Facebook was predominantly being used to promote brand awareness and not as a medium to acquire customers.

You might be wondering what had prompted Portea to even consider trying out Facebook as the primary choice for acquiring customers. Let me explain.

*Search Volume*
Home medical care is a very niche segment. When Portea's digital marketing efforts started out, there was not enough search volume on Google for home medical care, so there was a need experiment with other channels. This necessity led Portea to try out Facebook marketing and it succeeded. But the greater lesson was that even platforms that do not seem ideal can yield fabulous results. It's just a matter of trying!

*Reach and Targeting*
Portea's research showed that no other digital medium in India has better reach and targeting options than Facebook. With the ability to target specific cities and even more specific sections of the audience, social media marketing professionals at Portea were able to reach out to a lot more people and achieve preset goals at a phenomenal pace.

### *Creativity Has No Bounds*

Whether in the real or virtual world, advertising success depends on creativity. For a segment such as health care, the scope for creativity is much less than that, say, of the food industry. But with the right combination of text and images, Portea gets the message across. The challenge with Facebook and other social media channels is that the space for sponsored ads (text and image) is very limited, so ads have to be short yet creative enough to stand out and grab the viewers' attention.

**Portea Medical**

Written by mahipal.saini@portea.com [?] · July 2 at 6:13pm ·

Proper care is critical for the first few months for the new baby and mom.

Our post natal home support by experienced staff will give you care and breathing space to enjoy this new stage of life.

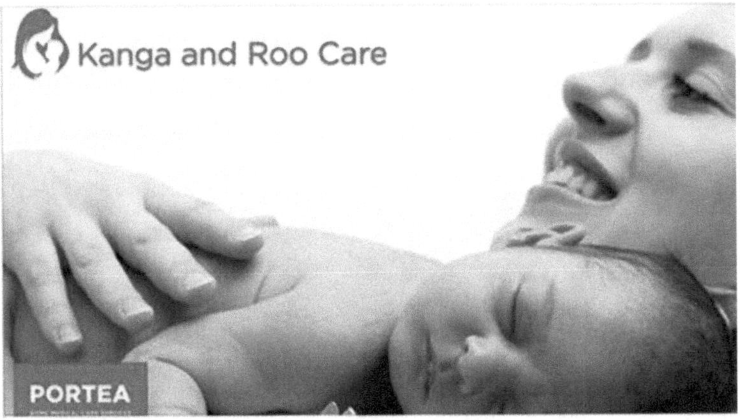


**Experienced Post Natal Care & Support at Home**

Portea Medical offers professional health care services at home. Contact us to get qualified & experienced staff for home healthcare.

PORTEA.COM

### *Targeting Makes It Easy*

Facebook, LinkedIn, Twitter and other social media platforms have different targeting options, and explaining all of them would be time consuming and difficult. So for ease of understanding let's take Facebook.

Facebook supports two types of ad format: right-hand side (RHS) and News Feed. RHS ads are easier to set up and cheaper, so they are good to start with.

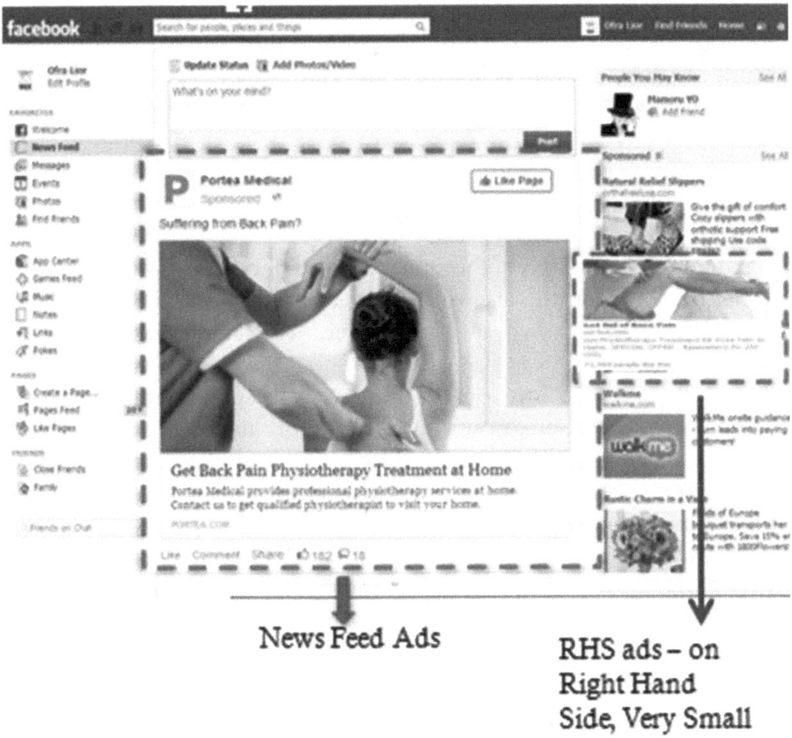


Even while setting up Portea's first Facebook campaign, our social media marketers were experimenting with different images and communication themes. I also remember that campaigns were initiated with a broad user base and as data built up, campaigns were fine-tuned.

### *Tweak, Tweak, and Tweak Some More*

This is the most important contributor to Portea's social media marketing success. Portea has a very strong in-house social media marketing team that takes care of optimization down to minute levels, monitoring each campaign individually with clockwork precision.

Any business using social media marketing needs to be data driven and interpret the language of data so as to understand user behavior.

Portea social media marketing team tweaks campaigns on a daily basis, ensuring success irrespective of changing trends. As with any new marketing channel, brands will take some time to figure out what works on social media, but when they do, the time and effort will be well worth it.

#### *Your Ads Can Be Your Number-One Enemy*

Ad fatigue can ruin even the most creative, potent advertisement. Ad fatigue occurs when the click-through rate drops because the ad's target audience has seen the ad too many times. Ad fatigue can significantly lower the quality of a campaign, so ads should always be kept fresh with periodic changes in color, copy, and clear call-to-action statements.

For Portea, Facebook now contributes more new customers than any other channel. There is a latent need for home-health-care services such as physiotherapy, but people do not search for them online. They rely on information provided by friends, and as a result, have no knowledge of information about other available services. Even for very niche services, such as those provided by nursing attendants, Facebook is allowing Portea to reach the target audience and acquire new customers at a significantly lower cost.

### Portea Facebook Strategy: What Worked

If you ask me to name one reason why Portea's Facebook marketing campaigns produced phenomenal results, I would have to answer with one word: analytics. Portea has a very strong analytics team that is dedicated to continuous testing, data interpretation, and improvement of campaigns. I know that Portea uses multiple targeting options such as look-alike audience and remarketing, but I've never deep-dived into what goes on behind the scenes because the team does their job exceptionally well and results are evident.

#### *Portea's Key Success Factors*

- refining target audience
- continuous optimization by campaign performance
- efficient use of Facebook tools and reacting to changes
- responding and engaging with customers to improve services
- improvement of creatives, landing pages and messaging

### *Lessons Learned from Portea's Facebook Marketing Campaigns*

- Portea has been able to consistently acquire customers at about one-fifth of the projected cost of above-the-line (ATL) marketing.
- Facebook marketing works with local businesses. This was a major revelation!
- Using Facebook, Portea's business grew to fifteen cities without having to set up any local marketing teams.
- Advertising on Facebook needs continuous optimization with frequent changes in images, copy, and messaging.
- I cannot overstate the contribution of good creatives to the success of a campaign.
- RHS ads work well for brand building, but for ROI conversion, News Feed ads are 50 percent more effective than RHS ads.

### *Why Portea (Heart-Image) Uses Facebook*

- Requests for services (leads) increased from around 30/day to 600/day in six months.
- Lead to patient conversion has been in double digits.
- Rate of acquiring new patients increased tenfold in six months.
- Facebook produces many more new customers than conventional online marketing methods such as search engine marketing (SEM).
- Cost of acquisition is surprisingly lower than SEM, whereby people search for a service with an intent to purchase.
- Number of "likes" on Facebook page went from 500 to 70,000 without doing any ads for "likes."

Facebook has given Portea the visibility and growth I had hoped for when Portea's Facebook marketing experimentation began. Now I know for a fact that social media marketing works at a local, state, and international level and provides great insights into customer profiles such as demographics, location, marital status, education, and interests. With lower marketing costs, social media marketing can help turn even a new brand into a force to be reckoned with.

## Future of Social Media Marketing

When I look back at the evolution of social media and the future possibilities, I think social media marketing is still in its infancy. Platforms that are popular today have the potential to generate much more value (for users and marketers). Social media platforms such as Facebook are testing some very exciting features, and I can definitely see great things in the offing.

### *Wallets*

Facebook has introduced a friend-to-friend payment feature via Messenger, which enables users to connect with Visa/Mastercard and transfer money with zero fees. Why this sudden interest in a payment gateway? It could be because Facebook sees competition from the likes of Apple Pay, Square, and Stripe, and the company does not want to be left behind. With payment integrated into the platform, users would be able to shop directly, which could mean easier conversions.

### *Buy Button*

Sometime back, Facebook and Twitter started beta testing the Buy button, which enables users to make quick purchases. Google has also confirmed that it will be introducing the Buy button, which is going to create a lot of new opportunities for marketers. Buy buttons integrated with wallets will augment "recommended" purchases, and we could very well see the dawning of a new social media marketing era.

## What Else to Expect?

### *Mobile Will Reign Supreme*

Mobile already has made a significant impact on digital marketing, and in the future, traffic from mobile devices will most likely take over the reins from the desktop. As more and more users log on to social media platforms from mobile devices, marketers will need to optimize their campaigns for mobiles if they are to stay relevant.

### *Content Will Still Be King*

Content is a very broad term and we've all heard it before that content is king. From the looks of it, I see this king's reign continuing. As Google and social media platforms evolve, relevant content will become more important than ever. Through useful content, brands will educate their customers and the importance of helpful, user-generated content will emerge on social media platforms in a big way.

### *Campaigns Will Be Data Driven and Hypertargeted*

As better data analysis tools and techniques emerge, marketers will be more data driven than ever before. Future digital marketers will be able to match traffic with exactly what they are looking for and enhance sales through hypertargeted ads.

Whatever the future brings, one thing is certain: social media is here to stay. Many new platforms might emerge, new advertising techniques will be discovered, and connectedness between future social media users will be stronger than ever. I expect the growth story and reach of businesses that use social media marketing to be on a scale we've never witnessed before. These are very exciting times ahead. Let's buckle up!

CHAPTER 15

# Qwikcilver's Experience: Why Social Marketing Drove Digital Gifting Growth in India

*T. P. Pratap*

Social media has played a strategically important role in driving a new consumption segment in the Indian environment over the last five years. The digital gifting category has kicked off and grown by over 300 per cent year-on-year over the last five years, due to relevant awareness, salience and buzz built on social media by the key brands across categories.

Social media has played the most important role, with a share of over 70 per cent of the resources of brands devoted to this medium to leverage the power of referrals and engagements with fans and followers to drive the advantages of digital gifting, so much so that social media has become the single go-to market approach for most of the leading brands in this domain.

Analysis of the social media activities of fifty brands across twenty consumer categories over the last four years showcases some interesting insights.

## Growing the Base of Fans and Followers

Brands have leveraged the power of social media effectively to scale up their fans and follower base in the first phase. Digital gift cards were launched by brands across their ecosystem of physical stores, e-commerce

T. P. Pratap (✉)
Qwikcilver, Bengaluru, Karnataka, India



G. Heggde, G. Shainesh (eds.), *Social Media Marketing*,
https://doi.org/10.1007/978-981-10-5323-8_15

portals, mobile apps and institutional business teams. This portfolio was scaled up through effective programmes on social media driving social media users to follow brand activities.

Brands like Café Coffee Day, Fastrack, Titan, and PVR Cinemas have made effective use of social media to grow a base of over 10 million fans and followers who are today aware of the benefits of digital gifting compared to traditional modes of gifting. Such benefits

- afford recipients the freedom to choose their own gift
- afford technological superiority to gift vouchers
- allow consumers to load variable value
- allow part-redemption
- allow an adequate, real-time management information system (MIS) and easy account reconciliation
- afford high-security—no pilferage threat

In order to plan the marketing programme dynamics, it is important for brands to analyse the fan base on the various social platforms used. This is enabled by the insights and profiles that the platforms provide.

In this phase, it is important to track and monitor, on a daily and weekly basis, the growth of the number of relevant fans garnered from brand activities on various offline, online and social media. Growing this base, however, is time consuming.

## Social to Local Marketing

Social media tools provide strong means for brands to track the demographics and psychographics of their fans and consumers. In order to analyse this audience, brands need to analyse the page engagements and app engagements. Facebook, Pinterest, Instagram, and Twitter enable brands to track and promote specific marketing messages effectively.

Marketing analytics enable deeper insights into consumer profiling using metrics like

- Sex
- Interests
- Profession
- Location
- Age group

These social media insights and details have enabled gift-card-powering brands like Woohoo to drive 400 percent ROI on transaction-specific engagements to local merchants and stores in targeted markets in Tier 2 and Tier 3 cities, based on segmented business objectives. The ROI of such social to local marketing has enabled brands to drive ROI far more effectively for their marketing spends and to boost engagements.

## Consistency of Relevant Engagements

The engagement quality of brand-specific posts plays a significant role in ensuring the ROI of social media campaigns. Tonality, time and relevance to specific audiences play a key role and allow brands to further tailor content to ensure it's the type of content their fan base engages with.

Facebook and Twitter have been the key platforms that brands have used to drive engagements in their digital gifting campaigns. The objectives have been made all the more complex to drive effective engagements with Facebook and Twitter's updates to their platforms.

Brands leveraged the first phase of their Facebook presence to strongly drive organic reach. With the updates made, brands have recalibrated their strategy to drive engagements by boosting posts intended to appeal to the desired targeted audience. For example, cinema brands, like PVR, have partnered with the mobile gifting brand Woohoo to drive effective engagements on Facebook and Twitter on Fridays, after the release of new films. This has enabled the engagement quality with their fans to be more effective as more fans look forward to engaging on Fridays to learn about new film releases and provide digital gifting options to their loved ones.

Analysis shows that Facebook videos get the highest level of engagements in the form of shares, while images and links get engagements mostly in the form of "likes" and comments. Brands like as Amazon and Myntra strategically mix their social media content to achieve their targeted reach and engagements in their specific gift card campaigns.

Twitter has been a far more viral platform, with tweets spreading quickly. Brands like Café Coffee Day make their gift card tweets stand out by adding interesting animated GIF images and memes that have produced an increase in retweets by over 200 percent.

## Social Loyalty Through Conversions

In today's milieu it is important for brands to ensure emotional and social loyalty rather than purely transactional loyalty. While not all engagements are intended to drive sales and footfall, it is necessary for brands to set up metrics to ensure that engagements are tracked.

Top brands with a widespread retail network like Titan, Fastrack and Helios have integrated their social media presence into their store systems to ensure that transactions and footfall can be tracked and managed in real-time so that the effect of social media campaigns for digital gifting are analysed with regard to:

- digital gift card value activated
- digital gift card value redeemed
- digital gift card reloaded
- time elapsed between activation and redemption
- product purchase value versus gift card value
- non-redeemed and unused value of gift card

Engagements can also be nontransactional in nature and developed by brands based on specific objectives. Some of the types of conversion that have been adopted by brands like Woohoo for its gifting app are

- driving fans and followers to download the Woohoo app from the play store;
- view a new brand's video film on YouTube
- drive trials of a gifting product launched for specific markets
- drive awareness of a new e-commerce gifting portal
- drive corporate customers' awareness of their reward needs

It is important for brands to drive ROI in accordance with their specific objectives.

Retailers should also find a means of asking customers who buy their services how they found the retailer's site and what made them decide to purchase from it. This is usually pretty straightforward for creative and marketing services, which usually have the customer fill out a form that lets the retailer understand more about the customer's transactional experience.

## Consistency of Social Persona

It is invariably observed that social media consumer behaviour is at variance with actual product consumer behaviour. Brands observe a significantly high level of transactional loyalty but low levels of social media loyalty from their consumer base. This implies that the social media persona does not match the expectations of brand users. Hence, brands need to recalibrate and develop content that resonates with both audiences.

The brand persona as perceived by fans and followers plays a very key role in the long-term effectiveness of the social media strategy. Deploying effective social media tools to analyse this trending metric is important in order to take stock and plan ahead. Particularly, attention needs to be paid to the tone of responses to customer comments and customers' grievances, and to social media referrals.

## Love Your Critics

Brands that are successful in driving their digital gifting products on social media are seen to be those that have supported dissatisfied fans and followers. Happy consumers don't respond with as much passion on social media as dissatisfied consumers do. Brands have leveraged this insight to convert their critics into fans with the quality of their responses, speed of responses and building a genuine sense of caring about the complaints of their fans.

Rather than being diffident about criticism on social media or being defensive in their responses, successful brands have been able to convert their social media problems into a strength.

## Relevant Content Is Ace, King, and Queen

Successful social media presence requires brands to drive their fans and followers into discussions where they share their points of view. This is at variance with the traditional concept of brand advertising. Brands that have shared a logical point of view on topics and been able to offer rational explanations that appeal to their fans have seen faster growth in their social media engagements.

Brands need to be seen as approachable and accessible, with a point of view on subjects of relevance to their consumer base. Digital gifting with gift cards is a positive emotional state of mind which brands have communicated with their fans with the necessary vibrancy. Occasions like Raksha Bandhan, Mother's day, Father's Day, Teachers Day and festive occasions like Diwali, Durga Puja, Onam, Pongal and Sankranthi have been celebrated by brands like Allen Solly and Arvind Brands in ways that appeal to their audiences, and they emphasise the relevance of gift cards for gifting to friends and family on these occasions.

## Users Generate the Best Content

Successful brands have also leveraged their fan base to generate a vibrant content base that is used for specific occasions to drive virality. On the lines of how Google allows external contributors to design the Google Doodle for certain events, brands like Shoppers Stop have leveraged their social media vehicles on specific occasions like Valentine's Day and Friendship Day to motivate their fans to share and develop content in the form of videos and images, thereby engaging and showcasing the benefits of digital gifting to their user base.

Woohoo, a new mobile gifting brand, drove more than 1200 interactions among consumers in their target segments during Friendship Day, sharing such user-generated images on social media.

## Clarity of Value for Users

In the midst of the era of information overload, consumers, users and followers of brands are strapped for time in their daily activities. In this context, it is necessary for brands to convey the message of value relevant to the user. Brand-related updates and information on promotions and offers need to be presented in a meaningful and interesting manner that is instantly appealing to social media users. Lifestyle department store chains maintain interesting communications in their digital gift card portfolios on Facebook, Twitter and Instagram. This has enabled users to drive transactions at their stores by leveraging the information shared on social media.

# Index[1]



[1] Note: Page numbers followed by 'n' refers to notes.



G. Heggde, G. Shainesh (eds.), *Social Media Marketing*,
https://doi.org/10.1007/978-981-10-5323-8

FSC
www.fsc.org
MIX
Papier | Fördert
gute Waldnutzung
FSC® C083411

Kolibri 360 GmbH
Ferdinand-Jühlke-Straße 7
99095 Erfurt, Deutschland
produktsicherheit@kolibri360.de